J. G. Ballard

Andrzej Gasiorek

Manchester University Press
Manchester and New York
distributed exclusively in the USA by Palgrave

Published by Manchester University Press
Oxford Road, Manchester M13 9NR, UK
and Room 400, 175 Fifth Avenue, New York, NY 10010, USA
www.manchesteruniversitypress.co.uk

Distributed exclusively in the USA by
Palgrave, 175 Fifth Avenue, New York,
NY 10010, USA

Distributed exclusively in Canada by
UBC Press, University of British Columbia, 2029 West Mall,
Vancouver, BC, Canada V6T 1Z2

British Library Cataloguing-in-Publication Data
A catalogue record for this book is available from the British Library

Library of Congress Cataloging-in-Publication Data applied for

ISBN   0 7190 7052 X   *hardback*
EAN   9780 7190 7052 5

ISBN   0 7190 7053 8   *paperback*
EAN   9780 7190 7053 2

First published 2005

14 13 12 11 10 09 08 07 06 05   0 9 8 7 6 5 4 3 2 1

Typeset in Scala with Dax display
by Northern Phototypesetting Co Ltd, Bolton
Printed in Great Britain
by Bell & Bain Ltd, Glasgow

J. G. Ballard

Blackburn
llege

Manchester University Press

⊙ Contemporary British Novelists

Series editor Daniel Lea

already published

Irvine Welsh Aaron Kelly

Contents

Series editor's foreword

Contemporary British Novelists offers readers critical introductions to some of the most exciting and challenging writing of recent years. Through detailed analysis of their work, volumes in the series present lucid interpretations of authors who have sought to capture the sensibilities of the late twentieth and twenty-first centuries. Informed, but not dominated, by critical theory, *Contemporary British Novelists* explores the influence of diverse traditions, histories and cultures on prose fiction, and situates key figures within their relevant social, political, artistic and historical contexts.

The title of the series is deliberately provocative, recognising each of the three defining elements as contentious identifications of a cultural framework that must be continuously remade and renamed. The contemporary British novel defies easy categorisation and rather than offering bland guarantees as to the current trajectories of literary production, volumes in this series contest the very terms that are employed to unify them. How does one conceptualise, isolate and define the mutability of the contemporary? What legitimacy can be claimed for a singular Britishness given the multivocality implicit in the redefinition of national identities? Can the novel form adequately represent reading communities increasingly dependent upon digitalised communication? These polemical considerations are the theoretical backbone of the series, and attest to the difficulties of formulating a coherent analytical approach to the discontinuities and incoherencies of the present.

Contemporary British Novelists does not seek to appropriate its subjects for prescriptive formal or generic categories; rather it aims to explore the ways in which aesthetics are reproduced, refined and repositioned through recent prose writing. If the overarching architecture of the contemporary always eludes description, then the grandest ambition of this series must be to plot at least some of its dimensions.

Daniel Lea

Acknowledgements

I owe debts of gratitude to many people. I would like to thank Daniel Lea for asking me to write this book on Ballard, and Matthew Frost, my editor at Manchester University, for overseeing the whole process. Peter Brooker and Patrick Parrinder were kind enough to read most of the book in manuscript and their comments and suggestions were enormously helpful. I would like to thank the School of Humanities at Birmingham University for giving me a sabbatical in the autumn of 2003 and the Arts and Humanities Research Board for awarding me a Research Leave in the spring of 2004; the freedom this gave me from other academic duties enabled me to finish the book. Various colleagues and friends have over the last couple of years helped me in innumerable ways. Thanks especially to David Aers, as ever; also to Maureen Bell, Steve Ellis, Alex Hughes, Alan Munton, Deborah Parsons, Max Saunders, and Marcus Walsh; and to Christine, David, Małgosia, Roger, Suzanne, Zbyszek; and Staś, whose scatological humour kept me entertained throughout. Without Basia and Lidia there'd scarcely be any point to it all.

Abbreviations

AE	*The Atrocity Exhibition* (1970) (London: Flamingo, 2001).
C	*Crash* (1973) (London: Vintage, 1975).
CI	*Concrete Island* (1973) (London: Vintage, 1994).
CN	*Cocaine Nights* (1996) (London: Flamingo, 1997).
CS	*The Complete Short Stories* (2001) (London: Flamingo, 2001).
CW	*The Crystal World* (1966) London: Flamingo, 2000).
D	*The Drought* (1965) (London: Flamingo, 2001).
DC	*The Day of Creation* (1987) (London: Flamingo, 1993).
DW	*The Drowned World* (1962) (London: Victor Gollancz, 2001).
ES	*Empire of the Sun* (1984) (London: Flamingo, 1994).
HA	*Hello America* (1981) (Reading: Triad, 1983).
HR	*High-Rise* (1975) (London, Flamingo, 2000).
KW	*The Kindness of Women* (1991) (London: Flamingo, 1994).
MP	*Millennium People* (2003) (London: Flamingo, 2003).
RP	*Rushing to Paradise* (1994) (London: Flamingo, 1995).
RW	*Running Wild* (1988) (London: Flamingo, 2002).
SC	*Super-Cannes* (2000) (London: Flamingo, 2001).
UD	*The Unlimited Dream Company* (1979) (London: Flamingo, 2000).
UG	*A User's Guide to the Millennium: Essays and Reviews* (1996) (New York: Picador, 1996).
VS	*Vermilion Sands* (1971) (London: Vintage, 2001).

Introduction

Terrestrial and psychic landscapes

In *The Kindness of Women* (*KW*; 1991), which offers a fictionalised version of aspects of J. G. Ballard's life, the young protagonist is informed by his father that after the Second World War ends he will go to live in England, a country he has never visited. The boy's response is a telling one: 'Already I feared that the England I visited after the war would be a larger version of Lunghua camp, with all its snobberies and social divisions, its "best" families with their stran-gled talk of "London town" brandished about like the badges of an exclusive club, a club I would do my best to avoid joining' (*KW* 41). And so it proves. But this proleptic reading of a social milieu he has experienced only in a distanced and debased form is a projection cast in the language of oedipal revolt. A classical narrative is already under construction here: independence will be achieved by an act of disaf-filiation from the paternal country of origin, which is 'known' before it has actually been encountered. Doubtless a defensive strategy of this kind, which nonetheless bristles with an edgy aggressiveness, vouchsafes various secondary gains, not least freedom from restric-tive social norms, a sense of intellectual autonomy, and a non-con-formist mind-set. Ballard the writer has been refusing to conform ever since, adopting a libertarian and anarchic stance *vis-à-vis* social life, which is related in complex ways not only to the exacerbation of an already febrile imagination under the unsettling conditions of a prisoner-of-war camp but also to the unbalancing of perspectives and frameworks that such conditions can bring about, when adults 'lose their belief in themselves, like actors in a play whose run is about to be cancelled ... a disturbing lesson that lasts a lifetime' (*A User's Guide to the Millennium*; *UG* 251).

Above all, this disturbing lesson offers instruction about the vulnerability of human beings and the fragility of their institutions. If the adolescent protagonist of *The Kindness of Women* is determined – in advance of getting there – to reject England and its entire social structure, then this is in part a symbolic rejection of the familial heritage and in part a defiant assertion of scepticism about all communal laws. Taken together, rejection and scepticism form a combustible package, a fiery amalgam of attitudes that can scorch accepted cultural platitudes. Just as his fictional alter ego intended, they position the writer as an outsider, as an unclubbable refusenik, as a dissenting voice. And this is how Ballard has always positioned himself rhetorically, insisting in interview after interview that because England was to him a completely foreign country (as with the past, they do things differently there) he viewed its landscape, its people, its social forms and its cultural codes from an alien perspective. Thus despite his alter ego's confident prognostications that Lunghua Camp will provide a key to England, the transition from a colonial and significantly Americanised reality to a parochial and largely decaying English milieu proves that mapping one in terms of the other is fraught with difficulties. The slippage between these two imaginative worlds opens up the creative space in which Ballard's fiction operates. It gives rise to a series of indeterminate, liminal zones that permit the writer to engage in an exploratory, speculative cartography of the contemporary everyday, which has over time drawn on the estranging resources of science fiction, Surrealism, and Pop Art. If it has proved difficult to 'place' Ballard within a 'map' of post-war British fiction (a difficulty to which every one of his critics attests) then this is because his work engages in an idiosyncratic 'mapping' process of its own; Ballard's oeuvre insists that neither the history of the twentieth century nor the significant features of the contemporary landscape can properly be grasped in the terms of conventional narrative forms. For Ballard, it is not just a question of cross-breeding genres and unsettling the boundaries between them – although this kind of disturbance, so ably analysed by Roger Luckhurst, is a key feature of his work – but of tackling the overdetermined and hybridised nature of late-twentieth-century life in literary forms that can do some sort of justice to its confusions, ambiguities and perhaps unresolvable dilemmas.[1]

Uneasiness characterises Ballard's relationship with his adopted country and with all the literary modes he has deployed. He has repeatedly expressed his disapprobation of the prevailing literary culture of the 1950s, and he has heaped scorn on the overt moralism associated with the then hegemonic Leavisite tendency (*UG* 138). This hostility is in turn bound up with that wider sense of alienation from England as a whole touched on above. In response to a question about the British landscape, Ballard responds bluntly: 'Didn't like that. Didn't like the English psychology, the class system ... Didn't like anything about it at all ... still don't!'[2] Ballard's hostility to post-war English life manifested itself more specifically in his rejection of a socially rooted fiction based on psychological realism, the development of character, and the close observation of cultural codes. These were for him out-dated and parochial literary forms incapable of engaging with the far-reaching changes that were taking place at a dizzying speed. Ballard admired Graham Greene for his engagement with a world beyond English shores, but he considered extreme modernist experimentation (instancing Joyce's *Ulysses* as an example) to be a self-defeating preoccupation with technique at the expense of subject matter, and his lack of patience with this kind of innovativeness extended to Robbe-Grillet's experiments with the *nouveau roman* and to Abstract Expressionism's focus on the surface of the painterly canvas. Neither social realism nor modernist self-reflexivity could in his view adequately respond to the transformation of post-war life visible in a burgeoning youth culture open to the popular and the new; the gradual transformation of male–female relations in both the public and private spheres; the growing openness about sexuality; the increasing visibility of a drug culture; the psychological influence of the United States on the English imaginary, especially with respect to the Cold War, atomic bomb tests, and its powerful popular iconography; above all, perhaps, the tentacular spread of the communications industries. To engage with these ambiguous phenomena within the parameters of a stable literary form characterised by narratorial omniscience, psychological depth and linear progression was a contradiction in terms. Thus Ballard praised William Burroughs, a great influence on his own work, for his unflinching acceptance not just of the sleazy realities of contemporary life but of the need to express the multiple sociolects through which those realities are articulated: 'Whatever his reservations about some aspects of the mid-twentieth century, Burroughs accepts that it can be fully described only in terms of its own language, idioms and verbal lore. Dozens of different argots are now in common currency; most people speak at least three or four separate languages, and a verbal relativity exists as important as any of time and space' (*UG* 126). Noting that Ballard's persistent traversal of generic boundaries makes him hard to classify, James Goddard and David Pringle settle for describing him simply as a 'contemporary' writer, a fair epithet.[3]

Science fiction provided one escape route from the social limitations and stultifying conventions of literary realism. It opened the door to preoccupations typically ignored by the mainstream writers from whom Ballard was alienated, and it enabled him to align himself with a 'popular' genre that mocked the overweening pretensions of so-called 'high' art. Science fiction, Ballard has insisted, is the authentic literature of the twentieth century: it is a form of writing that occupies the middle ground between the death of the written word and the dominance of the visual image, concentrates on the far-reaching implications of technology for everyday social life, invents new myths through which contemporary existence can be given imaginative shape, and offers a powerful means of accessing the unconscious. Ballard's earliest short stories made a quick impact on the science-fiction scene and helped to establish him as an important new voice. He was lauded as a leading representative of the New Wave school of British science-fiction writers who were published by *New Worlds*, the innovative magazine principally associated with the editorship of Michael Moorcock. Ballard's first short story was published in 1956, to be followed by around fifty further stories in the next decade. This frenetic pace gradually slowed down thereafter, partly because Ballard was now also writing novels. *The Wind from Nowhere* was published in 1962, and was soon followed by *The Drowned World* (*DW*; 1962), *The Burning World* (1964) – later retitled as *The Drought* (*D*; 1965) – and *The Crystal World* (*CW*; 1966). Ballard was from the early 1960s publishing short stories and novels in tandem, but the latter began to predominate after 1970. Of all the works he has written since the 1950s, *The Wind from Nowhere* is the only one from which he has distanced himself.

One way of thinking about Ballard's career trajectory is to see it in terms of a shift away from the short story (a shift linked to the economics of book and magazine publishing) toward the novel. This is too tidy a view, which reveals a partial truth but obscures the fact that Ballard has continued to write short stories and that some of his most interesting work may be found in stories such as 'The Ultimate City' (1976), 'The Index' (1977), 'The Intensive Care Unit' (1977), 'Motel Architecture' (1978), 'Zodiac 2000' (1978), 'Memories of the Space

Age' (1982), 'Answers to a Questionnaire' (1985), 'The Enormous Space' (1989), and 'A Guide to Virtual Death' (1992), all of which were written when he was already well established as a novelist. No less problematic is the notion that Ballard abandoned science fiction, not only because several of the late stories clearly belong to the genre but also because several of the novels that are not overtly science fictional in orientation continue to draw on the genre's techniques and preoccupations. All kinds of complex negotiations and renegotiations of forms, themes, styles and genres are in play here, and it is a mistake either to blend them into some over-arching unity or to impose a chronology on the oeuvre that sees it in clear-cut phases. Ballard's works are more profitably seen as engaged in a mapping enterprise that is both diachronic and syntagmatic; his corpus reveals him to be both a historian of the post-war era, who is interested in the unfolding of social developments over time, and a cartographer of the contemporary period, who is committed to forging connections between phenomena that for most observers are unrelated. Inasmuch as these two imperatives drive Ballard's work they take it in all sorts of unexpected directions precisely because, as with Burroughs, the hybrid nature of late-twentieth-century life demands a flexibility of approach and an openness of form. Each of Ballard's texts is an experiment (although he dislikes the term) – an exercise in coming to terms with and elaborating some aspect of the contemporary world that seems to require this particular structure or that particular mode, all in an attempt to do justice to the heteroglossic chaos of present-day existence, marked as it is by 'the overlapping, jostling vocabularies of science, technology, advertising, the new realms of communication.'[4] Ballard has noted that his 'inventions of imaginary landscapes' are attempts to 'place oneself, to find oneself, to give oneself a certain sense and a set of map references, so one knows where one is', but this form of cartography is not prescriptive – it creates 'road signs' that 'point to possible directions', a way of thinking that aligns this process with the Deleuzian 'map' rather than with the 'tracing', a point I develop more fully in my second chapter.[5]

Ballard's adoption of science fiction underscored his rejection of a certain version of 'England', but this seemingly filiative act was no less troubled than that of his initial disaffiliation, for he has always been an awkward presence within the science-fiction fold, pretty much from the outset chafing at the genre's constraints and, as a key member of the science-fiction New Wave, pushing it in new

directions. The writers associated with the New Wave sought to
extend the range of science-fiction writing and to align it with experimental, modernist, and/or avant-garde practices. In Ballard's case,
this led to polemical calls for a decisive move away from fantasy evocations of outer space, which he considered juvenile and uninterest-
ing, and a conscious turn to the fast-moving and explosive reality of
1960s culture. Hence his call, as early as 1962, for an experimental,
abstract, analytical, and formally 'cool' science fiction that would have
nothing at all to do with outer space but would function as a speculative ideas laboratory.[6] This was hardly the kind of rallying cry to appeal
to most practising science-fiction writers or to their hard-core fan
base, but it revealed the extent to which Ballard (along with several
other writers) was something of a maverick with regard to science fiction, a fact about him that is brought out by his observation to David
Pringle that although he believes 'that sf is the true literature of our
day ... in a way the trouble with science fiction is that the wrong people
have written it' – namely those who refused to extend its
possibilities.[7]

Irony succeeds to irony here, for Ballard's election of science fiction
as a valid literary mode turns out to be predicated on his refusal of the
very features that made it successful and popular, but this refusal, an
attempt to kill off an earlier manifestation of the genre, is fully in
keeping with the hidden history of science fiction, which in Luckhurst's powerful analysis attempts to attain the legitimacy of the 'literary' by repeatedly killing off its earlier avatars, especially those
associated with the tightly coded, formulaic products of the pulp era.[8]
Yet if Ballard's work cannot easily be subsumed under the rubric of
science fiction then this is only in part because of his dissatisfaction
with what he saw as its generic constraints; of equal significance is his
concern to distance himself from its enthralment to a future of unlimited possibilities, which he countered with a number of end-of-the-
road fictions that depicted an entropic, depleted world in which the
future had failed to materialise and was now nothing but a derelict
zone bestrewn with abandoned ruins, discarded machines, and cryptic icons. Consider, for example, this opening to 'The Dead Astronaut'
(1968):

> Cape Kennedy has gone now, its gantries rising from the deserted
> dunes. Sand has come in across the Banana River, filling the creeks and
> turning the old space complex into a wilderness of swamps and broken

concrete. In the summer, hunters build their blinds in the wrecked staff-cars; but by early November, when Judith and I arrived, the entire area was abandoned. Beyond Cocoa Beach, where I stopped the car, the ruined motels were half hidden in the saw grass. The launching towers rose into the evening air like the rusting ciphers of some forgotten algebra of the sky. (*The Complete Short Stories; CS* 760)

A typically Ballardian opening, this description of a junk-ridden, deserted, but strangely evocative landscape calls for an act of decoding through which the lineaments of a failed future, now consigned to history, may be glimpsed. As in several of Ballard's stories, it is the psychological and cultural importance of the space programme that is at issue here, and the characters who arrive on this scene of disaster are witnesses to its overweening but perhaps laudable ambitions. Such stories adopt a fictionalised historical perspective: narrated from the vantage-point of an imagined future, they tease out the inner meaning of the attempt to compass space and explore the implications of its abandonment. The half-submerged buildings and launch-pads, over-run by a mineral world indifferent to human aspiration, are the poignant remnants of a language that needs to be reconstructed from the available fragments. Reconstruction of this kind, along with the subversion of assumptions, are marked features of Ballard's writing style. In his stories and novels he makes use of two techniques that contribute to these processes of reconstitution and defamiliarisation: the opening *in medias res*, which plunges the reader straight into a series of events that are already under way, before tracking back to the beginning; and the adoption of a perspective that portrays the central protagonist as though he were misguided, while the conventionally accepted reality is depicted as though it were entirely unobjectionable, an ironic strategy that invites readers to question their habitual acceptance of social norms, especially when the central character is in the end shown to be far from deluded. It is a technique that enables the writer to exploit ambivalence and uncertainty, as Ballard makes clear in an interview: 'Is your doctor really trying to cure you or is he a sinister psychopath who is actually trying to maim you? Are the police defenders of right, or are they naturally professional criminals? Science fiction is full of these reversed roles, and you can play on these ambiguities'.[9]

Ballard's early stories and novels played on such ambiguities by inventing a hallucinatory present that exaggerated the dominant characteristics, pressures and agendas underlying everyday social life. He was 'interested in the real future' that he 'could see approaching, and less in the invented future that science fiction preferred' (*CS* ix). When it was objected that the exotic desert resort in which several early stories are set was an implausible depiction of the future, Ballard responded by insisting that he was drawing on contemporary life to construct a parallel reality that tried to reconceptualise the world from an oblique angle of vision: '*Vermilion Sands* isn't set in the future at all, but in a kind of visionary present – a description that fits the stories in this book and almost everything else I have written' (*CS* ix). Because realism seemed inadequate to the task of creative mapping Ballard was drawn to a style of writing that communicated much of what it had to say through its evocation of physical landscapes with symbolic, mythic and psychological connotations. Influenced by the Surrealists' insistence that the prosaic world concealed realities that were inaccessible to the fettered rational mind, Ballard shared their conviction that one of art's appointed tasks was the revelation of hidden links between ostensibly unconnected phenomena. This insistence on connections that were difficult to perceive – not least because they were subjected to cultural and political repression – led in two directions: on the one hand, to investigative, analytical texts that anatomised social life in an attempt to uncover its motive forces, a kind of angry imaginative assault on numerous perversions of the truth about contemporary reality; and, on the other hand, to rhapsodic, restitutive texts that integrated the prosaic with the marvellous in an effort to escape the constraints of a finite space-time continuum with all its brute phenomenological reductiveness. The first of these trajectories focused on issues such as urbanisation, the death of cities, population explosion, environmental damage, scientific and technological change, the influence of the mass media, the destructiveness of war, the proliferation of atomic weapons, and the effect on everyday life of an increasingly image-based culture. The second tendency explored themes of metamorphosis and transfiguration in texts that tried to evade the tyranny of linear time or to overcome the strife of a conflict-torn world.

Science fiction, Surrealism, Pop Art

Ambivalence and uncertainty feature prominently in Surrealist art and writing, which, along with Pop Art, have been major influences on Ballard's writing. Surrealism has been a marked presence in his

work from the outset, while Pop Art proved to be particularly influential in the late 1960s and early 1970s when Ballard produced two
ground-breaking and still largely unassimilated texts: *The Atrocity
Exhibition* (1970) and *Crash* (1973). There are, of course, obvious links
here. Those associated with Pop Art drew for their images on popular
magazines, and some, such as Roy Lichtenstein and Eduardo
Paolozzi, were influenced by science fiction especially. Nor is there
any necessary incompatibility between Surrealism and science fiction, unless the latter is restricted to the inter-galactic themes that Ballard disavowed. For Ballard there was in fact a resonance between the
analytic and psychologically charged science fiction he was writing
and the exploration of the wayward interactions between the unconscious psyche and an unfathomable external world that was associated with Surrealism. Science fiction and Surrealism could both be
read as forms of a resolutely non-sentimental artistic naïve, which
offered a means of departing from accepted norms and received
accounts of reality (*UG* 97), and thus produced the kind of 'cognitive
estrangement' that critics such as Darko Suvin have seen as an indispensable feature of science-fiction writing.[10]
   Science fiction offered Ballard a way of exploring and perhaps
coming to terms with the unprecedented scale of twentieth-century
social and technological change, a way of grasping how and why
human life had developed in the ways that it had. Surrealism provided
a technique for generating insights into the hidden logics that motivated these developments; in yet another version of estrangement, it
laid bare the unconscious processes that informed key aspects of
external public life. At the same time it sought to overcome divisions
– between self and world, the rational and the irrational, the conscious and the unconscious – sublating them in a liberatory synthesis. When Casey Fredericks describes the mythic dimension of
science fiction as an attempt to transcend or to reject 'the breach
between fantasy and cognition, or between myth and reason, or
between intuitive imagination and rational intellect', which then combines the 'analytical/critical' with the 'mystical/visionary', he might
just as well be referring to Ballard's work as to Breton's.[11] The latter
famously wrote: 'I believe in the future resolution of these two states,
dream and reality, which are seemingly so contradictory, into a kind
of absolute reality, a *surreality*, if one may so speak.'[12] The new forms
of expression sought by the Surrealists through dream association,
automatic writing, and collage were to free the mind from the unitary

control of reason, and co-workers in the Surrealist *recherches* such
as Pierre Reverdy insisted that the turn to dreams represented a
deepening of thought, not its antithesis.[13]

Ballard, in turn, writes of Surrealism's invocation of 'a heightened
or alternate reality beyond that familiar to our sight or senses' as follows: 'What uniquely characterizes this fusion of the outer world of
reality and the inner world of the psyche (which I have termed "inner
space") is its redemptive and therapeutic power' (*UG* 84). He linked
this enterprise with the form of science fiction that he himself was
trying to create, arguing 'that speculative fantasy, as I prefer to call the
more serious fringe of science fiction, is an especially potent method
of using one's imagination to construct a paradoxical universe where
dream and reality become fused together' (*UG* 200) – a quintessential Surrealist aspiration, as Ballard acknowledged in an interview: 'I
am interested in the surrealists altogether, because I am a great
believer in the need of imagination to transform everything, otherwise we'll have to take the world as we find it, and I don't think we
should ... We should re-make the world ... The madman does that ...
The psychopath does that ... But the real job is to re-make the world in
a way that is meaningful, you see ... And that's what surrealism
does'.[14] As in Blake's *The Marriage of Heaven and Hell* (1792), a poem
whose themes resonate through several of Ballard's texts, the aim
here is not to synthesise opposites but to maintain the invigorating,
creative tension between them in order to open up new ways of
seeing. Blake's claim that if 'the doors of perception were cleansed
everything would appear to man as it is – infinite/For man has closed
himself up, till he sees all things through narrow chinks of his cavern'
chimes with Sanders's insight in *The Crystal World* into the significance of the crystallising forest: 'There the transfiguration of all living
and inanimate forms occurs before our eyes, the gift of immortality
a direct consequence of the surrender by each of us of our own
physical and temporal identities. However apostate we may be in
this world, there perforce we become apostles of the prismatic sun'
(*CW* 169).[15]

The Surrealist attempt to overcome the debilitating duality of subject and object by merging the visions of the unfettered unconscious
with the experience of mundane life was animated by a desire to unite
the sacred and the profane in a marvellous lyricism. Central to the
quest for this higher synthesis – a *sur-realité* – was the rejection of
constraining limits, the insistence on thinking and experiencing the

world anew in order to untrammel desire and to open the self up to as yet unimagined ways of perceiving and being. Breton's description of the required state of receptive wonder captures the spirit of several of Ballard's texts, perhaps most notably *The Crystal World* and *The Unlimited Dream Company* (*UD*; 1979): 'Behind ourselves, we must *not let the paths of desire become overgrown*. Nothing retains less of desire in art, in science, than this will to industry, booty, possession. A pox on all captivity, even should it be in the interest of the universal good, even in Montezuma's gardens of precious stones! Still today I am only counting on what comes of my own openness, my eagerness to wander *in search* of everything, which ... keeps me in mysterious communication with other open beings, as if we were suddenly called to assemble.'[16] Several of Ballard's early novels and short stories portray the period of waiting (*l'attente*) not as dead Beckettian time in which nothing happens but rather as the necessary prelude to far-reaching change. Mary Ann Caws notes that for Breton the 'readiness for an undefined event, in all its openness, permits the advent of the marvelous', and in much of Ballard's work such openness is explicit in the 'zones of transit' through which his central protagonists willingly pass.[17]

Ballard's early works are near obsessed with themes of metamorphosis. The post-apocalyptic worlds they envisage, in which so-called civilised life is stripped bare by drought, deluged by floodwater, or frozen in time by the crystallisation of living matter, are all in limbo, awaiting rebirth to a radically new dispensation. The search for some path out of a seemingly endless purgatorial present manifests itself most obviously in the behaviour of the early novels' central protagonists, each of whom is at once an outsider who refuses to accept the existing situation and a questor eager to meet the challenge that it offers. In *The Drowned World* Kerans disassociates himself from the community of scientists who cling to an out-moded rationalism and heads into the heart of the danger, in full knowledge 'that his own life might not long survive the massive unbroken jungles to the south' (*DW* 174); in *The Drought* (1965) Ransom embraces the new reality emerging around him, thereby proclaiming 'his involvement with the changing role of the landscape and river, their metamorphosis in time and memory' (*D* 40); and in *The Crystal World* Sanders returns to the forest that almost killed him, unable and unwilling to abandon the dream of regeneration exemplified in his 'curious premonition of hope and longing, as if he were some fugitive Adam chancing upon a

forgotten gateway to the forbidden paradise' (*CW* 79). Metamorphosis in these novels is not just a question of theme, functioning like an
easily evulgated plot-strand; it is integral to the entirety of their textual
constructions. The style in which Ballard's early texts are written is a
key feature of their ambivalent power: it evokes the slippery elusive-
ness of the border-zone that lies between the real and the fantastic,
persistently blurring them together and refusing to commit to the
over-riding validity of one over the other. This style proclaims its affinity with Rimbaud's 'alchemy of the word' and with the Surrealists'
dream of raising human life out of a deadening drudgery through the
transformative power of a marvellous lyricism.

An expanded conception of the mind lies at the heart of Ballard's
early novels and stories. In these works the strange, haunting landscape exteriorises inner experiences that are otherwise inarticulable.
It is above all these experiences – and the psychological changes to
which they give rise – that interest the writer. This points to another
parallel with Surrealism, namely that its drive to release repressed
desires – which drew on depth models of the mind principally derived
from Freud – was orientated toward the experience of the individual
rather than the social group, and this in spite of its chequered and
largely unproductive relationship with the Communist Party. Surrealism shared Dada's contempt for the over-valuation of human reason
and endeavoured to give free rein to fantasy. Raymond Williams cor-
rectly sees in this tendency a 'celebration of creativity which finds
many of its sources in the irrational, in the newly valued unconscious,
and in the fragments of dreams', and it should be noted that this celebration reflects a kind of apotheosis of the individual, the *self* becoming the most important reference point for change of any kind.[18]
Eugene Jolas, the editor of the avant-garde 'little magazine' *transition*,
and a Surrealist fellow-traveller, articulated this view when he
described creativity as the gateway through which 'a new type of man
… a universal being, an harmonious being, synthesizing in himself
the impulsions of the spirit and the social sense of the twentieth century' would emerge.[19] A similar view of creativity and of the need for
psychological transformation motivates much of Ballard's writing.
He has referred to himself as 'a kind of pilot … a sort of representative
of the free spirit, the imagination', and there is here a concern to
envisage both how an alternative world might look and how the mind
might change in response to the challenges the new world would represent.[20] Early novels such as *The Drowned World* (1962), *The Drought*

(1965), *The Crystal World* (1966), and the *Vermilion Sands* (*VS*; 1971) stories – discussed in the next chapter – put a positive gloss on this process of self-exploration while later works such as *The Unlimited Dream Company* (1979), *The Day of Creation* (*DC*; 1987), and *Rushing to Paradise* (*RP*; 1994) – analysed in my third chapter – provide a darker reading of self-deification as the expression of the untrammelled monstrous ego, a reading that looks ahead to Ballard's exploration of nihilism in *Millennium People* (*MP*; 2003).

But despite Ballard's oft-repeated alignment of his writing with Surrealist painting, his work should not be seen as little more than an off-shoot of Surrealism. Surrealism plays a role in his imaginative landscapes and offers potent ways of seeing through the surface truths of social phenomena but is not the master-key that unlocks the door to his fictional world. Pop Art is an equally significant influence on Ballard's writing, and it is in the course of a discussion with Paolozzi that he explains why Surrealism can no longer be an exact model for the contemporary writer:

> Surrealism moulds the two worlds together, remakes the external world of reality in terms of the internal world of fantasy and fiction. Now what has happened, and one reason why there are really no Surrealist painters in the true sense of the term today, is that this position has been reversed. It's the external world which is now the realm, the paramount realm of fantasy. And it's the internal world of the mind which is the one node of reality that most of us have. The fiction is all out there. You can't overlay your own fiction on top of that. You've got to use, I think, a much more analytic technique than the synthetic technique of the Surrealists. Eduardo does this in his graphics. He's approaching the subject-matter of the present-day exactly like the scientist on safari, looking at the landscape, testing, putting sensors out, charting various parameters.[21]

Remaking the world imaginatively has always been a key feature of Ballard's writing, but it has also been motivated by a strong analytic tendency, a drive to uncover and to understand the hidden logics that inform everyday social life. When writing in this mode Ballard conducts inquests or post-mortems. He dissects the body of contemporary culture with scalpel-like precision, deploying a deliberately 'cold' technique that has often incorrectly been seen as lacking moral engagement and emotional passion. The point is worth stressing, as Ballard himself did in his interview with Alan Burns: 'I regard myself as a very emotional writer. I write out of what I feel to be a sense of great urgency and commitment ... the moral and psychological pres-

sure is very strong ... I use the language of an anatomist'.[22] Surrealism
was in Ballard's view of limited use in this respect, partly because the
reversal of the fiction–reality dyad meant that the external world had
become the phantasmatic realm previously associated with the
hidden depths of the unconscious, and partly because its desire to
overcome division, to bring about a synthesis of disparate psychological and phenomenological elements, threatened a premature resolution of contradictions. For Ballard, to superimpose a private
mythology onto an already heavily fictionalised social reality was then
not to uncover its inner truth but rather to proliferate further fantasies. A more distanced, abstract and constructivist technique was
needed if the real force-fields at work in present-day culture and society were to be traversed.

Pop Art provided a corrective not only to Surrealism but also to the
parochialism of a fictional tradition (the social novel) that was in Ballard's view blind to the material reality and cultural iconography of
contemporary life. Because this tradition, especially through its preoccupation with class, made sense of the present in terms of the long
shadow of the past, it was retrospective in orientation. Ballard was
hostile to this way of thinking: 'I wasn't interested in the English past
– and the reason why, which I discovered when I first came here, was
that the English past had led to the English present. One wanted to
press the plunger and blow the whole thing up'.[23] Ballard experienced
Pop Art as an imaginative liberation because it refused to disavow the
materiality of culture, treating the growth of technology, consumerism and the mass media as the everyday data to which the arts
should respond, and as the substance out of which their works should
be assembled. Pop was also linked to science fiction. It was an art of
the now, and for Ballard science fiction was an art form that should
be (even if it often was not) an art form concerned with interpreting
the present. The iconography of Pop, its interest in the charm but also
the expendability of technological products – as ephemeral media
images, as gleaming and erotically charged fantasy objects, as frivo-
lous gadgets doomed to obsolescence – encapsulated the day-glo
allure of a fast-moving contemporaneity that was at the same time
destined to end up as just so much junk. Lawrence Alloway's view that
the media provided 'an inventory of Pop technology' in which 'the
missile and the toaster, the push-button and the repeating revolver,
military and kitchen technologies' collided calls to mind Ballard's
claim that 'the subject matter of science fiction is the subject matter

of everyday life: the gleam on refrigerator cabinets, the contours of a wife's or husband's thighs passing the newsreel images on a colour TV set, the conjunction of musculature and chromium artefact within an automobile interior, the unique postures of passengers on an air-port escalator – all in all, close to the world of the Pop painters and sculptors, Paolozzi, Hamilton, Warhol, Wesselman, Ruscha, among others' (*UG* 207).

But at the same time, Pop was committed to 'looking at subtexts and hidden agendas in the consumer landscape' just as Ballard was doing in his 'early science fiction', and it was the constructivist nature of Pop Art's collages and assemblies that especially influenced the form Ballard's own writing would take in the late 1960s and early 1970s.[24] In emphasising this aspect of Pop Art Ballard downplays what was also a Surrealist preoccupation, but it seems as though Bal-lard felt that Surrealism's emphasis on the individual unconscious deflected attention away from a social unconscious that was being exteriorised on a daily basis in the realm of public life, and that Pop Art's interventions were better able to analyse its constellations. It would not be an overstatement to say that Ballard's writing is obsessed with the hidden codes that determine contemporary life, nor to suggest that his oeuvre represents an exercise in decipherment. Equally important, however, is the use of what Ballard, following Chomsky, has called 'transformational grammars' – linguistic sys-tems that recode the ciphers once their hidden meaning has been exposed. Crucially, however, this recoding does not take the form of creating a new fixed system out of the old one but rather of breaking the latter up into numinous fragments and then juxtaposing these in speculative collage-like assemblages that are provisional and open. As Paolozzi elliptically put it in *The Metallization of a Dream* (1963): 'Assembly decided on the floor of the workshop; creative decision on several levels. Spontaneity meets discipline and so these simple objects grew in assembly into new positive forms.'[25]

It is here that Surrealism meets Pop Art in Ballard's work. Christo-pher Finch usefully draws attention to the linguistic dimension of Pop Art when he describes its artists as entering 'the field of com-parative linguistics – correlating dialects, searching for unexpected structural links between styles, uncovering portmanteau images', a description that chimes with Ballard's account of the multivocality found in the novels of Burroughs.[26] Paolozzi, a close friend of Ballard's, not only utilised the techniques of the assembly in his

sculptures but also created a series of works inspired by Wittgen-
stein's philosophical reflections on language. In Paolozzi's work, as
in Pop Art more generally, the content of everyday life in the form
of mass-produced objects is inseparable from a semiology of their
multiple meanings in an increasingly commodified and mediated
culture. Referring to Paolozzi's interest in the media landscape of the
1960s, Finch emphasises the fusion of materiality with language in
his work: 'His method ... has been to programme material drawn
from this landscape – from Mickey Mouse to transistor circuits –
re-energising this material in new contexts. Language structures are
superimposed upon one another to produce new patterns of syntax'.[27]
The production of original patterns of syntax, in an effort to lay bare
the grammars of a technological and media-dominated world, lies at
the heart of Ballard's work in texts such as *The Atrocity Exhibition* (*AE*;
1970), *Crash* (*C*; 1973) – the subject of my second chapter – as well as
Concrete Island (*CI*; 1974), and *High-Rise* (*HR*; 1975), which I analyse
in my fourth chapter. Hence Ballard's observation that although the
Pop painters 'liberated the external environment' in that they 'perceived it at first glance', it had become necessary 'to look at the external environment at second glance and look beyond the worlds of
consumer goods and mass iconography', a task on which he himself
embarked with an uncompromising rigour.[28]

Wayward logics

Ballard's most notorious and difficult texts are without question *The
Atrocity Exhibition* and *Crash*, both of which have provoked reactions
of distaste and revulsion. Robert Scholes and Eric S. Rabkin describe
Ballard's work as 'a fiction of extremities, in which the horrible is
commonplace', and their uneasiness with *The Atrocity Exhibition* is
clear from their claim that 'the ghastly collages of Ballard have
brought the form as far as possible toward encompassing its potential
terror.'[29] Both books are apocalyptic renderings of the hidden and
possibly deviant logics of the technological age, focusing on its implications for human subjects in a fictional study of violence, psychopathology and perversion. But whereas *Crash* is formally a
straightforward first-person narrative, *The Atrocity Exhibition* is an
experimental work, a collage of 'condensed novels', each of which is
in turn a fragmented text divided up into sections that resonate with
each other thematically but eschew all the traditional props of realist

narrative: linearity, psychological consistency, social context, authorial omniscience. Every chapter functions as a self-enclosed entity in
its own right, but interacts in suggestive ways with all the other chapters. By cutting out what he considers to be the unnecessary building
blocks of narrative, Ballard produces a multi-perspectival work in
which scenes are rotated so that 'each episode can be inspected from
a number of angles' and the text is not looked at solely 'from one ele-
vation'.[30] The chapters are all linked by shared preoccupations, which
run through the novel: the celebrity culture of the 1960s; the power
of the telecommunications industries to mediate reality; the assassinations of iconic figures (most notably John F. Kennedy and Marilyn
Monroe); the phenomenology of space-time; the death of affect; the
social significance of the space programme; and the prevalence of violence in a society increasingly in thrall to an apocalyptic imaginary
haunted by images of an impending World War Three, which is figured here as a possibly redemptive conceptual cataclysm. But
although these preoccupations are run together, they do not explain
each other, as though one might provide a key to another, but rather
are made to rub up against each other – as in Surrealist automatism
– the resultant friction producing new combinations of meaning. Ballard describes the effect of this technique as achieving a 'critical mass'
that generates 'crossovers and linkages between unexpected and previously totally unrelated things, events, elements of the narration,
ideas that in themselves begin to generate new matter.'[31]

But inasmuch as most critics have found both texts hard to stom-
ach, it is *Crash* that has caused the greatest problems, largely because
its lapidary depiction of 'the nightmare marriage between sex and
technology' (*C* 6) refuses to flinch from the implications of its thesis,
whereas the fractured structure and estranging modality of *The Atrocity Exhibition* produce a more distanced representation of its no less
disturbing subject. And a veritable cottage-industry of criticism has
developed around *Crash*, initially in response to Baudrillard's account
of the text as a morally neutral testament to the dissolution of all distinctions between fiction and reality, which then translates both
realms into 'a kind of hyperreality that has abolished both', and more
latterly in response to Cronenberg's film version of the novel.[32] Critics
who have objected (often vociferously) to Baudrillard's reading of
Crash have argued that he not only interprets it as the fictional exem-
plification of his own theories but also ignores its moral critique of the
psychopathology it dramatises. Thus for Vivian Sobchak, *Crash* is self-

evidently a cautionary tale, which 'is vigorously about the human body abstracted, objectified, and literalized as techno-body – and Ballard's vision sees this techno-body as driving us, quite literally, to a dead end', while Nicholas Ruddick suggests that the 'death-oriented sexuality in *Crash* is an extended metaphor for this insatiable cultural death-lust.'[33] The claim that *Crash* is not based on the articulation of desire but is structured around the principle of the death-drive has also been eloquently made about the film of the book.

I have a good deal of sympathy with these views, and I shall offer similar arguments (although for somewhat different reasons) in my discussion of *Crash*. But I want to note here that the text is more ambiguous than these critics are willing to acknowledge. The novel's brilliance derives in part from its overdetermined nature: it can never finally decide what kind of text it is – a moral tract, or a paean to the joys of sexual violence? This indecision makes it a liminal work that blurs the boundary between the moral and the immoral, and it keeps crossing back and forth between these discourses. It is neither a ludic nor a fashionably relativistic text but rather a serious and unsettling exploration of the ambiguities that arise when easily agreed distinctions between these categories break down. To complicate matters still further, buried within the text is a debate over the respective claims of the domains of morality and aesthetics. How far is the literary imagination entitled to go in its speculations, and to what extent can its productions be said to lie outside the ethical realm altogether? Two antithetical orders of discourse meet in a head-on pile-up here: the crash is as much about this collision between incommensurable value systems as it is about the wrecked cars it describes in such clinical detail. This is a latter-day replay of the Wildean dilemma and its outcome is no less messy. Nor is it the text alone that discloses the difficulty. Ballard's own uneasiness about *Crash* is clear from his shifting pronouncements about it; he himself can never quite decide if it is a cautionary tale with a moral purpose, a deeply immoral and corrupting book, or a dispassionate forensic examination of a repressed cultural logic.[34] Those critics who move quickly to the view that *Crash* is a moral text, a warning against deviant human impulses that are exacerbated by the technological realm, are no less reductive in their reading of what remains a baffling work than Baudrillard is when he reads it as the valorisation of a hyperreality in which the tough moral questions the novel raises are simply air-brushed out of the picture.

After the nightmarish visions of *The Atrocity Exhibition* and *Crash* Ballard produced several dystopian evocations of urban life in texts such as *Concrete Island* (1974), *High-Rise* (1975) and *Running Wild* (*RW*; 1988); the much lauded *Empire of the Sun* (*ES*; 1984), a fictionalised autobiographical account of his experiences during the Second World War, which he followed up with *The Kindness of Women* (1991), a second instalment, as it were, which offered a compelling depiction of England's post-war cultural milieu; and the novels *Cocaine Nights* (*CN*; 1996), *Super-Cannes* (*SC*; 2000) and *Millennium People* (2003), all of which offer intriguing variations on the genre of detective fiction. Some critics have read *Empire of the Sun* and *The Kindness of Women* as source texts for the Ballardian fictional world, treating them as a form of self-analysis that opens up both the writer and his literary works. This is a naïve view that misconstrues the nature of both books, which are subtle and teasing explorations of narrative form as much as they are accounts of the writer's life. But even with respect to this second aspect of *Empire of the Sun* and *The Kindness of Women* it must be noted that both texts offer highly self-conscious and distanced representations of the life they narrate, and that this life is in turn *read* through the fictions that Ballard had already written. These works are thus involved in two complex dialogues, one between the man and his memories of his earlier self, inseparable now from the sediment of forty years further experience, and the other between the author and his literary oeuvre. If *Empire of the Sun* focuses on a young boy's experiences, humorously exploiting the discrepancy between his insights into his situation and his illusions, then *The Kindness of Women*, which begins by reworking the earlier narrative from yet another perspective, stages a potentially explosive confrontation between these two texts before defusing it in the form of domestic pastoral. The over-excited protagonist of the first text is shown in the second to be rushing headlong to meet the oncoming culture of the 1960s, which seems to have been invented to fulfil his psychic needs. Once these two narratives – the private and the public – finally coincide, the older character is depicted as beginning to understand how cultural and personal pathologies can be mapped onto one another, and the text moves more clearly to the detached language of critique. But it is not so easy to move away from a powerfully embedded psychological trajectory, one that the text has traced with such acuity. It can be deflected onto an all too convenient alter ego (David) but that dark other will always return to haunt the scene, an unquiet memory of the repression upon which this domestic peace rests.

The sense of an ending

Ballard's late novels lay bare the psychopathologies of everyday life in a post-humanist world. The sense of an ending, a historic ending, haunts these books. Time has contracted down to a depleted present stretching out towards a blank future; change is ceaseless and ever more rapid, but it takes place within a globalised, technology-driven system that seems uncannily adaptable and fearfully resolute. This is postmodernity as end-game and terminal zone, the site of a late capitalist colonisation so complete that temporality has been evacuated from it and can only be conceived in terms of spatial extension: more buildings, roads, airports, shopping malls, car parks. Look closely, remarks a Ballardian figure, pointing towards an advancing estate, 'and you can see the future moving towards you' (*MP* 133); beached up on the Costa del Sol, another character describes the 3,000-mile-long Mediterranean leisure-city as 'Europe's future', adding that 'everywhere will be like this soon' (*CN* 23); and a gleaming, computerised corporate estate is simply 'a huge experiment in how to hothouse the future' (*SC* 15). This is the future as more of the same, the future as an interminable present that cannot be imagined as other, the future as post-history. Flexible, decentralised, and geared to the reinvention of its institutions and bureaucratic structures, thus ensuring that it survives by way of mutation, late capitalism is in these texts shown to be both reflexive and static.[35] In Lutz Niethammer's formulation its 'reflexivity signals not the termination of a dynamic structure but dispersal of the hope associated with it'; stasis is not imputed to the system but to its effects, which produce the picture 'of a mortal life lived without any seriousness or struggle, in the regulated boredom of a perpetual reproduction of modernity on a world scale.'[36]

The fear of a life without meaning connects the narratives of *Cocaine Nights* (1996), *Super-Cannes* (2000), and *Millennium People* (2003). Of course, this had been a prevalent theme in much of Ballard's writing, but there is a subtle shift in these novels; whereas the earlier works depict social collapse as originating in the failure of the system, here, with the exception of *Millennium People*, it is the result of the system's *success*. No more the crazed crises provoked by rotting tower-blocks or decaying industrial wastelands, no more the extremism unleashed by the specularisation of atrocity or the violence promoted by the sexualisation of a car-crash culture. In both *Cocaine Nights* and *Super-Cannes* we are in a realm of high-tech perfection, a

cool, plate-glass world in which virtually every aspect of the individual's life is subject to a routine, all human needs have been anticipated, and the entire social mechanism has been calibrated to
minimise friction and disturbance. *Cocaine Nights* is set in a luxury
resort on the Costa del Sol and focuses on a leisure society in which
nothing happens until, unexpectedly, five murders are carried out. A
sun-drenched paradise whose decorticated residents inhabit 'an
eventless world' (*CN* 33), Estrella de Mar is a place of sleep and drift,
a place in which the future has 'come ashore … lying down to rest
among the pines' (*CN* 33) and enforcing 'a special kind of willed
limbo' (*CN* 34) upon its hapless inhabitants. *Super-Cannes* takes the
highest echelons of corporate existence as its subject, exploring a
world devoted to and dominated by work, a world in which the individual is subordinated to institutional logics. With the office turned
into an ersatz 'home', and the business-estate providing all necessary
amenities, life is almost entirely controlled by economic imperatives,
houses being reduced to 'service stations, where people sleep and
ablute' and the human body being treated 'as an obedient coolie, to be
fed and hosed down, and given just enough sexual freedom to sedate
itself' (*SC* 17).

    Millennium People differs from these novels in that it is overtly con-
cerned with the apocalyptic imaginary. It returns to the theme of
social breakdown, depicting a middle-class revolt against the values of
bourgeois ideology, and it explores the implications of the nihilist philosophy that underpins the particular variant of terrorism dramatised
here. But this is really just a difference in emphasis, because all three
novels are preoccupied with modernity's failure to deliver its emancipatory promises. *Millennium People* focuses on a will-to-destruction,
which manifests itself as an atavistic response to the fear of absurdity,
and which the novel locates in the mind of a character so outraged by
the world's arbitrariness that he attempts 'to find a desperate meaning in nature's failings' (*MP* 215). *Cocaine Nights* and *Super-Cannes*
alter the angle of vision, locating this destructiveness in the social
realm itself and then tracing its corrupting effects on the lives of those
caught up within it. All three novels are studies in alienation. They are
peopled with characters who are alienated not from the products of
their labour but rather from a depthless, pointless existence in which
the belief that social life could be different in any significant way has
been lost. In an eternal present, no imaginable alternative exists, and
the dream of revolutionising socio-political life melts into the air.

Ballard may be regarded as a compulsive chronicler of the hidden agendas lying behind the most significant developments of the twentieth century, a writer so devoted to uncovering the links between apparently unconnected historical events that at least some of his narratives, especially those of the late 1960s and early 1970s, exhibit a paranoia and a pessimism in keeping with the strange, unsettling occurrences of that period, so brilliantly caught in films such as *The Parallax View, The Manchurian Candidate, Dr Strangelove* and *Blow-Up*. Traven in 'The Terminal Beach' (1964) – the story most closely linked with the preoccupations that would be developed in *The Atrocity Exhibition* – literalises this paranoia in the blockhouses of Eniwetok Island, when 'with a sort of drugged stride, he set[s] off into the centre of the blocks, breaking into a run and darting in and out of the corridors, as if trying to flush some invisible opponent from his hiding place' (*CS* 590). But in another sense, Ballard is an optimist who values many of the achievements of this technological century and is as excited by the energy implicit in its transformation of the world as any of the Italian Futurists ever were, refusing to see its technophilic idealism as nothing but a promethean aberration. Halloway – in 'The Ultimate City' – offers a contrast to the paranoid. Invigorated by the power and beauty of the combustion engine and the skyscraper, he is dismayed by the pallid security of his ecologically responsible community: 'The whole bucolic landscape of Garden City, this elegant but toy-like world of solar sails and flower-filled gardens, the serene windmills and gently nodding reduction gear of the tidal-power machines – all these cried out for a Pearl Harbour' (*CS* 875).

This is a deliberately shocking image, and although 'The Ultimate City' does not endorse this will to destruction, it does suggest that a benign, peaceful world designed on Morrisian lines lacks the gritty textures and edgy uncertainties that make human existence, with all its glorious ambiguities, worth living. This paradox lies at the heart of Ballard's work. His writing cannot simply be regarded as an assault on the technological landscape, although it contributes to a critique of that landscape, because it is not only enamoured of the opportunities opened up by science but also keen to hold onto the benefits it has vouchsafed. Ballard objects to a world that has become mechanised, affectless and aggressive, but he is exhilarated by its electric dreams, so potent, glamorous and unpredictable. Inasmuch as his writing traces the sinister trajectories often taken by a potentially world-annihilating technology, it also explores the emancipatory hopes and the uneasy pleasures unleashed by the juggernaut of modernity.

Implicit in Halloway's death-dealing fantasy is the Conradian belief that immersion in the destructive element offers the only chance of confronting these ambiguities head-on. The protagonists who receive authorial approval in Ballard's texts embrace the challenges with which they are confronted, welcoming them as portals to new experiences. Some of the ambiguities in Ballard's stories may be traced to this question of response, for inasmuch as they contain cautionary elements, which warn of the dangers of capitulating to technological power, they also insist not just that these dangers must be passed through but that they may, despite appearances and ethical considerations, be beneficial and liberatory. Ballard has suggested that 'our talent for the perverse, the violent, and the obscene, may be a good thing' and that we 'may have to go through this phase to reach something on the other side, it's a mistake to hold back and refuse to accept one's nature'.[37] This commitment to the logic of the quest can then be read as a form of optimism, and this is what enables Ballard to claim that his is 'a fiction of psychic fulfilment' because it encourages his characters to discover 'the truth about themselves' even if this process of discovery culminates in their deaths.[38]

It is a compelling view with a long intellectual history behind it. But it is also a view that, despite the author's pronouncements, is problematised right through his paradoxical oeuvre, an issue to which I return in the 'Coda' to this book. There is an enormously complex interplay in his writing between the notion of an authenticity of selfhood and the recognition that human beings have been transformed into subjects, terminal clusters who exist by virtue of the machines that program them and the codes that inform them how to think and act. What it might mean to speak of an authenticity or truth to the self in this context is not at all clear. This is not just because we are in the realm of what Scott Bukatman calls terminal identity, a 'doubled articulation' that marks 'both the end of the subject and a new subjectivity constructed at the computer station or television screen' through which, as Darko Suvin puts it, 'Debord's and Burroughs's addictive image-virus is reproducing within all of us, manipulating our takes on reality.'[39] It is also because the innate perversity that Ballard attributes to human organisms seems to destine them to embrace this decentred, cybernetic subjectivity as though it were the perfect conduit for their most wayward fantasies, individuals willingly (insofar as it is meaningful to invoke will in this context) jacking into the systems that already control them. And if one trajectory within this nightmare imaginary culminates in subjects who are simply channels for the technological and media logics that articulate them and speak through them, then its other trajectory can only result in the absolute negation of the symbolic realm through acts of meaning-defying terror, the final signs of a desperate desire to find psychic peace in a zone of nothingness.

Notes

1 See R. Luckhurst, 'The Angle Between Two Walls': The Fiction of J. G. Ballard (Liverpool: Liverpool University Press, 1997).
2 C. Bresson, 'J. G. Ballard at Home', Métaphores 7 (March 1982): 5–29, p. 5.
3 J. Goddard and D. Pringle (eds), J. G. Ballard: The First Twenty Years (Hayes, Middlesex: Bran's Head Books, 1976), p. 1.
4 E. Paolozzi, Writings and Interviews, ed. R. Spencer (Oxford: Oxford University Press, 2000), p. 204.
5 A. Burns and C. Sugnet, 'J. G. Ballard', in A. Burns and C. Sugnet (eds), The Imagination on Trial: British and American Writers Discuss their Working Methods (London: Allison and Busby, 1981), pp. 16–30, p. 18; W. Self, 'Conversations: J. G. Ballard', in Junk Mail (London: Penguin, 1996), pp. 329–71, p. 341; G. Deleuze and F. Guattari, A Thousand Plateaus: Capitalism and Schizophrenia, trans. B. Massumi (Minneapolis and London: University of Minnesota Press, 1996), pp. 3–25.
6 See 'Which Way to Inner Space?' in Ballard, UG, pp. 195–8.
7 D. Pringle, 'J. G. Ballard', Interzone (April 1996): 12–16, p. 15.
8 R. Luckhurst, 'The Many Deaths of Science Fiction: A Polemic', Science Fiction Studies 21. 1 (March 1994): 35–50.
9 Burns and Sugnet, 'J. G. Ballard', p. 24.
10 For 'cognitive estrangement', which Suvin derives from Brecht, see D. Suvin, Metamorphoses of Science Fiction: On the Poetics and History of a Literary Genre (New Haven and London: Yale University Press, 1979), pp. 3–16.
11 C. Fredericks, The Future of Eternity: Mythologies of Science Fiction and Fantasy (Bloomington: Indiana University Press, 1982), p. 176.
12 A. Breton, Manifestoes of Surrealism, trans. R. Seaver and H. R. Lane (Ann Arbor: University of Michigan Press, 1972), p. 14.
13 See M. Nadeau, The History of Surrealism, trans. R. Howard (London: Jonathan Cape, 1968), p. 93, footnote 16.
14 Bresson, 'J. G. Ballard at Home', p. 7.

15 W. Blake, *The Complete Poems*, ed. W. H. Stevenson (London: Longman, 1990), p. 114.
16 A. Breton, *Mad Love*, trans. M. A. Caws (Lincoln: University of Nebraska Press, 1988), p. 25.
17 M. A. Caws in Breton, *Mad Love*, p. 126, footnote 1.
18 R. Williams, *The Politics of Modernism: Against the New Conformists* (London: Verso, 1990), p. 52.
19 E. Jolas, 'Super-Occident', *transition* 15 (February 1929): 11–16, p. 12.
20 Bresson, 'J. G. Ballard at Home', p. 8.
21 Paolozzi, *Writings and Interviews*, p. 199.
22 Burns and Sugnet, 'J. G. Ballard', p. 19.
23 Self, 'Conversations', p. 339.
24 Self, 'Conversations, p. 334.
25 E. Paolozzi, *The Metallization of a Dream* (London: Lion and Unicorn Press, 1963), p. 5.
26 C. Finch, *Pop Art: Object and Language* (London: Studio Vista/Dutton Pictureback, 1968), p. 20.
27 Finch *Pop Art*, p. 158.
28 Paolozzi, *Writings and Interviews*, p. 202.
29 R. Scholes and E. S. Rabkin, *Science Fiction: History, Science, Vision* (Oxford: Oxford University Press, 1977), pp. 89, 96.
30 Burns and Sugnet, 'J. G. Ballard', p. 24.
31 J. Goddard and D. Pringle, 'An Interview with J. G. Ballard', in Goddard and Pringle (eds), *J. G. Ballard: The First Twenty Years*, pp. 8–35, p. 30.
32 J. Baudrillard, 'Two Essays', *Science Fiction Studies* 55. 18. 3 (November 1991): 309–19, p. 312.
33 V. Sobchak, 'Baudrillard's Obscenity', *Science Fiction Studies* 55. 18. 3 (November 1991): 327–9, p. 328; N. Ruddick, 'Ballard/*Crash*/Baudrillard', *Science Fiction Studies* 58. 19. 3 (November 1992): 354–60, p. 357.
34 Goddard and Pringle, 'An Interview with J. G. Ballard', p. 31; Burns and Sugnet, 'J. G. Ballard', pp. 22–3; Bresson, 'J. G. Ballard at Home', pp. 24–5.
35 For a good discussion of these issues, see R. Sennett, *The Corrosion of Character: The Personal Consequences of Work in the New Capitalism* (New York: W. W. Norton, 1998).
36 L. Niethammer (in collaboration with D. Van Laak), *Posthistoire: Has History Come to an End?* trans. P. Camiller (London: Verso, 1992), pp. 2, 3.
37 Burns and Sugnet, 'J. G. Ballard', p. 23.
38 Bresson, 'J. G. Ballard at Home', p. 17.
39 S. Bukatman, *Terminal Identity: The Virtual Subject in Postmodern Science Fiction* (Durham and London: Duke University Press), p. 9; D. Suvin, 'Novum is as Novum Does', in Karen Sayer and John Moore (eds), *Science Fiction, Critical Frontiers* (London: Macmillan, 2000): pp. 3–22, p. 6.

1

Cryptic alphabets

Ambiguity and ambivalence are the hallmarks of J. G. Ballard's short stories. Not for Ballard the simple resolution or the comforting coda. The economy of form offered by the short story has enabled him to concentrate tightly on particular topics while opening them to further speculations. His stories bristle with ideas and images that linger long after the tales have been read, sparking off new trains of thought and inviting considered reflection. Many of the stories return to certain abiding preoccupations, which they rework from alternative perspectives, as though trying to get at some tantalising truth that has still to be captured. Ballard has referred to 'their snapshot quality, their ability to focus intensely on a single subject', pointing out that they are 'a useful way of trying out the ideas later developed at novel length' (CS ix), something he did with great success when he developed 'The Illuminated Man' (1964) into *The Crystal World*. The short stories are a laboratory for the exploration of themes to which Ballard returns again and again, both in later stories and in longer novels, and the reworking of themes – which occurs from yet another perspective (that of fictionalised autobiography) in *Empire of the Sun* and *The Kindness of Women* – is a major feature of all his writing.

Many of Ballard's stories extrapolate from present-day conditions in order to create plausible possible futures by trying to envisage how key aspects of late twentieth-century life might develop if their hidden inner logics are exposed. The 'real future' that Ballard 'could see approaching' (CS ix) is evoked in the visionary present of the Vermilion Sands stories, which look ahead to a world dominated not by work but by leisure. Described by Ballard as 'largely the product of advanced technologies of various kinds', Vermilion Sands is 'an exurbia of the future', and the main characteristic of this strange realm is 'that everything is over'.[1] This is a resort that has itself been beached up, since its 'past lies behind it, and nothing that can happen in the future will substantially change it again.'[2] Some of Ballard's earliest stories, such as 'Prima Belladonna' (1956) and 'Venus Smiles' (1957), both published in *Science Fantasy* magazine, are set in Vermilion Sands, a zone out of time and a dream of lassitude. There is nothing shabby or dull about Vermilion Sands, which rather 'celebrates the neglected virtues of the glossy, lurid and bizarre' (*VS* 7), glorying in a garish aesthetic influenced by Art Deco chic, Hollywood kitsch, and Pop Art glitziness. Even when its days of splendour have long passed, the resort's love affair with a fabulous hedonism is blazoned forth by its exotic architecture. Already an atemporal holiday zone, Vermilion Sands becomes a limbo in the early stories, the events narrated in it occurring during a period of complete inactivity, a 'world slump of boredom, lethargy and high summer' (*CS* 1). The resort is thus transformed into a liminal space in which the normal laws of reality are temporarily suspended, and this permits interlopers such as the exotic Jane Ciracylides ('Prima Belladonna'), the enigmatic Lorraine Drexel ('Venus Smiles'), or the mystical Aurora Day ('Studio 5, The Stars') to weave their disruptive magic.

In keeping with the resort's atmosphere of decadent glamour, the representation of these mythical and celluloid figures has a stylised *fin-de-siècle* air about it. All these stories are concerned with the themes of metamorphosis and transfiguration that also dominate *The Drowned World*, *The Drought* and *The Crystal World*. Jane Ciracylides, an archetype projected by the unconscious, is 'poetic, emergent, something straight out of the primal apocalyptic sea' (*CS* 2). At once ominous and captivating, she is an image of inexplicable sexual potency with the capacity to destabilise social relations and a dream-figure who offers to re-enchant the world through the visions she induces. But her real interest lies not with the ineffectual men who live out a desultory existence in Vermilion Sands but with the narrator's sonic plants, especially his rarest exhibit, a Khan-Arachnid, and when the passionate consummation between flower and woman finally takes place it culminates in an embrace of death. Jane Ciracylides is a typically ambiguous creation. The allure of her singing does not destroy the male figures haunted by her voice, but then they are not her principal addressees; like Prufrock's mermaids, singing each to each, orchid and siren have ears and voices only for each other, and this conjunction displaces the men altogether. If their lives are temporarily rejuvenated by the female archetype's metamorphic power, they themselves are bystanders of the real drama who are rendered insignificant by a scene of seduction that absolutely excludes them. With the woman's disappearance the interregnum within an interregnum comes to an end and the visionary, sensual realm that she briefly enabled the male figures to glimpse makes way for a lacklustre world in which labour reinstates the codes of masculinity that, significantly, prevent reflection on the meaning of the events that have just transpired: 'Not long afterwards the Recess ended, and the big government schemes came along and started up all the clocks and kept us too busy working off the lost time to worry about a few bruised petals' (CS 11).

'Venus Smiles' explores transfigurative female power in a different way. Lorraine Drexel, a famous sculptor, is commissioned to make a sonic sculpture for the resort's central square, but her stark metal construction is universally deplored. This unsettling work of art is a technological monstrosity: 'With its pedestal the statue was twelve feet high. Three spindly metal legs, ornamented with spikes and crosspieces, reached up from the plinth to a triangular apex. Clamped on to this was a jagged structure that at first sight seemed to be an old Buick radiator grille' (VS 40). A form of technological *bricolage*, this awkward metal machine deploys industrial materials in order to refuse an aesthetic of visual beauty and naturalistic representation, asserting its place as an object created out of other objects – those that make up the modern world. The narrator is shocked by the dehumanised sculpture that is revealed – the 'whole structure of scratched chromium had a blighted look like a derelict antenna' (VS 40) – and he is still more disturbed when this apparent parody of industrial waste starts to emit discordant, unmusical sounds that are indistinguishable from the noise of traffic. There follow a number of failed attempts to cut the statue down to size, to put a stop to its strident music-making, but like so many uncontrollable scientific creations the sculpture reconstitutes itself again and again, functioning as an industrial-gothic symbol of untrammelled technological voraciousness. When the statue is melted down, in an attempt to destroy it, the metal is recycled for industrial use and turns up in the girders of the town's new buildings, which start to hum and vibrate just as the sculptor had intended. But in a typical Ballardian twist, what had seemed to be a fearful deformity, a product of technological detritus, now turns out to be an instrument of beguiling beauty, no longer a threat but rather a portal to a new harmony. The visionary world briefly opened up by Jane Ciracylides is here linked to a transformed technology that is now associated not with mindless power but with aesthetic beauty. The initially discordant sounds emitted by the sculpture turn into a music that is perfectly attuned to the technological world out of which it comes and to which it belongs, and the narrator is elated by its implications: 'Did you say it was all over? Carol, it's only just beginning. The whole world will be singing' (CS 49).

The theme of transformation crops up again in 'Studio 5, The Stars' (1961), which associates the mythic figure of Aurora Day with Dalí's 'Cosmogonic Venus' in its exploration of how creativity is returned to a group of poets whose verse is being written by machines. 'Studio 5, the Stars' draws on the story of Melander and Corydon, creating a narrative that hovers between realism and fantasy. The story makes use of one of Ballard's favourite techniques – the reversal of perspectives – in order to mock the narrator's assumptions about creativity and poetic value. Aurora Day is an overdetermined figure who inundates the narrator with scraps of poetry that reprimand him for his unthinking belief that contemporary poetry, which is churned out mechanically by Verse Transcribers, should be nothing more than a series of elaborate technical exercises. This empty conception of writing seems fitting for an ennui-filled existence in which all aspiration has been stifled. Aurora Day is the avatar of an alternative realm – that of myth in this case – the illusions of which are more real than the simulacrum of life within which the story's characters waste their days. At stake here is the question of what role art might play in a post-technological age: is its relevance to life so negligible that it has been reduced to mannerism and pastiche, capable of nothing more than mechanical reproduction of once auratic forms? Aurora Day offers an alternative vision in which the revivifying power of words transforms everyday existence by overspreading its every dimension, an ambition that is hinted at in the story's opening paragraph, when the narrator finds 'fragments of the poems everywhere' (CS 208), and that is fulfilled when he finds that everything is 'covered with the same fragments', including his own body, now become 'a living manuscript in which the ink still ran, the letters running and changing as if the pen still cast them' (CS 220). Initially horrified, the narrator eventually accedes to the goddess's vision and, in fulfilment of the myth, rejects the machined poetry produced by the Verse Transcribers and finds his creativity reborn.

The textual representation of all these female figures draws overtly
on a gendered symbolism based on the codes of myth, fiction and
cinema. David Pringle sees them as figures of the lamia, noting that
they 'are reminiscent of Jungian Anima figures' and suggesting that
they are prototypes of all the author's women characters, since the
lamia is 'the essential figure' in his fiction.[3] But Ballard's conventional
use of this gendered imagery has the double function of exposing the
self-defeating nature of male fantasy and the vulnerability of masculine social identity. In this future, men have been made redundant in
more ways than one; it is not only that the field of work, such a key
determinant of that identity, now lies permanently fallow, but also
that a life of enforced leisure has made them spectators of their own
lives. The twist here is that a world given over to leisure takes away the
traditional male *raison d'être* and reveals that masculinity, bereft of the
public props out of which it is constructed, is a redundant product, fit
only for the post-technological scrap heap. If some of Ballard's other
stories – such as 'The Overloaded Man' (1961), 'The Subliminal Man'
(1963) or 'The Enormous Space' (1989) – evoke a longing to resist
coercive and exploitative socio-economic systems then the Vermilion
Sands stories hint at one consequence of what might happen if this
dream of escape were to be fulfilled. The longing for escape is ques-
tioned and undermined in these stories for the quite precise reason
that it represents a threat to masculinity itself, a theme that Ballard
later developed in *Rushing to Paradise*. Inasmuch as the conventional
female figures of these early texts are predictably associated with a
threat to male identity, what emerges no less clearly is that the deeper
threat comes from technology, which will destabilise sexed identity
and human relationships more thoroughly than anything else. The
epitaph that might then be written for masculinity in this exurbia is a
simple one: no future.

Inner landscapes

Faith in the truth-telling power of dreams suffuses J. G. Ballard's
imaginative worlds. The events portrayed in his fictions have an
uncertain ontological status, their significance deriving less from
what occurs than from the meanings imputed to them by the novels'
protagonists. The symbolic atmospheres that surround and permeate
the events depicted in his works exemplify a form of Conradian technique: their meaning lies 'not inside like a kernel but outside,

enveloping the tale which brought it out only as a glow brings out a haze, in the likeness of one of these misty halos that sometimes are made visible by the spectral illumination of moonshine.'⁴ *The Drowned World* begins with a *tour-de-force* description of sweltering heat and of tentacular jungle vegetation smothering the last remaining outposts of a long-since drowned metropolis, creating an oppressive but hauntingly compelling scene. Kerans, the novel's main character, is temporarily trapped between two intersecting worlds, which exist both in physical space and in his own mind. An uncanny moment of recognition, akin to a form of 'fantastic hesitation', occurs when the text hints that it is a fictional elaboration of Surrealist art:

> Over the mantelpiece was a huge painting by the early 20th-century Surrealist, Delvaux, in which ashen-faced women danced naked to the waist with dandified skeletons in tuxedos against a spectral bone-like landscape. On another wall one of Max Ernst's self-devouring phantasmagoric jungles screamed silently to itself, like the sump of some insane unconscious.
>
> For a few moments Kerans stared quietly at the dim yellow annulus of Ernst's sun glowering through the exotic vegetation, a curious feeling of memory and recognition signalling through his brain ... the image of the archaic sun burned against his mind, illuminating the fleeting shadows that darted fitfully through its profoundest deeps. (*DW* 29)

Whereas the Delvaux canvas offers a proleptic glimpse of the violent, scapegoating carnival that will later pit Kerans against Strangman in 'The Feast of Skulls', Ernst's hallucinatory painting provides a visual counterpart to Ballard's atmospheric prose and functions as a gateway into Kerans's submerged mind. Both art-works are also metonymic representations of *The Drowned World*'s desire to meld different kinds of reality so as to escape the constraints of a worldview based on rationalism. The novel concocts a surrealist textuality in which inward dreams are superimposed onto outward realities: 'Just as the distinction between the latent and manifest contents of the dream had ceased to be valid, so had any division between the real and the superreal in the external world' (*DW* 74).

The Drought, Ballard's next novel, is drawn to a different strand within Surrealism – the cool, spectral forms of Tanguy and the fluid, deliquescing images of Dalí. Two paintings are important to its shape and texture: Tanguy's *Jours de Lenteur* (1937) and Dalí's *The Persistence of Memory* (1931). Whereas *The Drowned World* follows the journey of a man seeking to re-establish contact with the deepest archaic

memories of the human race, *The Drought* traces the path of a figure
trying to free himself from the past. Ballard is a spare, lucid writer,
but these two early novels differ from one another in register and
ambience, one luxuriating in imagery redolent of the lush, exotic and
bizarre, the other confining itself to a bleached prose evocative of the
parched, denatured world it depicts. The stripping down of a landscape gradually reverting to desert once again corresponds to an internal progress that is more significant than the external events
precipitating it. In this text the quest is for release from memory
through a kind of self-purging ascesis – a particular art-work (*Jours de
Lenteur*) standing as an emblem of this aspiration: 'With its smooth,
pebble-like objects, drained of all associations, suspended on a
washed tidal floor, this painting had helped to free him from the tire-
some repetitions of everyday life. The rounded milky forms were isolated on their ocean bed like the houseboat on the exposed bank of the
river' (*D* 11). Tanguy's painting is a talisman warding off the pain of
early trauma. Eroded over long aeons, its objects have had their dis-
tinguishing features erased, turning them into blank forms no longer
subject to the haunting of memory or the passage of time to come.
The gradual disappearance of water as the drought takes hold heralds
a process of questioning and sifting in which all redundant aspects of
the past will be discarded like unwanted scrap. Ransom, the novel's
main character, is mesmerised by this vision of evacuated time, which
signifies respite and peace. As with the visions of Delvaux and Ernst
in *The Drowned World*, so the imagery of the Tanguy and Dalí paintings that permeates *The Drought* suggests that the events depicted
exteriorise psychological adjustments and transformations: 'The
unvarying light and absence of all movement made Ransom feel that
he was advancing across an inner landscape where the elements of
the future stood around him like the objects in a still life, formless and
without association' (*D* 181).

From the outset of *The Crystal World* a similar blurring of boundaries between the outer landscape and the inner mindscape takes
place. Exterior reality reflects internal preoccupations and dilemmas.
The novel's characters project their own feelings and fantasies onto
the sombre scene in which they act their parts, and this blending of
perspectives gives it an eerie hallucinatory feel. Consider this depiction of Ventress, given as Port Matarre and the metamorphosing
forest draw near: 'he was looking out across the deserted starboard
rail into the mouth of the river, and at the distant forest stretching

away into the haze. His small eyes were half-closed, as if he were deliberately merging the view in front of him with some inner landscape within his mind' (*CW* 16). This merging unsettles realist assumptions. Figuring an imagined world that is believable but also inseparable from the minds of its characters, it weaves together a kind of fantastic realism in which the choice between visionary dream and veridical truth is suspended. That said, *The Crystal World* is of the early novels closest to the exuberant lyricism sought by the Surrealists. The novel's sombre opening, with its brooding portrayal of dereliction and darkness, is given a symbolic resonance when the apostate priest Balthus invokes Arnold Böcklin's painting 'Island of the Dead' as the fitting emblem of his sense of foreboding. But despite his fear that the changes taking place in the forest betoken a post-theological world, Balthus sees them as a Eucharistic consummation, while other characters view the crystallising forest as a return to a time before the Fall – to an edenic world in which all of creation pulses in harmony. *The Crystal World* glows with a sense of wonder at an ever-changing world full of unexpected, unlooked for possibilities, a theme developed more fully in *The Unlimited Dream Company*. Suffused with that longing for the marvellous that drove the Surrealist dream of a *surréalité*, its phantasmagoric avatar is the illuminated man:

> He turned to see a brilliant chimera, a man with incandescent arms and chest, race past among the trees, a cascade of particles diffusing in the air behind him. He flinched back behind the cross, but the man had vanished, whirling himself away among the crystal vaults. As his luminous wake faded Sanders heard his voice echoing across the frosted air, the plaintive words jewelled and ornamented like everything else in that transmogrified world. (*CW* 167)

The new environments depicted in the early novels are post-apocalyptic. *The Drowned World* creates a prescient vision of global warming, envisaging a geophysical transformation that raises the earth's temperatures so high that the polar ice-caps melt, deluging the planet with oceanic floods that sweep vast quantities of topsoil away, thus entirely remaking its geography and biosphere. *The Drought* depicts a parched, starving earth and traces the source of the calamity back to the routine dumping of industrial waste in the seas; *The Crystal World* offers a vision of what might happen if anti-time were to collide with time, their intersection resulting in stasis, a leaking away of temporality concretised in the novel through the crystallisation process that embalms all living things in a glittering carapace of frozen jewels. In these novels the changes that have already occurred are the preliminary stages of further transformations to come, but these are internal rather than external: they are responses to the challenge posed by altered environments, a challenge that enables them to remake their identities in a process of individuation. For Ballard, the willingness to confront catastrophe and to work through its consequences is indispensable to psychological growth:

> My characters behave in a paradoxical way. In many cases, they embrace Death, but that doesn't mean I am pessimistic. In fact, they find fulfilment. I think that all of my fiction is optimistic because it's a fiction of psychic fulfilment ... The characters find after a long journey of self discovery, gradually, the truth about themselves. They find a logic with this running. They realize that to find themselves, they must follow that logic, even if it means their own death.[5]

Archaeopsychic time

The question of identity lies at the heart of *The Drowned World*. It is bound up with scepticism as to the validity of the scientific outlook, which the novel, focalised through Kerans's consciousness, presents as the cornerstone of a superseded modernity. Two perspectives are thus placed in opposition to each other, and the disjunction between them is central to the text's *modus operandi*. The mobile scientific testing station for which Kerans works maps the emerging land-masses and lagoons, studies the new ecosystem, and evacuates the various remaining refugees, carrying them to safety as it moves northwards, away from the life-threatening heat of the south. The testing station combines two public functions: scientific and administrative. In its scientific capacity it endeavours to get to grips with the changing nature of the world in order to adapt to it; in its administrative role it polices the movements of individuals. A roving government outrider aiming to gain control over the environment through its cartographic project, it tries to bring order to the civic life that has been destroyed. Kerans is detached from these imperatives. Although he is one of the scientists on the testing station, he is sceptical about its purpose, since he believes that the environmental changes taking place portend transformations of a more significant order. For Kerans, the work of the testing station is a ruse of power, a government-sanctioned obfuscation of the true issues that need to be faced: 'The

biological mapping had become a pointless game, the new flora
following exactly the emergent lines anticipated twenty years earlier,
and he was sure that no one at Camp Byrd in Northern Greenland
bothered to file his reports, let alone read them' (*DW* 8–9).

There is a shift here from the exigencies of public policy to the free-
doms of private speculation, always for Ballard the guarantor of the
imagination's autonomy and power. But the idea that a science
focused on external manifestations (climate change, biological mutation, topography) cannot engage with their hidden effects on the
psyche is equally significant. The contrast between these perspectives
is established when Kerans chooses to live in what is left of the Ritz
hotel instead of remaining on the testing station: 'He had comman-
deered the Ritz the day after their arrival, eager to exchange his
cramped cabin among the laboratory benches at the testing station for
the huge, high-ceilinged state-rooms of the deserted hotel. Already he
accepted the lavish brocaded furniture and the bronze art nouveau
statuary in the corridor niches as a natural background to his existence, savouring the subtle atmosphere of melancholy that surrounded these last vestiges of a level of civilisation now virtually
vanished forever' (*DW* 9).

The testing station's spartan, functional habitat is all bustling
activity, while the Ritz glows faintly with a languid opulence that
emblematises Kerans's inner frame of mind and signals the final dissolution of the submerged world. Kerans has at this stage neither
grasped what is taking place nor understood his own role within it,
but in choosing the hotel he reveals an emotional readiness to come
to terms with the past, which he implicitly recognises must be left
behind. Whereas the scientists' work is a form of denial, a psychic
defence against change, Kerans's affinity with the hotel's melancho-
lia suggests that he has begun the process of mourning and will reject
the confining mentality of Camp Byrd and the north just as he has
removed himself from the restrictive living conditions of the testing
station. The incompatibility between these two viewpoints is articulated more directly when Kerans's acceptance of his destiny is shown
to mark him out from those who hold onto superseded techniques of
living and pointless habits: 'What completely separated them now
was the single fact that Riggs had not seen the dream, not felt its
immense hallucinatory power. He was still obeying reason and logic,
buzzing around his diminished, unimportant world with his little
parcels of instructions like a worker bee about to return to the home

nest' (*DW* 75). For Kerans, the United Nations assumption that social existence will continue on the old established lines is clearly wrong, leaving him to conclude that an entirely different kind of cartography is needed: 'A more important task than mapping the harbours and lagoons of the external landscape was to chart the ghostly deltas and luminous beaches of the submerged neuronic continents' (*DW* 45).

Kerans is fascinated by and drawn to the aquatic realm, although he recognises that the hold it exerts over him may be feeding regressive fantasies of a return to uterine bliss and thus preventing him from moving forward. The fantasy of a return to a pre-conscious state of undifferentiated unity leads him to make a near fatal dive, leaving him unsure if he has been the victim of an accident staged by Strangman or if he has attempted to commit suicide. The question is finally unanswerable, but the drowning (in a chapter titled 'The Pool of Thanatos') is described in a way which suggests that the pull of the ocean is connected to a desire to pass from waking life into the soothing embrace of death. The ambiguity that surrounds the drowning lies at the heart of the novel, for the lure of the water is associated with threat and succour in equal measure. Immersion in the lagoons may gesture towards the safety of the womb, but it is also a passage into the domain of the lizards. The link is forged in Kerans's dreams of this nightmarish, prehistoric landscape in which 'the powerful mesmeric pull of the baying reptiles' (*DW* 71) is felt as an internal presence that pulls him to almost certain death. Although he is petrified of these giant amphibians, he identifies their braying calls with the rhythmic movements of his own heart. This suggests that the peace to be found in the amniotic sac cannot be disassociated from archetypal fears. It may then be that Kerans's complicity with his near drowning represents his last attempt to evade the challenge of confronting this transformed world.

The rationalist explanation for what is happening is provided by Bodkin, who argues that the massive rise in the earth's temperature has reversed evolution, driving the planet back through geological time until it has reached the Triassic period, a process accompanied by a parallel transition in the human mind that has returned it to the very origins of human consciousness. By recapitulating the biological history of the earth, the new environment has triggered mankind's most ancient and most repressed unconscious memories. The terrifying jungle dreams – Jungian archetypes – experienced by the novel's characters are race memories dredged up from

the unconscious and embodied in physical form by the giant, shriek-
ing reptiles that are once again becoming the lords of creation. For
Jung, the archetypes emerge out of the dark abysm of time, giving
rise to a 'collective unconscious' that 'is an image of the world that
has taken aeons to form' and in which 'the archetypes or dominants
have crystallised out in the course of time.'[6] And just as psychoanalysis demands that trauma be 'worked through' if it is to be
accommodated, so *The Drowned World*'s characters are given the
choice of confronting these archaic demons or of evading them.
Bodkin insists that the new psyche is undergoing 'a total reorientation of the personality', telling Kerans that if 'we let these buried
phantoms master us as they re-appear we'll be swept back helplessly
in the flood-tide like pieces of flotsam' (*DW* 44–5). Once Kerans
accepts the need to *act*, to meet the challenge of this internal conflict,
he is ready to break out of the larval state and undergo the necessary
psychological metamorphosis:

> The shattering of this shell, like the piercing doubts about his true
> unconscious motives set off by his near drowning in the planetarium,
> was the necessary spur to action, to his emergence into the brighter day
> of the interior, archaeopsychic sun. Now he would have to go forward.
> Both the past, represented by Riggs, and the present contained within
> the demolished penthouse, no longer offered a viable existence.
> (*DW* 147)

But before Kerans can commit to the future he must come to terms
with the aptly named Strangman, whose strange behaviour plays a
decisive role in Kerans's neuronic odyssey. Whereas Riggs is the stiff-
backed epitome of military rigidity, who represents a limited understanding of events, Strangman is a bizarre interloper from the
unconscious, as envisaged in Surrealist art: 'Suddenly he remembered the Delvaux painting, with its tuxedoed skeletons. Strangman's
chalk-white face was like a skull, and he had something of the skele-
ton's jauntiness' (*DW* 94). Strangman seems to have stepped straight
out of a canvas so as to assert himself in a world to which he does not
belong. Straddling the border between reality and artifice, the conscious and the unconscious, he is a spook come to haunt an emerging future, functioning as a figure of Freud's 'uncanny'. Vindictive
and malevolent, he is a warning from the depths of nightmare; with
his albino skin drained of blood and his preternaturally white suits, he
is a zombie-like avatar of death, a 'white devil out of a voodoo cult'

(*DW* 158). An obvious *Doppelgänger* – the despised dark side of Kerans's psyche – Strangman is also Kerans's symbolic opposite at the level of culture. The latter's lack of interest in the remnants of the civilisation that has been destroyed stands in contrast to Strangman's desire to reclaim the cities only in order to despoliate them. Strangman's looting is a pointless activity; he surrounds himself with the treasure of an extinct civilisation in a futile attempt to hang onto its material and cultural value, treating these residues of the past as the means by which he can accrue symbolic capital, a defensive strategy as misplaced as Riggs's rationalist faith in order and the scientific method. This avariciousness hints at the rapacious aspects of the old society, especially in relation to urban life, as is revealed when he drains the lagoon: 'With the reappearance of the submerged streets and buildings his entire manner had changed abruptly. All traces of courtly refinement and laconic humour had vanished; he was now callous and vulpine, the renegade spirit of the hoodlum streets returning to his lost playground' (*DW* 123).

The symbolic battle between Strangman and Kerans centres on the significance and relevance of the past to any future life. The reclaimed city is both the sign of this conflict and the site on which it is played out. Strangman stages a mythic confrontation between Kerans and himself, casting Kerans in the role of Neptune, while he positions himself as an earth-bound deity. Inasmuch as Riggs represents one version of a reliance on the displaced civilisation – with his commitment to social order, military discipline, and rationalism – Strangman signifies its hidden history, the repression of the primal violence on which these social norms have been erected, and is thus a fitting reminder of Benjamin's claim that for the historical materialist 'without exception the cultural treasures he surveys have an origin which he cannot contemplate without horror.'[7] In Strangman we witness the reversion of enlightenment to myth, a retrogression away from the achievements of civilisation back to inferior magics. His attempt to overthrow Kerans takes the form of a scapegoating ritual enacted through a carnivalesque feast of skulls that turns Kerans into a totem of abjection forced to take upon himself this culture's refuse and waste.

The obvious symbolic link between Riggs (control) and Strangman (chaos) suggests that they be read as opposed sides of the same dialectic: both belong to an older episteme and to the form of life that produced it. The differences between them only make sense *within* the terms of a conceptual system and a way of living that embraces them both. The bond between them is emphasised when Riggs notes that Strangman's act of reclamation will be praised in political circles since urban regeneration is what the government wants to promote. Fundamentally different versions of reality are at stake in a moment that is a textual crux: Riggs and Strangman may be buccaneer and policeman, but like the anarchists and police in Conrad's *The Secret Agent*, they are bound by the same law, the same system, and it is this over-arching framework that gives their roles any meaning that they might have. Caught up together in a shared conception of the old social habitus, they merely represent its opposed poles: chaos/order, crime/law, id/ego. Refusing (unable) to see any significance in the changes taking place and trying to restore modes of life that belong to a compromised past, they belong to the dialectic Kerans has broken away from in his views that these changes are so far-reaching that an entire re-orientation of the mind and of social life is unavoidable. There is a subtle twist here on the ending of William Golding's *Lord of the Flies*. In that work, the unexpected arrival of the naval officer, just as the descent into barbarism is reaching its brutal climax, effects a sudden *volte-face*, awakening Simon to reality; in *The Drowned World* the equally unexpected return of Riggs and Macready has the opposite effect, leaving Kerans 'unable to accept wholly the idea of Riggs' reality' and convinced that his crew are 'flat and unreal, moving about their tasks like intelligent androids' (*DW* 157–9). Kerans's self-transformation opens him up to an archaeopsychic dimension through which he will emerge renewed, whereas Strangman's and Riggs's desire to reverse time aligns them with a superseded civilisation whose dead puppets they are. Once Kerans has made the necessary paradigm shift, he is committed to his interior neuronic odyssey, even as the text's closing lines make it clear that his quest for a lost utopia may, perhaps fittingly, end nowhere but in the realm of mythic dream: 'So he left the lagoon and entered the jungle again, within a few days was completely lost, following the lagoons southward through the increasing rain and heat, attacked by alligators and giant bats, a second Adam searching for the forgotten paradises of the reborn sun' (*DW* 175).

The crying land

The Drought, Ballard's next novel, concludes in much the same fashion as *The Drowned World*, with the novel's central figure setting off once more on the next stage of his solitary quest. If anything, the inward significance of his journey is more marked than in the previous work, a point underscored in the text's penultimate paragraph and rammed home in its last line, which informs the reader that he has failed to notice the coming of the rain that has been absent throughout the entire preceding narrative. The final folding of exteriority into interiority not only emphasises that the two dimensions have been blurred in the story just narrated but also suggests that the inner reality has been the more significant of the two: 'To his surprise he noticed that he no longer cast any shadow on to the sand, as if he had at last completed his journey across the margins of the inner landscape he had carried in his mind for so many years ... An immense pall of darkness lay over the dunes, as if the whole of the exterior world were losing its existence' (D 233). The text's *terminus ad quem* is the fulfilment of a psychological odyssey.

Ballard's descriptions of physical expanses are a form of psychological notation, offering clues to often inarticulable emotional processes. *The Drought* takes this technique further. In this text the landscape is made to speak, a strategy that looks ahead to the semiotic concerns of a later text such as *The Atrocity Exhibition*. If *The Drowned World* urged a kind of breaking out from the husk of outmoded ways of thinking and living, then *The Drought* is more willing to accept the inescapability of historical residues. It is revealing that technology has no significant role to play in the earlier work; Ballard gives basic information about the work of the testing station but seems uninterested in either the impact or the future relevance of technology. This perhaps explains why he has suggested that these early novels are not so much allegorical works about the end of the British Empire but rather texts that explore 'the end of technology' and thus more properly 'the end of America'.[8] The passage through the psyche back to the origins of human life, in preparation for a metamorphosis of the mind that draws on archetypal patterns and the collective unconscious, encapsulates that novel's imaginative terrain. But although *The Drought* is equally concerned with the need for psychological change, it depicts a more obviously recognisable world, which is everywhere stained by industrial waste and strewn with technological detritus. This is a historicised landscape, the denatured creation of ecologically irresponsible practices. It is not just that the drought, which has been caused by large-scale environmental damage, acts as a scourge but that the earth has become the perverse *product* of this damage. Abandoned cars, collapsed dwellings, rusting machines, stranded boats, festering rubbish, smashed lightships, corroding iron, smouldering fires, parched reservoirs, derelict cities – these are the physical features of *The Drought*'s post-apocalyptic topography and its new vocabulary.

The point here is that *this* landscape, *this* reality, constructed out of industrialism's wreckage, must provide the starting point for imagining alternatives. No facile transition from one form of life to another is envisaged in this dark text. The technology that has made the world what it is thus seems to function both as blight and as source of renewed activity. There are numerous examples of this: Philip Jordan creating 'his own world out of the scraps and refuse of the twentieth century' (*D* 22); Ransom constructing a home out of 'rusty motor-car bodies' that have been 'piled on top of one another' (*D* 144); Johnson's community building a settlement with a distillery out of old, discarded equipment; and, most optimistically, Lomax with his fantastic pavilion 'constructed from assorted pieces of chromium and enamelled metal – the radiator grilles of cars, reflectors of electric heaters, radio cabinets and so on – fitted with remarkable ingenuity to form what appeared at a distance to be a bejewelled temple' (*D* 213). Yet the ambivalence of the novel's depiction of this post-technological *bricolage* is nowhere more clear than in the brutal irony with which Ballard treats Philip's lovingly reconstructed car. The vehicle is a hearse, fit only for carrying the dead to their burial grounds, and it is also non-functional; despite its shining bodywork, it cannot start because the battery no longer has any power. Appearing to Ransom 'like an embalmed fragment of an unremembered past' (*D* 171), the automobile mutely asks whether this particular past is re-usable in any form, a question that *The Drowned World* has already answered in the negative.

In *The Drought* the signs are not promising, as its world scarcely functions at all. The desolation of the land progressively closes life down, forcing its inhabitants to scrape a minimal existence, and a kind of frozen stasis ensues. People communicate less and less, each retreating into isolation in order to concentrate on survival, and their withdrawal leaves the earth to fuse with the remnants they scatter behind them. Ransom's shack has been reclaimed from the stern of a wrecked ship in which 'the engine room and gangways had rusted into grotesque hanging gardens of corroded metal' (*D* 143), and this bric-a-brac creation has taken on a gothic life of its own: 'Its bulging shell, puffed out here and there by a car's bulbous nose or trunk,

resembled the carapace of a cancerous turtle' (D 144). The journey
back to the city abandoned ten years earlier is punctuated by similar
sights: 'They stopped in the shade below the bridge, and looked out at
the endless expanse of the dry bed framed within its pillars. In the
afternoon light the thousands of shadows cast by the metal refuse covered the surface with calligraphic patterns' (D 183). Everywhere in evidence, these patterns have turned the landscape into a script
over-written by a far from beneficent technology, making it a
palimpsest through which a new, but scarcely intelligible, language
can be glimpsed. Thus the text is full of references to deformed natural objects that endeavour to communicate some sort of message,
from 'the dead trees' that form 'brittle ciphers on the slopes' (D 14) to
the plumes of black smoke that drift away 'like the fragments of an
enormous collapsing message' (D 42). Calligraphic patterns, brittle
ciphers, collapsing messages – all attempts at communication, but
with no easily decodable meaning, as though this topographic inar-
ticulacy is in itself a rebuke to the arrogance of human speech. Perhaps this is the impulse behind the image of 'the crying land' (D 37),
which discloses its suffering wordlessly and inaugurates linguistic
conventions that call the entire human enterprise into question: 'She
was looking out over the bleached bed of the river, and at the brittle
trees along the banks, ciphers suspended in the warm air. Ransom
began to speak, but this cryptic alphabet seemed to overrule anything
he might say' (D 97).

And little is indeed said in this novel, the blighted landscape
appearing to supersede and to silence human speech altogether. Its
ultimate meaning may be cryptic, but this ruined topography appears
to signify a post-humanist order clearly enough. Tanguy's *Jours de
Lenteur*, that achromatic vision of denatured objects suspended in
some time-stripped void is a key reference point, representing as it
does a dream of erasure, a forgetting attainable only when long aeons
have passed. This painting is a mediating presence in the text, offering an imaginative alternative to the two kinds of disaster that have
overtaken its central protagonist: the despoliation of the earth, and the
shattered relationships that he wants to cast from his mind. Both
forms of damage provide a sharp reminder of the depredations of
public and private history, whereas the Tanguy offers a vision of stasis
and peace. This may be a distant aspiration, but in the here and now
human identity is already slipping away, to be folded back into the
stark landscape that shapes and defines it. Consider these reflections

of Ransom's: 'The four people with him were becoming more and more shadowy, residues of themselves as notional as the empty river. He watched Catherine and Mrs Quilter climb on to a fallen steel girder that spanned the stream, already seeing them only in terms of the sand and dust, the eroding slopes and concealed shadows' (D 112).

The determining role of landscape in the formation and sustenance of identity is a major theme in the second part of the novel – the ten-year period of subsistence on the beach. During this transitional period of waiting the external trappings of identity are stripped away, leaving only the most hard-won, recalcitrant aspects of the self in place:

> Like all purgatories, the beach was a waiting-ground, the endless stretches of wet salt sucking away from them all but the hardest core of themselves. These tiny nodes of identity glimmered in the light of the limbo, the zone of nothingness that waited for them to dissolve and deliquesce like the crystals dried by the sun. (D 146)

The beach is a purgatory because it represents a volitionless and eventless horizon. The awaited translation of the self into some new form, which first requires its disintegration, cannot occur in this dead zone. But the dissolution of subjectivity that takes place in this zone is reminiscent of the ground-down, depleted Surrealist canvas, although there is a subtle difference:

> The beach was a zone without time, suspended in an endless interval as flaccid and enduring as the wet dunes themselves. Often Ransom remembered the painting by Tanguy which he had left behind in the houseboat. Its drained beaches, eroded of all associations, of all sense of time, in some ways seemed a photographic portrait of the salt world of the shore. But the similarity was misleading. On the beach, time was not absent but immobilized; what was new in their lives and relationships they could form only from the residues of the past, from the failures and omissions that persisted into the present like the wreckage and scrap metal from which they built their cabins. (D 147)

This suggests that the strategy of *bricolage* that has been deployed with respect to the environment now needs to be adopted in the realm of human relationships, which must be rebuilt from the fragments into which they have fractured. The Tanguyan escape from temporality would then be read as an impossible fantasy, a dream of translating the restlessness of the human into the stasis of the inorganic. Ransom's attempt to break with the past, whose residues, like the rust

shimmering on the surface of the landscape, are for him the signs of
an inescapable taint, thus represents a desire for uncontaminated
relationships. The trauma of personal suffering and extreme environmental damage (from which the Tanguy painting offers release)
have coalesced to produce a vision of purity, a *tabula rasa* out of which
an entirely new identity, freed of all past history and limiting communal ties, may be forged in an unalloyed form. This radically inner,
radically isolated reality is in turn an emblem of Tanguy's haunting
landscape, as seen in the post-technological world that everywhere
surrounds Ransom and that makes him feel that he is 'advancing
across an inner landscape where the elements of the future stood
around him like the objects in a still life, formless and without
association' (*D* 181).

There is, however, another aspect to this search for a new identity
untarnished by previous associations, namely that it also represents a
dream of reconciliation. Towards the end of the novel Ransom makes
reference to a possible merging and resolution of the residues of the
past, an idea that reverses the previous Tanguyan trajectory: 'he now
felt that the white deck of the river was carrying them all in the opposite direction, forward into zones of time future where the unresolved
residues of the past would appear smoothed and rounded, muffled by
the detritus of time, like images in a clouded mirror. Perhaps these
residues were the sole elements contained in the future, and would
have the bizarre and fragmented quality of the debris through which
he was now walking. None the less they would all be merged and
resolved in the soft dust of the drained bed' (*D* 186). As it turns out,
absolution will depend on a final coming to terms with the wounds of
the past and of forging conciliatory relationships in an as yet
unknown future. Ransom reads the purging experience of the
drought as a necessary prelude to change – it is a cleansing of individuals that permits them to recreate themselves and their relationships with others. What I have already described as his purist fantasy
of self-fashioning should then be seen not as narcissistic solipsism
but rather as a passionate desire to forge a utopian community in
which the old dominative bonds no longer have any sway, and this
gives the novel a social dimension that is entirely lacking from the
radical individualism of *The Drowned World*. The religious significance of Ransom's name, and the desert-like environment, should
not go unnoticed here. Associated variously with the Old Testament
Jonah and with the figure of Christ, Ransom is the only character who

brings succour to others, and he does so in ways that are symbolic: giving water to Grady after Johnstone, a Christian minister, has refused it; freeing Jonas from the burning pulpit and salving his brow; carrying his adopted family away to the sea and then, ten years after their exodus, safely bringing them back again. It is Ransom who at the start of the novel is committed to the river community and who at its end dreams of a new communal dispensation: 'Simultaneously he would become the children's father and Quilter's brother, Mrs Quilter's son and Miranda's husband' (D 226).

But in sounding these religious echoes, the novel signals its distance from their point of origin, treating them as little more than the faint reverberations of a belief system that has long passed into desuetude. If Ransom is in any way a salvific figure, he is not a redeemer with the personal power to transform others but rather a reinterpreter of a discredited way of life. Central to this dimension of *The Drought* is its complex re-working of Shakespeare's *The Tempest*, a play preoccupied with questions of power and dominance. In Shakespeare's play Prospero and Miranda exert a control over Caliban that goes beyond physical enslavement, since they position him as a being different not in degree but in kind, insisting that their gifts of language and culture have released him from a brutish existence. Caliban's revolt against this munificence leads to the charge of ingratitude and to the claim that because he belongs to a different order of creation he is fundamentally irredeemable. Although Prospero renounces power and attempts to reconcile all parties to one another, Caliban remains a failed project, a 'demi-devil' and 'thing of darkness' for whom Prospero ambiguously admits responsibility, leaving it unclear how far he blames himself for Caliban's behaviour, and although Prospero proposes to break his staff and drown his book, he never questions the hierarchy of human relations that he has imposed on the island.[9]

The Drought inverts this hierarchy. The characters who correspond to *The Tempest*'s protagonists are parodic versions of their textual models: Lomax is a demented narcissist who is completely unable to connect with reality; Miranda is an obscene travesty of the naïve girl in Shakespeare's play and is associated with the corruption originally attributed to Sycorax; the Caliban-like Quilter, despite his physical deformity, is a vatic figure gifted with great perceptiveness; and Mrs Quilter is a benign Sycorax in whom the traditional image of the witch is reversed. Eric Cheyfitz's view that *The Tempest* dramatises a difference in power that is technological as much as it is linguistic is

pertinent to the post-apocalyptic scenario in *The Drought*.¹⁰ The novel's
critique of the abuse of technology is also a critique of domination,
and this is where the intertextual connections with *The Tempest* are
most salient. For there is a subtle link not only between Prospero as a
figure of coercive power and the ravages wrought by the technology
with which Cheyfitz associates him, but also between Prospero as the
instigator of social hierarchies based on the concept of innate differences and the instrumental logics that have devastated the earth.

   The Drought rejects the uses to which this kind of language of difference can be put. A crucial part of Ransom's internal journey concerns the distance he must travel from the feelings of fear and
revulsion he experiences in Quilter's presence. Initially repelled by
what he sees as 'this grimacing parody of a human being' (*D* 68), he
is later told by Mrs Quilter that he looks like Quilter (*D* 182) and finds
himself hoping they will meet again. Whereas his first impulse is a
dissociative one, which resists any identification with the physically
grotesque Quilter, he is eventually able to acknowledge the shared
commonality between them. Similarly, Prospero's prohibition of any
sexual relationship between Caliban and Miranda is overturned in
this text, and their children, far from being the cretinous whelps of
Lomax's diseased and rivalrous imagination, appear to Ransom as
illuminati, as the first signs of a remade world. Like Riggs and Strangman in *The Drowned World*, Lomax stands committed to the old dispensation; unable to see that the dissolution of the old hierarchies is
potentially emancipatory, he is the 'serpent in this dusty Eden' who is
trying to preserve 'the world before the drought' (*D* 217). When Quilter kills the demented Lomax he knows inner peace for the first time
in his life, and the brave new world over which he presides is finally
aligned with the vision in Tanguy's *Jours de Lenteur*.

   The Drought suggests that human subjectivity must be transformed if social relations are to be remade in a way that will not
repeat its cataclysmic history. It also depicts identity as formed by
and out of the external world, insisting that the individual is an infin-
itesimal part of a much wider reality. The novel suggests not just that
people are like the tiny grains of sand that are a ubiquitous feature of
its imaginative terrain but also that they should submit to a process
of wearing away that adapts them to their environment. The erosion
of differences between the text's main characters erases the wounds
caused by dominative relationships (hence the re-working of *The
Tempest*) and subordinates all the protagonists to the landscape that

has been ravaged by an instrumental view of social existence. As in *The Drowned World* this historically determinate past and the modes of life it embodied offers nothing more than a baleful warning. Human beings are thus seen as interchangeable, their much prized individuality the meaninglessness residue of an outmoded conception of the self: 'He had expected the beach to be crowded, but not the vast concourse below, a meaningless replication of identity in which an infinite number of doubles of himself were being generated by a cancerous division of time' (*D* 115). On the long view taken by Ballard in this work, man appears as a recent entity belonging to a particular order of things and as one who could and perhaps should pass away. *The Drought*'s vision of a post-apocalyptic world in which a previous way of life has been shattered hints at a post-humanism that has affinities with Foucault's now infamous prediction: 'If those arrangements were to disappear as they appeared, if some event of which we can at the moment do no more than sense the possibility ... were to cause them to crumble ... then one can certainly wager that man would be erased, like a face drawn in sand at the edge of the sea.'[11]

The artifice of eternity

The Crystal World completes Ballard's first quartet of books in a visionary finale, depicting apocalypse not as cataclysm but as redemption, and offering another variation on themes already explored in tales such as 'The Waiting Grounds' (1959) and 'The Voices of Time' (1960). The latter takes place in a future in which scientists have activated the silent genes present in living organisms by radiating them; the results have been both bizarre, giving rise to creatures who seem to belong to 'a monstrous surrealist' (*CS* 178) world, and catastrophic, causing them to die in horrible ways. These hybrid fauna warn of the dangers of scientific interference in the natural order, but they also offer a glimpse into the future. They represent an evolutionary advance guard which suggests that their 'silent genes are a sort of code, a divine message that we inferior organisms are carrying for our more highly developed descendants' (*CS* 179). On this view, *homo sapiens* is already in irreversible decline, a trajectory seemingly revealed by human beings' need for more and more sleep, and by the catatonic states into which they constantly fall.

'The Voices of Time' is centrally concerned with entropy, the gradual winding down of the cosmos functioning as the counterpart to the
degeneration of the human species. But as so often in Ballard's work,
cataclysmic events that might be presented as pure disaster offer portals to alternative ways of seeing and being. The diminution of
humankind depicted here thus represents the death of one form of
life while the path to another opens up. In the case of Powers, the
story's main character, awareness of entropy results in an entirely different way of conceiving temporality, enabling him to 'explore the lat-
eral byways now, the side doors, as it were, in the corridors of time'
(CS 170). For Kaldren, the troubled chronicler of humanity's past, the
way out of the old world lies in the 'terminal documents' he is obses-
sively collecting. Convinced that the Mercury Seven astronauts were
informed by 'mysterious emissaries from Orion that the exploration
of deep space was pointless' (CS 185) because the universe is virtually
extinct, Kaldren believes that he has decoded a message from the
stars, which represents a countdown to its end, and he enjoins Powers
to listen the voices of time that are urging human beings to see themselves as part of a continuum that lies outside time. When Powers
dies he is convinced that he is being pulled to eternity by a 'majestic
current' that is 'the source of the cosmos itself' (CS 193), and he
undergoes an experience similar to that of the narrator of 'The Waiting Grounds', who imagines himself to be suspended '*at the threshold
of time and space, celebrating the identity and kinship of the particles
within our bodies with those of the sun and the stars of our brief private
times with the vast periods of the galaxies, with the total unifying time of
the cosmos*' (CS 93). Powers' vision seems to bear out Kaldren's asser-
tions, and the story concludes with this ambiguous figure – paranoid
psychotic or visionary seer? – thinking 'of Powers and his strange
mandala, and of the seven and their journey to the white gardens of
the moon, and the blue people who had come from Orion and spoken
in poetry to them of ancient beautiful worlds beneath golden suns in
the island galaxies, vanished for ever now in the myriad deaths of the
cosmos' (CS 194–5).[12]
    Taking the metamorphosis of all creation as its major theme, *The
Crystal World* portrays a transfigured world in which every living thing
shimmers with a new-found light. Its depiction of this rebirth draws
imaginatively on the resources of Romanticism, and perhaps especially on Wordsworth's iterations of a childhood sense of joy and
wonder in face of the natural world. In a reworking of the romantic

sublime *The Crystal World* neither evokes the feelings of awe and terror so often associated with the sublime nor emphasises its unrepresentability – the radical incommensurability between the felt emotion and its articulation, between the object of perception and its representation – but embodies an experience of ecstasy that harks back to Longinus. Wordsworth's 'sense sublime/Of something far more deeply interfused' haunts *The Crystal World*, and although the novel's imagery and verbal register are far removed from those of 'Tintern Abbey' or *The Prelude*, its descriptions of the natural world show that Ballard is equally concerned with the difficulties of grasping its meaning. The text's narrative structure is interesting with respect to this problematisation of perception. It begins as a science-fiction variant on the mystery/detective genre, with the text's main protagonist (Sanders), in the role of metaphysical detective given the task of investigating a series of strange events in order to unravel their meaning. But the second part of the novel undercuts the narrative drive that typically sustains this genre by beginning with a long letter from Sanders to a friend in which he explains the outcome of events that have yet to be recounted; this proleptic interruption of the plot's forward momentum diverts the reader's attention away from narrative suspense and directs it firmly onto the *significance* of what is being described. In this way the novel subverts the genre it has made use of, suggesting that the question 'what happened next' is trivial in comparison to the interpretative issue of how the occurrences about to be narrated are to be understood in terms of their metaphysical meaning. It is with the inner mystery of events that *The Crystal World* is principally concerned.

As might be expected of a Ballard novel, these events abound in ambiguities and unresolved tensions. Ballard has spoken of his admiration for Graham Greene's writing, and there are interesting parallels between *The Crystal World* and two of Greene's novels in particular: *The Power and the Glory* (1940) and *A Burnt-out Case* (1960). Ballard's apostate priest Balthus is close in conception to Greene's whisky priest; able to acknowledge God's existence on an intellectual level, Balthus cannot find it in himself actually to believe in him, and his sense of despair and unworthiness is similar to that of Greene's unforgettable anti-hero. Sanders, in turn, resembles Querry, the burnt-out case who sequesters himself in a *leproserie* in the African jungle, and the relationship between Greene's Rycker and his wife Marie may also be a source for the Ventress/Serena couple and the conflict over her between Ventress and Thorensen. More importantly, the mixed motives that characterise the behaviour of so many of Greene's protagonists, making his novels morally ambiguous, are very much in evidence in *The Crystal World*, with Sanders finding himself drawn to the deep forest on the grounds that 'here at last he might be free from the questions of motive and identity that were bound up with his sense of time and the past' (*CW* 17–18). And, of course, *A Burnt-out Case* raises the possibility that Querry could be a leprophil, drawn to the disease because it permits complete self-abasement. Whereas in Greene's novel leprosy may represent the embodiment of sin, in Ballard's text it has psychological implications, although uncertainty as to motive is a shared feature of both works:

> For some time he had suspected that his reasons for serving at the leper hospital were not altogether humanitarian, and that he might be more attracted by the idea of leprosy, and whatever it unconsciously represented, than he imagined. Suzanne's sombre beauty had become identified in his mind with this dark side of the psyche, and their affair was an attempt to come to terms with himself and his own ambiguous motives. (*CW* 19)

Pushed too far, such parallels can lead to readings that interpret one text in the terms set out by the other. But Querry and Sanders, just to take the two novels' main figures, are unlike each other in that the former is seeking to escape his past, whereas the latter is trying to confront it. Like so many of Ballard's protagonists, he is a questing figure who goes forward to meet his fate, and his willingness to do this – which requires him to acknowledge the double-sided nature of his motives – is central to *The Crystal World*'s concern with overcoming antinomies. The novel is structured around several doublings and oppositions, the most important being the Manichean light/dark divisions, which are balanced at the equinox, opening up a range of choices and possibilities, and which the novel ultimately seeks to reconcile to each other. The text's indebtedness to Manicheanism is obvious, as can be seen from Sanders's account of the significance of symbolic binaries: 'There may well be some fundamental distinction between light and dark that we inherit from the earliest living creatures ... For all we know, this division is the strongest one there is – perhaps the *only* one – reinforced every day for hundreds of millions of years. In its simplest sense time keeps going, and now that time is withdrawing we're beginning to see the contrasts in everything more clearly. It's not a matter of identifying any moral notions with light and dark' (*CW* 135–6). This symbolism is stripped of ethical significance – a naturalistic account derived from the biological origins of life explains the changes that are occurring – and the overcoming of divisive binaries, precipitated by the evacuation of time itself, is envisaged as a physical process. Its outcome is exemplified in the three frozen bodies of Ventress, Thorensen and Serena finally united together, and in the images of hybridity through which humans blend back into the environment from which they originally evolved.

The disease of leprosy provides a scientific parallel to the crystallisation process and hints as to its metaphoric significance. For Sanders, the morbid tissues studied under a microscope are 'a miniscule replica of the world [he] was to meet later in the forest slopes' (*CW* 84) in that the viral process of self-replication seen in the disease is a precursor of the infinite duplication of anti-time values (akin to anti-matter particles) which is emptying the entire universe of time and freezing it in a 'macrocosmic zero beyond the wildest dreams of Plato and Democritus' (*CW* 85). Leprosy is then the opposite of the alchemy taking place in the forest, its degenerative obverse. Metaphorically, leprosy symbolises the Jungian shadow that must be confronted: 'Of course there's a dark side of the psyche, and I suppose all one can do is find the other face and try to reconcile the two – it's happening out there in the forest' (*CW* 136). The crystallisation of the forest can thus be read in different ways. The scientific explanation of what is happening seems to co-exist with psychological, symbolic and religious accounts, none of which is decisively endorsed. The events narrated have a powerful significance for the novel's characters, acting as manifestations of their inner desires. But the transfiguration of the physical world is ultimately not reducible to the scientific thesis, which is treated as a discourse belonging to a cognitive paradigm of limited validity. Suzanne is from the outset transformed by her beatific response to a changing landscape in which people 'walk through the dark forest with crowns of light on their heads' while the 'light touches everything with diamonds and sapphires' (*CW* 18), while Sanders is only marginally interested in a scientific rationale:

> The beauty of the spectacle had turned the keys of memory, and a thousand images of childhood, forgotten for nearly forty years, filled his mind, recalling the paradisal world when everything seemed illuminated by that prismatic light described so exactly by Wordsworth in his recollections of childhood. The magical shore in front of him seemed to glow like that brief spring. (*CW* 69)

This vision of sublimity needs to be seen not in terms of the terror so often associated with the sublime but in terms of the wonder, awe and energy that, in Philip Larkin's words, is 'loosed with all the power/That being changed can give'.[13] *The Crystal World* is written out of a metamorphic reverie, a longing for a reconciliatory trans-formation of both self and world that has been glimpsed in an all but forgotten ecstatic experience of oneness with nature. This view of the sublime accords with Schiller's insistence that our 'demand that those objects that are existent be beautiful and good ... is consonant with the highest freedom of the spirit.'[14] Isobel Armstrong's descrip-tion of the sublime in 'Tintern Abbey' is of relevance to the depic-tion of it in *The Crystal World* and to Ballard's abiding concern with the interpenetration of external reality and inner perception: 'It comprehends the space and time of a dying universe: it is *made out of*, constituted by, the categories of space and time, matter, mind. The categories of sense and thought are constructed out of one another as the subsuming of thought by matter creates an interac-tive universe. Thus the sense sublime is not about being overpow-ered, as in Burke, or about the despotic subject/object relationship, but about the possibility of the transformation of categories, new knowledges.'[15] In contrast to the purgatorial landscape of *The Drought*, which demanded an ascetic withdrawal from life itself, prior to a re-awakening to new possibilities, *The Crystal World* envi-sions a re-enchanted world in which the division between life and death has been overcome, the animate and the inanimate integrated together in a new symbiosis. For Balthus it signifies Christ's resur-rection and the pantheistic presence of God 'in every leaf and flower' (*CW* 162). To Sanders it represents a gateway to paradise and the gift of immortality, while Suzanne sees in it a world-altering religious intensity; for both of them the significance of the forest lies in the fact that 'the only final resolution of the imbalance within their minds, their inclination towards the dark side of the equinox, could be found within that crystal world' (*CW* 173). The crystallisation process thus appears as the fulfilment of archaic dreams of unity in which the Jungian shadow is confronted so that division and strife may be healed and the world be sanctified. It is perhaps not insignif-icant that the painting presiding over this novel – Böcklin's *The Isle of the Dead* – was originally titled *A Quiet Place* and was commis-sioned by a widow who yearned for an image about which she could dream.

But we should be wary of placing a religious interpretation on *The Crystal World*. The text's imagery suggests that it is as much about the transformative dimension of art and the healing power of the imagination as it is about the metamorphosis of the world or the reconciliation of opposed parts of the mind. Consider the following lyrical description:

> He pointed up to the dome-shaped lattice of crystal beams that reached from the rim of the forest like the buttresses of an immense cupola of diamond and glass. Embedded at various points were the almost motionless forms of birds with outstretched wings, golden orioles and scarlet macaws, shedding brilliant pools of light. The bands of colour moved through the forest, the reflections of the melting plumage enveloping them in endless concentric patterns. The overlapping arcs hung in the air like the votive windows of a city of cathedrals. Everywhere around them Sanders could see countless smaller birds, butterflies and insects, joining their cruciform haloes to the coronation of the forest. (*CW* 162)

Is there a Yeatsian echo in this vision of an escape from the contingent world into an aesthetically transfigured reality, an image of purging that identifies life with art, which is asked to gather the soul into 'the artifice of eternity'?[16] The immutability of art functions as the emblem of a desired durability, which cannot be found either in nature or in history. What the philosopher Alfred North Whitehead referred to as a cosmological 'intuition of permanence in fluency and of fluency in permanence' is captured in *The Crystal World*.[17]

In celebrating what Balthus describes as the 'last marriage of space and time' (*CW* 162) *The Crystal World* imagines a mode of being that has been redeemed from the imperfections of life, but this redemption is conceived in aesthetic rather than sacral terms. For Suzanne, quoting from Shelley's *Adonais*, life 'like a dome of many-coloured glass, stains the white radiance of eternity' (*CW* 125), and of course the lines that follow, which she doesn't quote, read: 'Until Death tramples it to fragments.–Die/If thou wouldst be with that which thou dost seek!'[18] Those of the novel's characters who embrace the crystallisation that betokens death do so precisely because they seek this radiant eternity. The novel portrays it as a *return* – a journey back in time to a lost paradise that is associated not so much with the visionary gleam Wordsworth located in childhood but with deep, archetypal race memories of a unified time-space continuum. Once regained, this paradise can only survive if temporality itself comes to an end, which is why the crystal forest is described as a 'landscape without time' (CW 16) that leads to 'an ultimate macrocosmic zero beyond the wildest dreams of Plato and Democritus' (CW 85). This neo-platonic line of thought envisages immortality as the prize consequent on the loss of temporal and physical identity. Plotinus's *The Enneads* beautifully exemplify it. For Plotinus, eternity is opposed to life, which, being generated and not *sui generis*, is bound up in time and 'for this reason it keeps hastening towards its future, dreading to rest, seeking to draw Being to itself by a perpetual variety of production and action and by its circling in a sort of ambition after Essential Existence.'[19] Were this ambition to be achieved, producing an exact matching of essence and existence, then – impossible paradox – life would be absolute and unchanging: 'Suppose that Life, then, to revert – an impossibility – to perfect unity: Time, whose existence is in that Life, and the Heavens, no longer maintained by that Life, would end at once'.[20] This would be eternity, that is, 'a life limitless in the full sense of being all the life there is and a life which, knowing nothing of past or future to shatter its completeness, possesses itself for ever'.[21] The crystallised world of Ballard's visionary imagination points to just this kind of self-identity and self-possession, depicting its dream of stasis as redemption. But the novel's perfectly judged tone, its careful economy, and its lustrous imagery also enact through language the transformation from the impermanence of life to the permanence of art. This aesthetic dimension to the novel calls to mind another image, that of Breton's *éloge du cristal*: 'There could be no higher teaching than that of the crystal. The work of art, just like any fragment of human life considered in its deepest meaning, seems to me devoid of value if it does not offer the hardness, the rigidity, the regularity, the luster on every interior and exterior facet, of the crystal'.[22]

For the first two-thirds of Spielberg's *Close Encounters of the Third Kind*, before the sentimentalised aliens make their banal appearance, the film powerfully depicts a group of characters in the grip of an all-consuming compulsion. Blind to everything else, they strive to work out why they are obsessed with a particular image, and what its meaning might be. Nowhere is this uncontrollable obsession better depicted than in Richard Dreyfuss's manic attempts to build a ceiling-high replica of the image consuming his mind (in the living-room, no less) while his family life disintegrates around him. Ballard has little interest in space travel, believing that the task of exploring inner space is of more pressing importance. But the first part of Spielberg's film captures the same kind of internal pressure to which characters may be subjected by inexplicable events that is such a marked feature of Ballard's early novels, and which has led critics to emphasise the determinist nature of his fictional worlds. Ballard's protagonists, like Spielberg's in *Close Encounters*, are troubled by their inability to understand how far the events in which they are involved are projections from their own minds, and to what extent their own behaviour is the product of blind compulsion. *The Drowned World* explicitly foregrounds this issue by establishing an intimate connection between the sun and the burning images in Kerans's psyche, which seem to impel him forwards: 'the archaic sun in his mind beat again continuously with its immense power, its identity merging now with that of the real sun visible behind the rain-clouds. Relentless and magnetic, it called him southward, to the great heat and submerged lagoons of the Equator' (*DW* 161).

In Ballard's work the fusion of internal drives and external reality, mainly achieved by blurring the boundary between mental and physical prospects, creates the border zones in which his novels take place. These indeterminate fictional worlds are heterotopic spaces in which the complex interplay between the external environment and the inner compulsions takes place. By exploring this terrain from a variety of perspectives these heterotopic texts offer imaginative responses to the old antinomy of freedom versus necessity. The central protagonists of all these early texts embrace the compulsions that drive them on, and this raises the perhaps unanswerable question of the extent to which their actions are to be read as freely willed or externally determined. Although they are all in one sense *impelled* into action by something outside of themselves (environmental change, the psychic residues of the past, broken relationships), they accede to these external forces because they see them as the external manifestations of forgotten or repressed desires. In psychoanalytical terms their decision to confront what appears to be an external embodiment of the unconscious may be read as a 'working through' that requires the regression (the prelude to change and growth) they undergo. The trajectory undergone by these protagonists is in Jungian terms a form of 'individuation', a process of self-discovery and self-realisation. Ballard read Jung in his twenties, though he was drawn more to his imagery than to his account of psychoanalysis, and he refers to Jung in interview as someone who 'describes images of self-discovery'.[23] The narrative tra-jectories of these early novels are all variants on this theme, and they suggest that the determinism at work in them is what its victims are trying to evade. On this view, these texts are principally reflections on the problematics of agency.

Ballard sees this work as a form of psychological mapping: 'One descends into a sort of formless dark scene, one knows what's up in this well, the bottom of a shaft, goes through the tunnel and then you come out the other side with a sort of route'.[24] The process by which this route is found requires a coming to terms of the subject with external reality and of the ego with the id. These disjunctions are the *fons et origo* of these texts' narrative logics and of their visionary power. For Schiller, the contradiction between reason and sensuousness gave rise to the magic of the sublime. Extrapolating from this insight, we can see in Ballard's hybrid interzones a science-fiction sublime in which the creative impulse is inseparable from an awful compulsion to destruction, and this fateful union will become his great subject in *The Atrocity Exhibition* and in *Crash*. Schiller's words remain perti-nent to this context:

> Let us stand face to face with the evil fatality. Not in ignorance of the dangers which lurk about us – for finally there must be an end to igno-rance – only in *acquaintance* with them lies our salvation. We are aided in this acquaintance by the terrifying and magnificent spectacle of change which destroys everything and creates it anew, and destroys again.[25]

Notes

1 J. Goddard and D. Pringle, 'An Interview with J. G. Ballard', in J. Goddard and D, Pringle (eds), *J. G. Ballard: The First Twenty Years* (Hayes, Middle-sex: Bran's Head, 1976), pp. 23, 24.

2 J. G. Ballard, 'J. G. Ballard's Comments on His Own Fiction', *Interzone* (April 1996): pp. 19–25, p. 19.

3 D. Pringle, *Earth is the Alien Planet: J. G. Ballard's Four-Dimensional Night-mare* (San Bernardino, CA: Borgo Press, 1979), p. 42.

4 J. Conrad, *Heart of Darkness*, ed. Robert Hampson (Harmondsworth: Penguin, 1995), p. 18.

5 C. Bresson, 'J. G. Ballard at Home', *Metaphores* 7 (March 1982): 5–29, p. 17.

6 Quoted in A. Samuels, *Jung and the Post-Jungians* (London: Routledge, 1997), pp. 26–7.

7 W. Benjamin, *Illuminations*, trans. H. Zohn (New York: Schocken, 1978), p. 256.
8 Goddard and Pringle, 'An Interview with J. G. Ballard', pp. 11–12.
9 W. Shakespeare, *The Tempest*, ed. F. Kermode (London: Routledge, 1992): 5. i. lines 272 and 275.
10 E. Cheyfitz, *The Poetics of Imperialism: Translation and Colonization from The Tempest to Tarzan* (Oxford: Oxford University Press, 1991).
11 M. Foucault, *The Order of Things: An Archaeology of the Human Sciences* (New York: Vintage, 1973), p. 387.
12 For Jung, on whose images Ballard repeatedly draws, the mandala (or magic circle) symbolised a unitary world (*unus mundus*) in which psyche and physis were unified.
13 P. Larkin, *The Whitsun Weddings* (London: Faber and Faber, 1990), p. 23.
14 F. von Schiller, *Naïve and Sentimental Poetry* and *On the Sublime*, trans. J. A. Elias (New York: Frederick Ungar, 1980), p. 196.
15 I. Armstrong, *The Radical Aesthetic* (Oxford: Blackwell, 2000), pp. 99–100.
16 W. B. Yeats, *Collected Poems* (London: Macmillan, 1981), p. 218.
17 A. N. Whitehead, *Process and Reality: An Essay in Cosmology* (New York: Harper, 1957), p. 526.
18 P. B. Shelley, *Poetical Works*, ed. T. Hutchinson (Oxford: Oxford University Press, 1978), p. 443.
19 Plotinus, *The Enneads*, trans. S. MacKenna (Harmondsworth: Penguin, 1991), p. 217.
20 Plotinus, *The Enneads*, p. 231.
21 Plotinus, *The Enneads*, p. 219.
22 Breton, *Mad Love*, trans. M. A. Caws (Lincoln: University of Nebraska Press, 1988), p. 11.
23 Bresson, 'J. G. Ballard at Home', p. 16.
24 Bresson, 'J. G. Ballard at Home', p. 8.
25 Schiller, F. *Naïve and Sentimental Poetry* and *On the Sublime*, trans. J. A. Elias (New York: Frederick Ungar, 1980), pp. 209–10.

2

Deviant logics

The Atrocity Exhibition (AE; 1970) is Ballard's most demanding and most unsettling work. An experimental text that eschews the codes of realist narrative, it is a heteroglossic and open-ended artefact that works on multiple levels and refuses the closure of meaning. A text that does not conform to the patterns of a socially rooted, character-driven and chronological mode of narration demands an alternative practice of reading. One cannot make sense of it, if indeed making sense is the point here, by trying to construe it within the parameters it rejects; a paradigm shift of sorts is enacted in its pages, and it is incumbent upon the reader to work in terms of the new perspective thereby laid out. The text is a literary collage, a Surrealist potpourri assembled out of found objects taken from popular culture, images culled from elusive art-works, fantasies woven round representative political events, obsessions drawn from the fragmented psyche of its unstable central protagonist, and conceptual extrapolations from the hidden meanings of everyday events. Everything here works by way of suggestions, resonances, echoes. One can note speculative patterns or imagistic constellations, but this merely opens up transecting lines of thought that do not resolve themselves into an overarching synthesis.

The juxtapositional approach is fundamental to the practice of collage, but The Atrocity Exhibition is equally indebted to the example of frottage and decalcomania, the techniques that Max Ernst and Oscar Dominguez deployed so effectively. Decalcomania is especially relevant here, since it gave rise to defamiliarised art-works in which a strange, mineral-like world is revealed. These haunting paintings not only distance human beings from the world they inhabit but also evoke a pre-human past, with the result that an entirely different kind of reality is disclosed. This transformation of one order of being into another is central both to the Surrealist project and to Ballard's *The Atrocity Exhibition*, which draws repeatedly on the Surrealist legacy. As I have argued throughout this book, Ballard has long championed the Surrealist movement, emphasising the value of its fusion of 'the outer world of reality and the inner world of the psyche', a view that accords with Odilon Redon's claim, quoted by Ballard, that such art places 'the logic of the visible at the service of the invisible' (*UG* 84). In the key essay 'The Coming of the Unconscious' (1966) Ballard discusses several of the paintings that play an important part in *The Atrocity Exhibition*, noting that 'they have a direct bearing on the speculative fiction of the immediate future' (*UG* 86). Surrealism offered Ballard a way of accessing and then externalising the social unconscious of the 1960s, a way of tapping into what Salvador Dalí saw as the 'concrete irrationality' of human life, and this is why the book is indebted to the perceptions of those who are deemed to be 'mad' and why Ballard, in his later notes to the book, remarked that 'the hidden logic of that decade made complete sense in terms of [the Surrealists'] work' (*AE* 139). Dalí's own 'paranoiac-critical' method, through which he sought to reinterpret reality by *misinterpreting* it, is, as Roger Luckhurst has persuasively argued, of great importance to *The Atrocity Exhibition*'s oblique exploration of the insanity and paranoia that for Ballard informed this historical period.[1] Dalí sought to construe reality in terms of an internally cohesive but deliberately delusional system of thought, aiming by this means to produce an 'irrational knowledge' that would not consider 'phenomena and images in isolation, but, on the contrary, in a coherent whole of systematic and significant relations.'[2]

In *The Atrocity Exhibition* this questioning takes a number of forms: the construction of the narrative out of random 'found objects'; the reinterpretation of reality in terms of alternative geometries; the externalisation of the human central nervous system, one of the strategies by which the text inverts the inner and outer world; the removal of objects and people from a temporal frame, which reveals a 'very different world' in which the 'familiar surroundings of our lives, even our smallest gestures,' appear to 'have totally altered meanings' (*AE* 6); and the exploration of the gradually fragmenting mind of its core character (Traven) whose obsessions dominate the book. This protagonist's passage through the text in some way holds its multiple themes together, since so much of it is filtered through his consciousness, but he is a metamorphic figure whose name-changes in each chapter provide a number of variations on his character, which not only signal its radical instability but also track the path of his psychosis. A doctor who is haunted by his experiences as an air-force pilot and the death of his wife, Traven is on a doomed quest for meaning. He elaborates a series of ever more bizarre conceptual experiments in an attempt to reintegrate self and world, and he functions as a secularised apocalyptic Christ-figure who seeks to redeem a fallen world. The commentaries of the ultra-rational Dr Nathan are juxtaposed against Traven's obsessions, and an internally fissured, doubled narrative is the outcome. For if Nathan is the voice of reason whose ideas, as Ballard has said, 'are pretty close to my own, all the things Nathan says, I to some extent believe them too', he is also a symbol of the detached scientist who thinks that he can explain every-thing, whereas Traven articulates social and psychological anxieties that cannot so easily be foreclosed. Unlike the secure but limited Nathan, Traven is a split personality whose shifting identity cannot be pinned down. Like the doomed Lee Harvey Oswald, he is a troubled man 'struggling to make sense of the largest issues of his day' (AE 52), whereas Nathan is a figure who believes he has already explicated them. Thus Ballard describes the latter as 'an example of the pornog-raphy of science' because he is completely disengaged from the events happening around him', while Traven is 'the man, myself I suppose, who is aware of the nightmare, who is repelled by what seem to be the new logics unfolding ... but he's trying to understand what's happening'.[3] The Atrocity Exhibition is a profoundly dialogic work, and it is fitting for a text of this kind that Ballard's additional notes to it, which he inserted in 1990, add one more voice to its internal conversation.

The Atrocity Exhibition offers a recursive tour of a social uncon-scious given over to spectacularisation, dissociation of feeling, and apocalyptic violence in which the possibility of 'reading' reality is called into question. A series of proliferating boxes within boxes, rem-iniscent of Dorothea Tanning's painting The Birthday, with its reflect-ing mirror and its parade of doors within doors, it details one figure's obsessions with what he sees as the dominant but hidden issues of the day and his attempt to break the codes which appear to be this cul-ture's insoluble dreams. Ballard was particularly concerned with the mediating role of the telecommunications industries in the 1960s, which in his view concealed the real meaning of the significant events of the day, while at the same time they colonised all the channels by which information about the world was disseminated. He wrote in *The Kindness of Women*, for example, that 'the 1960s had effortlessly turned the tables on reality' and that the 'media landscape had sealed a technicolor umbrella around the planet, and then redefined reality as itself' (*KW* 185). And in his 'Introduction' to *Crash* he suggested that the 'most prudent and effective method of dealing with the world around us is to assume that it is a complete fiction – conversely, the one small node of reality left to us is inside our own heads' (*C* 5). Freud's distinction between the 'latent' and the 'manifest' is deployed here to suggest that the outer world has taken over the realm of fantasy – the dreamlike nature of social life functioning as the externalisation of a social unconscious – while the inner world of the psyche offers access to its latent meanings. In trying to unpack these meanings, the book works in a circuitous way that calls to mind Deleuze and Guattari's schizoanalytic cartographic method. In *The Atrocity Exhibition* we see a textuality that links the personal map to the impersonal tracing.[4] For Deleuze and Guattari, the map follows the modality of the rhizome, which 'ceaselessly establishes connections between semiotic chains, organizations of power, and circumstances relative to the arts, sciences and social struggles', and does not 'reproduce an unconscious closed in upon itself' but 'constructs the unconscious', whereas the tracing presupposes the existence of a deep structure, which it attempts to reproduce, a process that involves the stabilisation and organisation of the rhizome's multiplicity.[5] There is in *The Atrocity Exhibition* a tension between these two modalities, for if its exploration of Traven's disintegrating mind connects up seemingly random obsessions, then its juxtaposition of these preoccupations aims to uncover the deeper social logics that might unify them. We are then forced to ask whether 'the codes of insoluble dreams' (*AE* 1) with which the book opens may not be soluble after all.

Zones of twilight

Before attempting to address this question, it is worth pausing over Ballard's short story 'The Terminal Beach' (1964), which Ballard has described as 'the most important story I have written' and one that 'marks the link between the science fiction of my first ten years, and the next phase of my writings that led to *The Atrocity Exhibition* and *Crash*.'[6] A former military pilot named Traven maroons himself on the island of Eniwetok in an attempt to make sense of various apparently unrelated events, which nonetheless have an imaginative meaning that exceeds their ostensive significance. Traven's obsessive preoccupation with the death of his wife and son, the atomic bomb tests, the mind-set of military personnel, the Cold War, the synthetic and maze-like block-houses in which he cannot find his way, and an impending Third World War discloses apocalyptic (and seemingly paranoid) fears that the world is about to end. A highly charged choice of location, Eniwetok is both a labyrinth – symbol of a world in which all bearings have been lost – and a death-trap, a Böcklin-like 'Isle of the Dead', its 'ruined appearance' like 'an Auschwitz of the soul whose mausoleums contained the mass graves of the still undead' (CS 590). For Traven, Eniwetok is a kind of historical palimpsest through which it is the impending future rather than the past that is glimpsed. With a landscape that is 'covered by strange ciphers' (CS 589), the 'symbols of a cryptic alphabet' (CS 589), Eniwetok seems to hold the key to a violent present that is rushing towards a death-filled future. Traven's exhaustion from malnutrition and his illness from beri-beri push him into a fevered state of mind. Encountering a Japanese corpse, he has a vision in which the man counsels him to 'pursue a philosophy of acceptance' and to abandon his Ahab-like quest 'for the white leviathan, zero' (CS 603). Unable to follow this path, Traven appears to remain locked in a cycle of violence, and at the end of the story he is left 'thinking of the great blocks whose entrance was guarded by the seated figure of the dead archangel, as the waves broke on the distant shore and the burning bombers fell through his dreams' (CS 604).

Apart from its overt preoccupation with the theme of military apoc-alypse, 'The Terminal Beach' has other significant affinities with the concerns of The Atrocity Exhibition, not least its oscillation between a drive to decode contemporary reality and a desire to escape it alto-gether. Both tendencies should be read as alternative, but in some underlying sense twinned, responses to a contemporary crisis in which the sense-making imperative vies with the longing for libera-tion from an unbearable world, a theme that Ballard also explores in stories such as 'The Overloaded Man' (1961), 'Motel Architecture' (1978), and 'The Enormous Space' (1989). What aligns the decoding strategy with the escapist one is their shared source in Ballard's trans-formative aesthetic, which is not only fascinated by the passage from one mode of existence or order of being to another but also interested in translating the conventional terms in which social reality is understood into a new language, one that might make a different kind of sense. In *The Atrocity Exhibition* this transformative aesthetic is directed at both the *phenomenology* and the *sociology* of human existence, although I would argue that the text's preoccupation with both these realms is linked to its negotiation of a determinate historical conjuncture. As Luckhurst rightly insists, '*Atrocity* is a "punctual" text, of its moment'.[7] Ballard describes 'our notions of conventional reality' as 'a largely artificial construct' (*AE* 62), which offers severely limited insights into the nature of phenomenal reality or the underlying patterns of social life. *The Atrocity Exhibition* tries to 'decode' some of the 'transformational grammars' (*AE* 62) through which alternative structures of meaning are discovered in human existence, in an attempt to ascertain what sort of 'language could embrace ... or at least provide a key' (*AE* 134) to the disparate shards into which life has fragmented. But at the same time it is traversed by a powerful desire to disengage from this shattered reality altogether, to drain it of temporality in a drive to inorganic stasis or to turn time back in an attempt to regain the bliss of the pre-uterine state. Here, in Nathan's terms, an extreme alienation from self and world is in play. For Traven, 'the phenomenology of the world is a nightmarish excrescence' and human bodies are 'monstrous extensions of puffy tissue he can barely tolerate' (*AE* 86); the 'human organism is an atrocity exhibition' (*AE* 9) from which he seeks to avert his eyes, while his obsession with the conceptual parameters of World War Three represents his 'revolt against the present continuum of time and space' (*AE* 6–7), which is figured as a generalised phenomenological revulsion at the very conditions of life and, as Nathan has it, results in his desire to rediscover 'a symmetrical world, one that will recapture the perfect symmetry of the blastosphere ... In his mind World War III represents the final self-destruction and imbalance of an asymmetric world' (*AE* 9).

Traven's search for a way out of the space-time continuum is inextricably linked with his psychological breakdown, which opens up a fissure in profane reality. The gradual defamiliarisation of everyday life takes place as his psychosis takes hold, but this fragmentation of the prosaic world, which blurs the boundary between fantasy and reality, creates a liminal space in which buried memories begin to stir. Psychosis is thus linked to a dream of anamnesis: the shattering of conventional reality leads not to irreality but to remembrance of an alternative realm and a different way of being. This is an important thread in *The Atrocity Exhibition*, which draws out the implications of several Surrealist paintings – such as Ernst's *Eye of Silence, Europe After the Rain, The Robing of the Bride,* and *The Stolen Mirror,* Tanguy's *Jours de Lenteur,* de Chirico's *The Dream of the Poet,* and Dalí's *The Persistence of Memory* – but is also influenced by J. M. Marey's experiments with 'chronograms', which sought to capture the passage of time across the photographic plate. These artefacts are united by a shared preoccupation with the perplexing categories of time and space, and their attempts to represent and experience them in new ways, in the process uncovering or indeed forging alternative realities. This occurs in a variety of ways in *The Atrocity Exhibition.* Marey's chronograms, for example, expose the slow-motion effects of time on the body, which then appears in non-human form 'as a series of dune-like lumps' (*AE* 6), but Traven reverses Marey's procedure in order to bleach time from photographs of people or buildings, with the result that the minutiae of everyday life take on 'totally altered meanings' (*AE* 6). The huge billboards that dominate the book magnify isolated fragments of the body so many times that they are no longer recognisable but appear as geometric patterns, the full torso being transformed 'into a quantified sand-sea' (*AE* 12).

Time and space are reconfigured here in an attempt to overcome a deep phenomenological unease, which is comparable in certain respects to Sartre's account of nausea, but whereas in Sartre's thought it is above all oozing, viscous textures that prompt intense anxiety, in *The Atrocity Exhibition* it is memories of the evolutionary conflict between the organic and the inorganic that underlie this malaise, prompting a sense of alienation from a hostile mineral world. The use by Oscar Dominguez of decalcomania, for example, is not only related to the inversion of the body but also to human fear of a non-organic realm: 'The spinal landscape ... is that of the porous rock towers of Tenerife ... The clinker-like rock towers, suspended above the silent swamp, create an impression of profound anguish. The inhospitability of this mineral world, with its inorganic growths, is relieved only by the balloons flying in the clear sky' (*AE* 41). Estrangement from habitual perceptions leads in two directions, either to a view of urban space as in some sense anthropomorphic or to a view of the human organism as itself as a possible location of the inorganic. Thus Traven sees the 'concrete causeways' as forming 'an immense cipher, the templates of an unseen posture', while at the same time the 'flowering tissue' of Karen Novotny's mouth reminds him 'of the porous esplanades of Ernst's "Silence," the pumice-like beaches of a dead sea'

(*AE* 23). Dalí's characteristic inversions of hard and soft are also in play here, undermining the boundaries between the organic and the inorganic and thus destabilising fixed notions of subjectivity. Equally important is the preoccupation with mortality, the passage of the human organism through time, which will result in its eventual reduction to rigid bones and finally to compliant dust: 'Karen Novotny's body seemed as smooth and annealed as those frozen planes. Yet a displacement of time would drain away the soft interstices, leaving walls like scraped clinkers. He remembered Ernst's "Robing": Marilyn's pitted skin, breasts of carved pumic, volcanic thighs, a face of ash. The widowed bride of Vesuvius' (*AE* 56). All these concerns are summed up in Traven's wife's conclusion that her husband is being 'pursued by furies more implacable than the Four Riders – the very facts of time and space' (*AE* 48).

But why should time and space appear to be so threatening? One way of approaching this question is to note the apocalyptic reference to the book of *Revelation* above. In contrast to the technophilic optimism of a modernist text such as Marinetti's 'The Founding and Manifesto of Futurism 1909', which declared that 'Time and Space died yesterday', and asserted that we 'already live in the absolute, because we have created eternal, omnipresent speed', *The Atrocity Exhibition* is haunted by the implosion of space-time caused by nuclear fission, which destroys vast tracts of space and shatters the lived time of numberless individuals.[8] A very different outcome from Marinetti's martial dreams of technology as a cleansing tool was revealed in Hiroshima, Nagasaki, and the years of the Cold War, one that in the short story 'Zodiac 2000' (1978) Ballard described under the rubric 'The Sign of the Cruise Missile': 'The true zodiac of these people, the constellations of their mental skies, constituted nothing more than a huge self-destructive machine' (*CS* 987). It is the spectre of nuclear Armageddon, as much as the Hydra of the telecommunications industries, that hovers over *The Atrocity Exhibition* and that goes some way to explaining its obsession with alienation, destruction and death. Indeed, the book's title brings these two central features of the narrative together: for its concern is not just to itemise and to analyse the various atrocities (as events) that for Ballard dominated social and political life in the 1960s but also to show the extent to which atrocity had become an accepted part of the very fabric of life. Numerous real occurrences loom large in this text, and these constitute the topical references that situate it historically, but equally important is the fact that they are rendered almost banal by being treated as spectacles for the citizen–voyeur.

To put it like this is not at all to suggest that individuals subjected to the remorseless scopophilia of the visual mass media are incapable of resisting its representations (as, at times, Baudrillard seems to claim) but rather to emphasise the far-reaching nature of this cultural transformation, the full effects of which are impossible to calculate but certainly seem to encourage some sort of detachment from the reality of what is depicted. The bombings of Hiroshima and Nagasaki, the assassinations of John F. Kennedy and Martin Luther King, the Apollo disaster, the war in Vietnam, the multiple deaths caused by automobile accidents, the Manson murders, are all horrific events, but this text suggests that to exhibit them for the delectation of the public is to perpetuate atrocity. The book's title goes to the heart of its multiple ambiguities and ambivalences – it bodies forth, for public consumption, a series of 'exhibits' (the short chapters within chapters) that shock and disturb not just because of their content but because they too are turned into a form of textual display. The book deliberately treads the fine line between exploitation and critique, saving itself from the trivialisation of issues that is so often associated with the 'culture industry' and refusing to titillate its readership by adopting a lapidary tone. There is, in truth, no incitement to pleasure here.

All this notwithstanding, Ballard's take on the 1960s is in *The Atrocity Exhibition* an uncompromisingly bleak one. There is little in this text about those aspects of the period that might be read as socially emancipatory or culturally invigorating: a widespread social liberalisation, a gradual if piecemeal loosening of the bonds of censorship, the enormous impact of pop music, the women's movement and second-wave feminism, peace demonstrations against the Vietnam War, the anti-nuclear movement. In interview Ballard has described the 1960s as 'a wonderfully exhilarating and releasing period. All those energies, particularly of working-class youth, burst out' but none of this finds its way into *The Atrocity Exhibition*, which concentrates exclusively on the dark depths of this ferment, bringing to the surface its morbid and noxious undercurrents.[9] For Ballard, always fascinated by the concealed wellsprings of socio-cultural forces, it appeared as though at this historical moment 'the unconscious needs of the human race could only be fulfilled in an obliterating sexual apocalypse, replayed in an infinity of slow-motion photography' (*KW* 176–7). The extent to which this view of the 1960s should be seen as the product of Ballard's particular obsessions rather than as a social diagnosis is a question raised both by this text (principally through the Nathan–Traven pairing) and, more centrally, by *The Kindness of Women*, which is yet another text in dialogue with *The Atrocity Exhibition*. The paranoiac-critical method is of relevance here because it systematises a deliberately psychotic reading of 'the real', but, equally importantly, the text's melding of the private with the public makes it a rhizomatic map, which 'is entirely oriented toward an experimentation with the real'.[10] *The Atrocity Exhibition* focuses on a mutually reinforcing nexus of phenomena: sexual and physical violence; the loss of affect; the mediatisation of reality achieved by the telecommunications industries; scientific instrumentalism; celebrity culture; psychological breakdown; political paranoia; and the threat of nuclear war. These social realities are read as the surface manifestations of deep tectonic realignments, which require the exposure of the world's new subterranean faultlines. And this exposure brings to light logics that appear to be oriented above all to death and destruction.

The death of affect

In a book as wide-ranging and over-determined as *The Atrocity Exhibition* it is potentially misleading to over-emphasise any one strand over another, but the 'death of affect' is one of its most significant motifs. This process of emotional deadening is depicted here as unfolding in two possible directions: it is connected with the instrumental approach to phenomena associated with the scientific method, which produces detachment; and it is linked to the intense over-excitation of the psyche encouraged by the spectacularisation of society, which gives rise to over-cerebralised responses to reality that are coupled with dissociation from the emotions. Ballard homes in on the ways in which these two trajectories intersect in 1960s culture, highlighting the disengaged form of the Warren Commission Report on the assassination of Kennedy, the impersonal tone of car-crash test-reports, the deadpan commentaries of Masters and Johnson in their sexual case-studies, and the numerous experiments in which scientific detachment seems to be aligned with an almost pornographic obsessiveness. This bizarre fusion of disengagement with febrility was for Ballard especially apparent in mass-media representations of the nuclear arms race. Among the book's many ambiguities is its representation of spectacularised violence as at once a sign of atrocity and a source of social energy. The car-accident is, for example, deployed as a symbol of powerful libidinal currents. The 'Crash' chapter, which contains *in nuce* most of the themes Ballard would develop in the novel *Crash*, focuses not just on the libidinal potency of the automobile, the most obvious phantasmatic feature of this commodity, but also on the way its destructive power (literalised in the car-crash), induces excitement and unleashes energy. Taking this conceit to an extreme, the chapter suggests that the image of the car-crash plunges the spectator into the pleasures of polymorphous perversity, liberating 'sexual and machine libido' and 'mediating the sexuality of those who have died with an erotic intensity impossible in any other form' (*AE* 157).

The psychological and sexual implications of the car-crash are teased out here in a provocative manner that borrows from the previous chapter's deployment of a *faux*-scientific language. In 'Love and Napalm: Export U.S.A.' a series of imaginary 'scientific' studies explores the impact of the Vietnam war on the minds of various subjects, with a view to seeing how media representations of the war might be 'spun' in order to regularise social relations, improve economic productivity, and stabilise sexual behaviour. The complete emotional detachment from what is being articulated here is central to Ballard's ironic intent, as the text's parodies of scientific case reports make clear: 'Further studies are in progress to construct an optimum sexual module involving mass merchandizing, atrocity newsreels and political figures. The key role of the Vietnam war is positively indicated throughout' (*AE* 149). Later on it is coolly noted that comparison 'of Vietnam atrocity films with fake newsreels of Auschwitz, Belsen and the Congo reveals that the Vietnam war far exceeds the latter's appeal and curative benefits' (*AE* 151). An example of Bakhtinian double-voiced discourse, this savagely satirical chapter cloaks the author's subversive intent in its straight-faced deployment of scientific language, while exposing the role it plays in sustaining the military-industrial complex. Nathan's commentaries on the implications of this appalling scopophilia are informative, even if his breezy tone is not to be trusted. It is Nathan who sees that the proliferation of visual *displays* of violence has very different implications and consequences from those normally attributed to them. Instead of provoking revulsion and critique, they quicken desire and ratify its subsequent realisations, which suggests that the manifest content of these representations must be decoded so as to reveal its latent meanings. This analysis aims to deconstruct the near ubiquitous images of violence and sexual perversion:

> In terms of television and the news magazines the war in Vietnam has a latent significance very different from its manifest content. Far from repelling us, it *appeals* to us by virtue of its complex of polyperverse acts. We must bear in mind, however sadly, that psychopathology is no longer the exclusive preserve of the degenerate and perverse. The Congo, Vietnam, Biafra – these are games that anyone can play. Their violence, and all violence for that matter, reflects the neutral exploration of sensation that is taking place now, within sex as elsewhere, and the sense that the perversions are valuable precisely because they provide a readily accessible anthology of exploratory techniques. Where all this leads one can only speculate – why not, for example, use our own children for all kinds of obscene games? Given that we can only make contact with each other through the new alphabet of sensation and violence, the death of a child or, on a larger scale, the war in Vietnam, should be regarded as for the public good. (*AE* 119–20)

This calm disquisition merely traces the logical conclusion that follows from accepting the starting premise. If everything is sanctioned, if experiences and sensations are to be multiplied without any regard to their consequences, then all is permitted and may even be portrayed as socially beneficial. Both Nathan's tone and his controlling terms (game, anthology, technique, alphabet) reveal the extent to which he is himself in thrall to the logic he expounds with such apparent clarity. In this discourse these terms at once presuppose and *institute* the notion of a system in which experiential possibilities can be permutated at will. Value is attributed here solely to the intensification and extension of the subject's experiences, with no reference to anybody or anything else. What follows from this, as Nathan points out, 'is the psychopathology of sex, relationships so lunar and abstract that people will become mere extensions of the geometries of situations. This will allow the exploration, without any taint of guilt, of every aspect of sexual psychopathology' (*AE* 120). In Deleuzian terms, this perverse structure can be read as antithetical to the workings of desire, since the experiential subject described here is, as Deleuze would have it, 'no more a desiring self than the Other is, for him, a desired object endowed with real existence'; for Deleuze, a world peopled by such subjects is simply 'a world without Others, and thus a world without the possible. The Other is that which renders possible.'[11]

There is a recursive pattern here, for the vision that Nathan expounds is itself conceptual and cerebral, reproducing, as it were, the very logic that culminates in the death of affect he is supposedly analysing. Elsewhere, his language is both emotional and implicitly moral, as in this passage:

> Consider our most real and tender pleasures – in the excitements of pain and mutilation; in sex as the perfect arena, like a culture-bed of sterile pus, for all the veronicas of our own perversions, in voyeurism and self-disgust, in our moral freedom to pursue our own psychopathologies as a game, and in our ever greater powers of abstraction. What our children have to fear are not the cars on the freeways of tomorrow, but our own pleasure in calculating the most elegant parameters of their deaths. The only way we can make contact with each other is in terms of conceptualizations. (*AE* 116)

The terms to which Nathan has recourse in this speech (pain, mutilation, pus, fear) belong to a different order of discourse, which suggests that the earlier disengaged analysis is complicit in the phenomena it is itemising. This is further supported by the fact that the words Ballard gives to Nathan in the speech I have just quoted are the same words that he himself uses in 'The Innocent as Paranoid' (1969), in which Dalí is described as the great prophet of the social developments that *The Atrocity Exhibition* dissects: 'Voyeurism, self-disgust, biomorphic horror, the infantile basis of our dreams and longings – these diseases of the psyche which Dalí rightly diagnosed have now culminated in the most sinister casualty of the century: the death of affect' (*UG* 91).

Toxic imagery

The double-voiced strategy deployed in the critique of science is taken one step further in 'Why I Want to Fuck Ronald Reagan', which focuses on Reagan's subliminal sexual appeal, and the stories added as appendices ('Princess Margaret's Face Lift' and 'Mae West's Reduction Mammoplasty'). Ballard takes scientific descriptions of cosmetic surgery but replaces references to the 'patient' with the names of two iconic figures to draw attention to the anaesthetising effect of an impersonal scientific discourse – motivated by an 'anatomizing fascination' and a 'reductive drive' (*AE* 180) – which is by this method shown to be powered by an instrumental view of life. The

Reagan text emphasises the role played by the mass media in the representation of contemporary politics. It homes in on the disjunction between Reagan's sanitised public image and his policies, drawing attention to the packaging of political figures as commodities on a par with automobiles and washing machines. For Ballard, Reagan's success lay in the way he grasped that the content of political policies pales into insignificance when set against the manner of their presentation. It was not that the medium could disguise the message but rather that the medium could obliterate the message, rendering it irrelevant to the way that voters decided on their political allegiances. Operating within a vicious tradition of satire, 'Why I Want to Fuck Ronald Reagan' offered a brutal critique of the mass media and the political process. This calculatedly obscene story suggests that the packaging of a figure like Reagan (a mere cipher in this context) is as nothing compared with the real obscenity at work in contemporary culture – namely, the transposition of politics into the realm of the simulacrum – although we should note that politics is just one aspect of the more wide-ranging spectacularisation of society with which *The Atrocity Exhibition* is concerned.

In this context, the writing of the Situationist Guy Debord – especially in *The Society of the Spectacle* (1967), which preceded *The Atrocity Exhibition* by three years – resonates with Ballard's work, as does some of Baudrillard's writing on consumer culture. For Debord, the shift to a 'society of the spectacle' was to be understood in terms of a transformation of the social system; the spectacle was not a superstructural phenomenon but rather had become a fundamental part of the social infrastructure, permeating all its levels. The principle of mediation was at the heart of Debord's conception, as he makes clear in his opening paragraph with the claim that '[a]ll that once was directly lived has become mere representation', but he claimed further that this process undermined the separability of subject and object (or the representation from that which it represented), since the two were now interlinked:

> Understood in its totality, the spectacle is both the outcome and the goal of the dominant mode of production. It is not something *added* to the real world – not a decorative element, so to speak. On the contrary, it is the very heart of society's unreality. In all its specific manifestations – news or propaganda, advertising or the actual consumption of entertainment – the spectacle epitomizes the prevailing model of social life.[12]

Acknowledging that 'reality erupts within the spectacle, and the spectacle is real', Debord sought to elaborate a critique that could disrupt
the transformation of social life into appearance, arguing that 'any critique capable of apprehending the spectacle's essential character
must expose it as a visible negation of life – and as a negation of life
that has *invented a visual form for itself*'.[13]

The dominance of contemporary culture by such visual forms has
been a marked Ballardian concern, and the kind of logic that *The
Atrocity Exhibition* is attempting to trace is also brilliantly uncovered
in 'The 60 Minute Zoom' (1976). The story focuses on the voyeuristic gaze of the camera lens during a protracted zoom. A man secretly
films his wife's sexual infidelities, seeing her behaviour as a series of
stylised, abstract acts. His emotional detachment from the significance of what he is recording derives both from the fact that the
camera provides a kind of barrier (enabling him to shield himself
behind it) and from its aestheticisation of the real, by means of which
events and emotions are translated into distanced representations.
This creation of an alternative reality (that of the filmed image) results
in an etiolation of the experiencing sensibility, which is then unable
to connect emotionally with the events witnessed by the dispassionate
camera. But the camera is not a blank recording instrument, which
can provide access to the 'truth' of these events in some neutral or
objective manner, since it is deployed in the service of a cinematic language that casts reality in a certain form. The difficulty of establishing
the 'truth' of events is partly what is at issue in this text: the narrator
kills his wife, but it is not clear if she has been participating in an
elaborate sexual game, consciously co-creating the cinematic record
of her infidelities in a series of stylised actions, which unexpectedly
culminates in her death. In a parody of the all-controlling *auteur*, the
narrator is depicted as a lordly directorial figure, but the action is
shown to be influenced by the conventions of cinematic genre and
constrained by its technology, as this description of the filming
process suggests:

> I eliminate him, and move to his neighbour, a thirty-year-old Brighton
> antique dealer ... Engaging but unscrupulous, he too is taking in his
> opposition – principally Fradier ... But Fradier is moving out of frame,
> and by the logic of this film can be dropped from the cast-list. As the
> camera moves nearer I approach the main stage of this vertical drama ...
> Helen at the centre. Two floors below her, bare-chested in the fierce sun-
> light, is a minor Italian film actor ... His profession would make him my

chief suspect, but he too is about to move out of frame, exiting from this reductive fable. (CS 859)

The labour of the photo-lens is indeed reductive in this scenario, creating a fable peopled by bit-part actors playing out roles that appear to exist solely for the benefit of the camera that records them. This reductiveness eventually bleaches both reality and the imagined screen white, creating a blank undifferentiated space within which death makes its entrance: 'Only a white field is now visible, detached from all needs and concessions, a primed canvas waiting for its first brush stroke. Applauding, I see the screen fill with sudden red' (CS 863).

The suggestive remarks made by William Burroughs in his 'Preface' to *The Atrocity Exhibition* about the affinities between the book's preoccupation with the image and the Pop Art of Bob Rauschenberg are pertinent in this context. Burroughs sees Ballard's textual experiments as verbal counterparts to Rauschenberg's visual ones: both are 'literally *blowing up* the image' and since in Burroughs' terms 'people are made of image' this makes *The Atrocity Exhibition* 'literally an explosive book' (AE viii). Burroughs focuses on Ballard's fictional depiction of the interpenetration of appearance and reality, emphasising that the various defamiliarising strategies deployed in *The Atrocity Exhibition* disintegrate the realm of appearances, exposing what Ballard describes as the 'sensational and often toxic imagery [that] inundates our minds' (AE 145), and this process combines the techniques of Pop Art with those of Surrealism.[14] The toxicity of these images is here traced to a different kind of affectlessness from that which is brought about by science; the telecommunications industries, especially those that are predominantly visual, turn the social realm into a spectacle, thereby disclosing a negation that invents for itself a purely visual form in which simulation and replication are the norm. The proliferation of giant billboards on which the magnified picture of Elizabeth Taylor is blazoned forth is glossed as follows:

> Yet these designs were more than emormous replicas. They were equations that embodied the relationship between the identity of the film actress and the audiences who were distant reflections of her. The planes of their lives interlocked at oblique angles, fragments of personal myths fusing with the commercial cosmologies. The presiding deity of their lives the film actress provided a set of operating formulae for their passage through consciousness. (AE 13)

The conceptual system of sex

A direct corollary of the death of affect is that others are treated in
instrumental fashion as objects to be used. Reduced to the status of
inert commodities, human beings function in *The Atrocity Exhibition*
as interchangeable products or as tokens in conceptual games. But
although all are subjected to this economy, women occupy a particularly vulnerable place within it. Drawing on the Surrealist interest in
the objectification of women and on Pop Art's explorations of the
form such objectification took in post-war consumer society, *The
Atrocity Exhibition* takes the exploitation of the female sexed body to a
cruel extreme. This exploitation takes a range of forms: the treatment
of characters such as Catherine Austin, Karen Novotny and Margaret
Travis as moduli for the male protagonist's quest; the repeated
emphasis on the commodification of famous screen actresses; the
sacrifice of women in real or imaginary ('alternate') deaths as a way of
redeeming a tragic personal and public history; the troping of woman
as madonna (herald of a new annunciation) or as untimely sexual
temptress; and the objectification of women as sex-toys for the playing out of fetishistic games. In all these guises women appear as constructed entities, which can be assembled and re-assembled, and as
produced images, which can be manipulated and exploited.

In its exploration of these issues *The Atrocity Exhibition* is indebted
above all to Hans Bellmer's 1930s work with dolls and Tom Wesselman's 1960s series of paintings *The Great American Nude*. Ballard's
book thus establishes links between Surrealism and Pop Art, a combination of artistic traditions that were themselves based on the principle of combination, utilising the throw-away materials of everyday
social life as the source of new visual collocations. Bellmer's work in
particular has long been deeply controversial; it has been read by
some critics as a form of dehistoricised misogyny, and by others as a
form of historically specific socio-political resistance in which the
doll-like ideal woman of Weimar society is subjected to critique, and
the emergent fascism of post-Weimar Germany is deconstructed.[15]
Ballard acknowledges the problematic nature of Bellmer's work in his
notes to *The Atrocity Exhibition*, 'hovering as it does on the edge of
child pornography', but he considers that Bellmer's inversions of the
female anatomy are the reverse of sexually titillating, arguing that his
work is unsettling because it is 'far too close for comfort to the truth'
(*AE* 89). What truth is this? That men find girls sexually alluring and

that their relative powerlessness unleashes fantasies of abuse? Or that these obscene mannequins (inverting all the codes of 'femininity' inscribed on the plastic bodies of golden-haired and blue-eyed toy dolls) expose not only the processes by which a certain kind of sexed subjectivity is enforced but also condemn it as a deformity? The meanings of Bellmer's deeply ambiguous artefacts cannot easily be resolved (and are not likely to be agreed upon), but his work, like that of Wesselmann and several other Pop Artists (Andy Warhol, Richard Hamilton, Allen Jones, Peter Phillips), offers a point of departure for critical discussion of the conceptual system of sex and the particular libidinal economy to which it belongs that is elaborated in *The Atrocity Exhibition*.

In the work of all these artists contemporary representations of the female body (to which the whole of female identity is reduced) are depicted as commodified objects subject to the law of exchange. This is particularly clear in works such as Warhol's silk-screen prints of Marilyn Monroe's face in *The Twenty-Five Marilyns* (1962) or of her lips in *Marilyn Monroe's Lips* (1962); in Hamilton's *$he* (1959/60) and the enormously influential *Just what is it that makes today's homes so different, so appealing?* (1956); and in Jones's various paintings and sculptures of fetishised women-as-furniture (1960s). Such works run the risk of inciting the voyeuristic gaze and thus of being complicit with the objectification they depict, and Ballard runs the same risk in *The Atrocity Exhibition*, but in this book there are no visual cues for the potentially predatory eye, and its textual representation of the objectified female body needs to be seen in relation to its wider concern with commodity culture and means–end rationality. In *The Atrocity Exhibition* the disarticulation of the female body is associated with an assault on the mass media and the affectless realm of pornography. Traven's synthetic maze, which consists of a blown-up physical rendering of Elizabeth Taylor's body, a potent symbol of the cult of celebrity, comments on the disorientating effect on the mind of a world given over to images – significantly, Karen Novotny cannot find her bearings in this artificial labyrinth and is unable to 'break the code of this immense body' (*AE* 87). Equally importantly, the numerous magnified images of film actresses, of Jackie Kennedy, and the photographs of Catherine Austin and Karen Novotny that pervade the text all disclose the dominance of the social life-world by manufactured appearances, which in Debord's terms 'cause a world that is no longer directly perceptible to be *seen* via different specialized mediations', a form of cognition that reveals 'the true depth of society's dependence on images'.[16] Here it is the female body *as image* that is presented as the site of manipulations that make and re-make it in accordance with a complex range of cultural imperatives. The text's own objectifications of such images through its inventories, disarticulations and blow-ups are inevitably at some level complicit with the phenomena they anatomise, but I would suggest that this complicity is tempered throughout by the language of critique, which aims to grasp the misogynist rationale that informs such objectification and which shows just how deeply it is connected to scientific detachment, televisual spectacularisation and pornographic reductiveness.

Traven's responses to these mediated images of women are characterised principally by his alienation from the female body, which appears to him as an entity detached from lived relations, an artefact on a par with the built environment: 'Her naked body was held forward like a bizarre exhibit, its anatomy a junction of sterile cleft and flaccid mons. He placed his palm against the mud-coloured areola of her left nipple. The concrete landscape of underpass and overpass mediated a more real presence' (*AE* 20). The body is an object of detached scrutiny here, and this detachment will lead to a conception of the body as an unliving mannequin on Bellmerian lines: 'He looked at her body. Humped against his right shoulder, her breasts formed a pair of deformed globes like the elements of a Bellmer sculpture. Perhaps an obscene version of her body would form a more significant geometry, an anatomy of triggers' (*AE* 92). Alan Jouffroy has suggested that Bellmer's first doll 'might well be regarded as one of the most effective instruments of counter-magic ever devised by a human being to liberate himself from the system of surveillance whereby society oppresses the individual.'[17] Traven appears to be engaged in a similar process of self-liberation, except that here the source of power is a society of the spectacle. The obscene transformation of the female body inverts culturally dominant images of sexed femininity, the individual constructing a fetish that signals his refusal to be co-opted to a sexual system in which stereotypical representations of woman serve the voyeuristic male gaze. The production of an obscene fetish of this kind obviously involves a different form of objectification, which is perhaps more violent and more misogynistic than the kind of representation it wants to resist. Ballard's text hints at this, I think, but it also suggests that what might be read as straightforward misogyny is bound up with the wider question of a generalised phenomenological anxiety that is here projected onto the monstrous feminine. Traven's increasingly desperate attempts to free himself from one kind of logic (that of the spectacular) merely lock him into another (that of the death-drive). Susan Sontag, drawing on Bataille's account of pornography, suggests that it is 'towards the gratifications of death, succeeding and surpassing those of eros, that every truly obscene quest tends', and Traven's quest appears to seek just this end-point.[18] Here the obscene is reduced to an affectless geometric experimentation with bodily forms and sexual postures that is stripped of emotional valence and physical or libidinal pleasure: 'Soon the parallax would close, establishing the equivalent geometry of the sexual act with the junctions of this wall and ceiling' (*AE* 83).

In the realm of Travis's imagination the female body is desexualised. Stripped of the expected cultural associations with desire, his dissociation of the body from affective attachments leads to the assembly of a 'sex kit' that plasticises the female body and fetishistically dismantles it into its component parts, as suggested in a description of Catherine Austin as having 'the texture of a rubber mannequin fitted with explicit vents, an obscene masturbatory appliance' (*AE* 20). But inasmuch as this dismemberment of the body is shown to recapitulate the logics of pornography (a reduction of what is already a reduction) it is also shown to be outside the realm of desire – 'Amatory elements: nil. The act of love became a vector in an applied geometry' (*AE* 81) – and this suggests that the book is tracing the path by which the cultural production of women as manipulable objects finally leads to their complete negation.[19] There is here a strong element of what Barthes, writing about Sade, describes as the production of 'a kind of surgical and functional doll' that destroys 'Woman', but the objectification should not really be understood in Sadeian terms, for it has gone beyond the Sadeian logic in which masculine egoism is justified in terms of a male pleasure that makes no concession to the female: 'it must be a matter of indifference to him whether that object is happy or unhappy, provided it be delectable to him; in truth there is no relation between that object and himself.'[20] Delectation is entirely absent from Traven's objectifications; there is no fantasy here of the kind of sexual machine envisaged in Ian McEwan's *The Comfort of Strangers*.[21] Traven's misogynistic strategies are part of a wider phenomenological dread in which all desire has withered away. It is the human organism *tout court* that is for him 'an atrocity exhibition'

(*AE* 9), and he is indeed in 'revolt against the present continuum of time and space' (*AE* 6–7).

Elza Adamowicz's reading of George Hugnet's fetishistic collage *Le Sang en proverbe* (1936) is pertinent to this discussion; suggesting that Hugnet's work 'exploits media images critically', she argues that the disarticulated figure it depicts is not only 'an instance of the fetish' but also 'a self-reflective comment on the process of fetishization'.[22] *The Atrocity Exhibition* is, I am suggesting, similarly self-reflexive. It not only foregrounds the processes by which objectification and fetishisation are put into place but also exposes their disastrous consequences. Nathan's reductive view that the 'sex kit' provides an inventory that is 'an adequate picture of a woman, who could easily be reconstituted from it', and that 'such a list may well be more stimulating than the real thing' (*AE* 85), must be set against Catherine Austin's revulsion at Traven's transformation of 'everything into its inherent pornographic possibilities' (*AE* 118), which manifests a sexual violence that she reads as 'part of a new grammar of callousness and aggression' (*AE* 119). *The Atrocity Exhibition* uncovers the workings of a logic in which the dematerialisation of women precedes their erasure. As Nathan rather more accurately puts it later on: 'The inventory of the young woman is in reality a death kit' (*AE* 86). It is a death-kit that dismembers woman in order finally to kill desire itself. The commodification of sexuality enacted by the mass media (cinema, television, fashion, advertising) functions in this text just as Baudrillard suggests it does more generally, to 'refuse the status of flesh, of sex, of finality of desire, instrumentalizing rather the fragmented parts of the body in a gigantic process of *sublimation*, of denying the body in its very evocation' – a functioning that construes the subject solely in terms of its use- and exchange-value.[23] The entire spectrum of the sexual life is here folded into an isolating and objectifying process from which desire has been expunged. In this cultural imaginary 'psychopathology is the conceptual system of sex' (*AE* 117).

Maps and tracings

Roland Barthes' declaration in *Writing Degree Zero* that in the post-1850 period experimental writing would principally be concerned with 'the problematics of language' needs to be amended in relation to *The Atrocity Exhibition*, which rather exemplifies a concern with the problematics of narrative form. The question of finding an appropriate narrative form is implicit in Ballard's deployment of the latent–manifest distinction, which demands an act of translation: one order of discourse needs to be transposed into the terms of another. The problem of how to make use of Freud's classic distinction had already been faced by the Surrealists to whom *The Atrocity Exhibition* is so deeply indebted. For Breton, two of the most important Surrealist techniques for achieving this expression were psychic automatism, which aimed to release the mind from the fetters of rational control and thus to open up a channel to the unconscious, and collage, which took a range of materials from everyday life and juxtaposed them in order to transform them and thereby create new visions of reality.

Collage may be seen as a practice that is programmatically indeterminate, disrupting the boundaries between the work and the frame, the conscious and the unconscious, art and life. But Breton's emphasis on combination – the attainment of two separate realities – also implies the possibility of *synthesis*, an overcoming of divisions into a higher *sur*-reality. The tension between a practice that evades closure, refusing premature resolutions, and one that seeks synthesis lies at the heart of *The Atrocity Exhibition*, revealing itself most notably in the strain between its fragmented evocation of apocalyptic psychosis and Traven's attempts to build bridges between seemingly unrelated phenomena and to redeem a tragic present through an act of restitution. Equally importantly, the various transformational grammars that the text puts into play are attempts to translate the manifest content of a social unconscious into its latent meanings. This way of viewing social existence conceives it as a code to be cracked; the act of decipherment (or, in Ballard's terms, the act of translation by way of a transformational grammar) permits the underlying truth of phenomena to be revealed. On this reading, the text's collage structure would be oriented less towards indeterminacy and more towards epiphany. The fragments collected together in *The Atrocity Exhibition* would then carry a symbolic significance and would function as the luminous shards that cast light on the inner reality of the time. This, perhaps, is why Ballard has said that *The Atrocity Exhibition* discloses the 'essence' of the age, claiming that 'you could reconstitute the late sixties almost *in toto*, and get it all right ... the whole psychology, the landscapes, the sum total of living, dreaming, dying during that period'.[24] The suggestion here is that in a period of history that was seemingly undergoing seismic shifts and that fractured the social totality, it is only through the dispersed fragments thereby thrown up, what Scott Bukatman usefully describes as 'the cut-ups of a postmodern experience that's *already* cut up', that any sense of the period could be gained.[25]

The Atrocity Exhibition, I think, bears the hallmarks of Surrealism's doubled desire to acknowledge social contradictions and to resolve them: the awareness of radical indeterminacy confronts and vies with a commitment to utopian sublation. The book is at once a Deleuzian 'map' *and* a 'tracing'. It does attempt to uncover what Ballard refers to as the hidden logics and agendas of the 1960s, and it is in this sense a 'tracing' oriented towards the exposure of a deep genetic structure that could make sense of the phantasmagoric nature of contemporary culture. But it also offers a deeply personal and idiosyncratic interpretation of that culture, melding public events with private obsessions, and it is in this sense a 'map' that follows some highly unpredictable 'lines of flight' that cannot easily be systematised or unified. Guattari describes his and Deleuze's 'schizoanalytic cartographies' (in which the plural term is of great significance) as a form of deliberately unscientific *bricolage* that invites their 'readers to freely take and leave the concepts we advance',[26] and this description chimes with Ballard's claim that 'the writer knows nothing any longer' and 'offers the reader the contents of his own head, a set of options and imaginative alternatives' (C 5). The schizoid nature of contemporary society is in *The Atrocity Exhibition* disclosed through Traven's psychosis and through the text's fractured form. If there is a deep structure to be uncovered here, it is certainly *not* in the form of scientific truth but rather in the form of a rhizomatic reading that acknowledges the deterritorialisation of contemporary life and does justice to the incalculable obsessions of a delusional social realm.

Metallised dreams

Ilya Ehrenburg's *The Life of the Automobile* (1929), an impassioned assault on early twentieth-century technophilia and Taylorist reorganisations of the work-space, begins with death. Its opening scene stages a fatal crash in which a once placid life is abruptly ended when the delirium of speed produced by the car, that quintessential machinic symbol of freedom, sensation and eroticism, gains control of its driver and propels him off the road: 'It no longer had a thousand parts, it only had one cruel will ... With the lofty joy of self-oblivion it flew downward, into a pitiful dale filled with dry juniper ... Car No. 180A-74 – iron splinters, glass shards, a lump of warm flesh – lay unstirring beneath the solemn midday sun.'[27] Ehrenburg's title already signals the shift from the human to the mechanical that his text will explore in implacable detail, and this description of death attributes both agency and value to the machine, in a foreshadowing of the author's wider arguments about the social and psychological consequences of technology. *The Life of the Automobile* traces a history in which the car, so potent an emblem of individual fantasy and wish-fulfilment, displaces humanity from its life-world, leaving the machine in sole possession. The vignette with which Ehrenburg opens his text plays on early enthusiasm for the automobile, before calling them to a sudden halt: the death of one individual functions here as the sign of a wider psycho-social dislocation, a revaluation of values through which a humankind subordinated to the imperatives of the machines it has created is subjugated by them: 'Only cars existed in the city. They dashed, they passed one another, they got sick, they squabbled with brazen horns'.[28]

To anyone familiar with Italian Futurism's laudatory invocations of machinery, in which the motor car and the aeroplane figure promi-nently, Ehrenburg's crash reads as a riposte to Marinetti's 'The Founding and Manifesto of Futurism' (1909), in which a similar mechanical delirium results in an accident that leads not to death but to rebirth and to a techno-aesthetic devoted to the Dionysian exalta-tion of danger, revolt, speed, aggression and energy. The 'new beauty' discovered by Marinetti in the primordial power of motorised vehicles is 'the beauty of speed', which produces a reversal of aesthetic values: 'A racing car whose hood is adorned with great pipes, like serpents of explosive breath – a roaring car that seems to ride on grapeshot is more beautiful than the *Victory of Samothrace*'.[29] Programatically technophilic, Marinetti's writing aligns modernity's newness with the engine's dynamism, uniting them in a celebration of movement visi-ble in the typography of the page no less than in the energised rheto-ric. A masculinist dream of self-creation and self-overcoming through a fusion of the organic with the inorganic presides over this pertur-bation, finding its clearest expression in *Mafarka the Futurist* (1909), in which the Daedalian protagonist seeks to forge his son as a mech-anised body capable of embracing the stars and mastering space.[30] Marinetti declared in the 1909 manifesto: 'Time and Space died yesterday. We already live in the absolute, because we have created

eternal, omnipresent speed'.[31] The absolute is in *Mafarka* subordinated to the 'ruthless, lucid will' of the modernist artificer, which
projects it as the fulfilment of desire: 'My metallized brain sees clear
angles everywhere, in rigid, symmetrical systems. The days to come
are there, before me, fixed, straight and parallel, like military routes
plainly mapped out for the armies of my desires!'.[32]

This voluntarist, ego-driven enunciation of power and control
envisages a malleable world in which technology can be harnessed to
the will in order that reality be reconstituted according to the law of
desire. Ehrenburg's text reverses this trajectory, disclosing the
autonomous logics that unfold from within an industrialised technology, which functions in his work much as it does in that of Jacques
Ellul, who argues that 'the ideal for which technique strives is the
mechanization of everything it encounters'.[33] In these accounts the
psychic routes fantasised by Mafarka belong not to the realm of desire
but to the logic of an economy whose needs both precede and prede-
termine those of the individuals whose subjectivities are formed
within that economy's structures, and this is why, as Georges Benko
puts it, 'the idea of the subject cannot be separated from an analysis
of present-day society, not as postmodern but as post-industrial or
programmed'.[34] On this analysis, the multiple and overdetermined
connections between nature, technology and human beings assume
particular significance, since these give rise to various body–machine
formations within an urban space that itself functions as a key determinant of the forms subjectivity is able to take.

The deadliness of *Crash* lies in the uncompromising equation it
makes between the car's material destructiveness and the deeper
social issues disclosed by this destructiveness, especially in the
psycho-sexual domain. The book persistently operates on both these
levels. It is concerned with the maimings and deaths daily brought
about by the car and with the structural–institutional parameters that
permit this to happen.[35] But at the same time, by using the crash as a
symbol of the fusion between destructive human desires and no less
destructive technological imperatives, which interpenetrate and exacerbate each other (with neither able to take precedence), the text suggests that contemporary social existence is powered by the
death-drive. This aspect of the novel has duly been noted by various
critics, but it is important to point out that the critical debate over
Crash tends to revolve around the question of its moral rather than its
aesthetic value. Nor is this inappropriate, for the moral questions

raised by the book go to the heart of its still perplexing ambiguities. Baudrillard's reading, in particular, has provoked a good deal of hostility, since he construes the novel in terms of his own theory of simulation – 'the generation by models of a real without origin or reality' – arguing that in *Crash* distinctions between fiction and truth have been abolished by 'a kind of hyperreality' and claiming on this basis that the text is outside ethical categories altogether.[36] Responses to this reading have frequently emphasised that *Crash* is a cautionary work and that its depiction of a profound techno-cultural will to destruction marks it out as a modern morality tale.[37] These responses recapitulate Ballard's own uncertain views about *Crash*, which have rehearsed these positions well in advance of the critics. In some of his pronouncements he has aligned himself with the morally driven reading, describing the book as 'a warning against that brutal, erotic and overlit realm that beckons more and more persuasively to us from the margins of the technological landscape' (*C* 6), while in other statements he has said that this reading is mistaken because 'the moral dimension' is absent from the book.[38] He has, it should be noted, even described *Crash* as 'a psychopathic hymn', adding that 'it is a psychopathic hymn which has a point'.[39] On this reading, the search for psychic plenitude entails the destruction of the subject as a desiring entity – in other words, its dissolution into the machine, a dissolution that is figured as a redemptive cataclysm.

The difficulty of coming to terms with *Crash* may be traced to the metaphor around which the text is constructed, namely that the car crash is a symbol of sexual fulfilment. By this rhetorical move the phantasmatic potential of the car (its dynamism and eroticism) is physically embodied and objectified. Everything that the automobile emblematises in the realm of the imaginary is now externalised and literalised. Symbolic identification is translated into material assimilation, the car no longer functioning as an image of what is desired but rather as its actual embodiment. This desire to be an integral part of the machine (in and of it as it were) as a way of absorbing its superior power is a marked feature of technophilic modernism, which can be seen, for example, in Le Corbusier's impassioned response to the car: 'Motors in all directions, going at all speeds. I was overwhelmed, an enthusiastic rapture filled me. Not the rapture of the shining coachwork under the gleaming lights, but the rapture of power. The simple and ingenuous pleasure of being in the centre of so much power, so much speed. We are part of it.'[40] For Ballard, 'the twentieth

century reaches almost its purest expression on the highway', for here
we see 'the speed and violence of our age, its strange love affair with
the machine and, conceivably, with its own death and destruction'
(*UG* 262). The desire to be at one with an empowering technology is
in *Crash* taken to an extreme conclusion: the novel's characters treat
the Corbusian rapture *literally* and seek to fuse themselves with their
machines once and for all. In this structure of desire it is not the case
that the distinction between fiction and reality has been dissolved into
hyperreality but rather that the seductive allure of the image is chosen
over the prosaic dullness of the real. The book's subtlety lies in the fact
that what it treats as metaphor, its characters construe as quiddity.
They are, in short, poor *readers*, who prove incapable of interpreting
the sub-texts of a culture in which the car, a metaphoric object *par
excellence*, carries a potent psycho-sexual freight that needs to be
decoded. Within the realm of the hyperreal, in which all distinctions
between truth and falsehood collapse, this would be a doomed enterprise. But in *Crash* the characters' inability to read the social text
should not be confused with the novel's own subtle decoding of the
logics that drive their phantasmatic preference for the image over the
real.

Crawling from the wreckage of this demolition-derby text are characters so powerfully in thrall to the logics of a fantasy technology that
they are bereft of the ability to locate themselves in social space if they
are not somehow placed there by way of mediation. It is no accident
that everything in *Crash* is filtered through image-making systems
and techniques, principally those associated with photocopies, photographs, advertisements, television, ciné-films, and, of course, the
'screen' of the car windshield itself. The novel's opening chapter
already says all that needs to be said on this issue – the rest is just elaboration. For Vaughan, events have no meaning and do not even seem
to be phenomenologically present until they are captured and mediated by some means of mechanical reproduction. The image is at the
hands of the text's characters thus the subject of both fetishisation
and exorbitation: nothing is more real than the image, and without
the image there is no longer any real.[41] Thus Vaughan's identity
seems to reside in the photographs he keeps of himself; sexual activity is meaningless without the presence of the recording camera; violence is an aestheticised and stylised slow-mo tracking-shot; wounds
are photographic illustrations that make no reference to bodily pain;
and the individual is an actor starring in a screen-play of his own

devising. Nowhere is this interpenetration of the reproducible image and a reconstructive technology more clear than in the brilliant long description of Gabrielle, a hybridised automobile-woman who is at once a mechanical and a photographic construct (C 98–100). Will Self's observation to Ballard that people 'are not aware of the extent to which their view of their own identity has been compromised by film and the car windscreen', freeing them 'notionally to annihilate figures on [their] screen', captures the exact end-point of a powerfully disquieting work:

> I knew that Vaughan had retired finally into his own skull. In this over-lit realm ruled by violence and technology he was now driving for ever at a hundred miles an hour along an empty motorway, past deserted filling stations on the edges of wide fields, waiting for a single oncoming car. In his mind Vaughan saw the whole world dying in a simultaneous automobile disaster, millions of vehicles hurled together in a terminal congress of spurting loins and engine coolant. (C 16)

Body-machines

Mark Seltzer identifies three ways of construing what he terms 'the body-machine complex': the human entity as already some sort of machine; the machine as that which replaces bodies and persons; technology as a process that transforms people into machines.[42] These different construals of the interaction between the human and technological realms nonetheless 'communicate on another level' in a number of literary works through a 'radical and intimate *coupling* of bodies and machines'.[43] The trope of coupling, with its boundary-blurring, and identity-shifting resonances, points not only to the erotic implications of such fusion but also to the vulnerability of the soft, pliable body when it is brought into conjunction with the hard, resistant surfaces of the machine. For how, one might ask, can these fragile textures withstand the importunities of those burnished minerals in any physical encounter between them? The coupling of the body and the machine in *Crash* is not of course restricted to that of the human being and the car. To be sure, crashes inscribe the body with the marks of their passing, a brutal fact upon which the novel insists repeatedly, with its references to the wound-scars that 'Ballard' – the text's narrator – describes as 'signatures, inscribed on my body by the dashboard and control surfaces of my car' (C 178), but the crashes are themselves situated within a mediatised 'society of the spectacle' in which the individual is subjected to inscription on another plane of existence: 'I thought of being killed within this huge accumulation of fictions, finding my body marked with the imprint of a hundred television crime serials, the signatures of forgotten dramas which, years after being shelved in a network shake-up, would leave their last credit-lines in my skin' (C 60). These two passages indicate the multiple ways in which both psyche and body are traversed by the technologies that inform social life, a traversal that in Deleuzian terms renders 'the nature–artifice distinction' irrelevant and suggests that desire 'is made up of different lines which cross, articulate or impede each other and which constitute a particular assemblage on a plane of immanence.'[44] Deleuze's critique of the Freudian and Lacanian emphasis on desire as lack is pertinent here because *Crash* persistently depicts desire as an assemblage built up within, and in relation to, the conjunction between the pulsions of the psycho-sexual body and the socius in which it has its being. Deleuze tends to downplay the role of historical determinants in this conjunction, whereas in *Crash* Ballard's emphasis falls decidedly on the power of independent logics to mould that individual, but the Deleuzian claim that desire 'is always assembled and fabricated, on a plane of immanence or of composition which must itself be constructed at the same time as desire assembles and fabricates' accords with the novel's depiction of the forms desire takes in a mediatised technological world.[45]

Burroughs's Doctor Benway observes in *Naked Lunch* that 'Western man is externalizing himself in the form of gadgets'.[46] This externalisation is ubiquitous in *Crash*, taking a doubled form: it manifests itself both in an extreme identification of subjects with machines, such that the two become interchangeable, the subjects' desires being not just mediated by the machine but subordinated to its imperatives; it reveals itself in the domination of subjects by a mechanised environment that has been handed over to the demands of technology. This doubling then discloses itself in what Seltzer usefully terms 'the psychotopography of machine culture' in which 'the crossing paths of the natural and the technological, the crossings between interior states and external systems' play the decisive role in identity formation.[47] It is only after the novel's narrator has a horrific car accident, in which another man is killed, that he is jolted out of a kind of dreamless sleep and begins to see his environment as though for the first time. What had previously been a scarcely observed urban space now appears in a defamiliarised form as a strange, dehumanised world in which the human individual is a nugatory presence:

On the first afternoon I had barely recognized the endless landscape of concrete and structural steel that extended from the motorways to the south of the airport, across its vast runways to the new apartment systems along Western Avenue. Our own apartment house at Drayton Park stood a mile to the north of the airport in a pleasant island of modern housing units, landscaped filling stations and supermarkets, shielded from the distant bulk of London by an access spur of the northern circular motorway which flowed past us on its elegant concrete pillars ... I realized that the human inhabitants of this technological landscape no longer provided its sharpest pointers, its keys to the borderzones of identity ... all the hopes and fancies of this placid suburban enclave, drenched in a thousand infidelities, faltered before the solid reality of the motorway embankments, with their constant and unswerving geometry, and before the finite areas of the car-park aprons. (C 48–9)

The phrase 'borderzones of identity' captures the indeterminate, shifting 'space' in which this novel's exploration of subjectivity plays itself out, and we might note, with a passing nod to Marinetti's Mafarka, that the 'constant and unswerving geometry' of the motorways is portrayed as a domineering reality, which diminishes the individual's significance. Later still, 'Ballard' grasps that there is no longer any meaningful distinction to be made between some inner authenticity and an alienating external reality, since the individual exists in an environment that has been penetrated through and through by the forces and forms of technology: 'Looking closely at this silent terrain, I realized that the entire zone which defined the landscape of my life was now bounded by a continuous artificial horizon, formed by the raised parapets and embankments of the motorways and their access roads and interchanges' (C 53). Within this space it is the conjunction of urban and bodily geometries opened up by technology that is of principal interest, producing a stylised sexuality which takes its cue from curtain-walled office-blocks, ferrous motorway intersections, rectilinear apartment buildings, anonymous airport concourses, and abandoned car parks. This is sex as laboratory experiment, the sexual researcher a detached figure manipulating human subjects as though they were so much mechanical equipment. In this enclosed environment technology opens up new paths for desire to track, creating circuits, relays and couplings that construct unexpected assemblages. On the one hand, it is the blocked energy of a technology brought to standstill in traffic-jams and gridlocks that unlocks the psyche, since this stasis seems 'to be a unique vision of this machinic landscape, an invitation to explore the viaducts of our minds' (*C* 54); but on the other hand, it is the shock of the car crash – a profoundly dynamic collision of body and machine – that unleashes desires that are now inescapably bound to technology. Imagining himself after the accident as 'some huge jointed doll, one of those elaborate humanoid dummies fitted with every conceivable orifice and pain response' (*C* 40), a machined conception of the body far removed from an anthropomorphic view of the human organism, 'Ballard' finds that his sexual responses both turn to, and are expressed through, a tooled environment.

The flowering of wounds

The crash has multiple resonances: it excites to violence and exacerbates desire; couples the body with the machine; produces physical pain and proclaims human mortality; transforms lives through the arbitrariness of the roadway collision; stages theatrical street-happenings for the voyeuristic gaze; and gives rise to an aesthetics of destruction characterised by unsettling techno-human sculptures. Above all else, the crash is the traumatic event, the rent in the social fabric, that shatters habituated lives and uncovers a repressed social unconscious, displaying the individual's fantasy life as the conduit for a perverse technology that embodies a potent will-to-death. 'Ballard' recuperates his crash as 'the only real experience [he] had been through for years' (*C* 39), and he points out that his 'obsession with the sexual possibilities of everything around me had been jerked loose from my mind by the crash' (*C* 29). His experience of wounding opens up a path to his unconscious from which Vaughan emerges to preside over the novel's quest for meaning. But inasmuch as Vaughan is an emanation of the narrator's psyche – as suggested by his conviction 'that Vaughan was a projection of my own fantasies and obsessions' (*C* 220) – he cannot be contained by the role of double, since he is a manifestation of a broader *social* unconscious. He functions as a reversed figure who externalises the dark interiority and bizarre logics of the technological dream: 'Now that Vaughan has died, we will leave with the others who gathered around him, like a crowd drawn to an injured cripple whose deformed postures reveal the secret formulas of their minds and lives. All of us who knew Vaughan accept the perverse eroticism of the car-crash, as painful as the drawing of an exposed organ through the aperture of a surgical wound' (*C* 17).

The image of the aperture in the body, which reveals what was concealed, is a *mise-en-abîme* for the novel as a whole. Everything in this text is turned inside-out, so that what was hidden and ignored is exposed and flaunted, giving rise to an inverted or upside-down reality in thrall to the productions of the unconscious. This reversal not only allows the unconscious to hold sway over the narrative but also treats it as the key to the social realm. The entire novel conforms to this 'nightmare logic' (*C* 23), which it unfolds with cold precision, but it is particularly evident in the opening scenes in which Vaughan's celebratory fantasies of elaborate road-deaths are itemised in remorseless detail, and in the narrator's hallucinatory vision of a reversal of humane behaviour. It is the wound that makes this possible, the novel emphasising that the characters drawn into Vaughan's phantasmagoria belong to a cabal of accident survivors who have been re-made by the technology that almost destroyed them. But what is interesting here, and it is a key part of the novel's purpose, is that the trauma of the accidents leads not to repression but to a heightened awareness of their possible meanings. In another reversal, this time of the influential psychoanalytic account of responses to trauma, the novel is peopled with characters who not only remember their traumas but also use their reminiscences as a means of confronting the inner significance of the logics that produced the trauma in the first place.[48] Thus in *Crash*, far from leading to a repetition compulsion attributable to repression of the unconscious, the trauma of road accidents is a stimulus to a *conscious* exploration of all their parameters. Hence the remorseless itemisation of the variations that can be worked around the relations of bodies with each other and with the technological world in which they have their being. And always, the 'headiness' thus provoked is the goal: 'The hard jazz of radiator grilles, the motion of cars moving towards London Airport along the sunlit oncoming lanes, the street furniture and route indicators – all these seemed threatening and super-real, as exciting as the accelerating pintables of a sinister amusement arcade released on these highways' (*C* 49). The desires unleashed by the trauma of the crash correspond to a violence implicit in technology itself, human sexuality willingly plugging itself into the electrifying realm of the machine. The exorbitation of consciousness all the way through the book is significant because it draws attention to the erosion of taboos, the deadening of affect, and the spectacularisation of social life at the heart of this deviant logic.

In *Crash* it is self-evidently a psycho-social unconscious that is visible through the aperture of the wound. Dynamic in structure and manifesting multiple relays and links, it functions as an assemblage that attests the novel's moral ambivalence. Body and psyche exist in mutually generative relations with a machined environment in which they produce and are produced in turn, and in this overdetermined transection of torsos, minds, cities and technologies any notion of alienation is called into question. The relationship between human and machine is so interwoven here that the appeal to a 'natural' realm or to a pre-technological system of values is closed off. But this is not depicted in some straightforward way as a state of affairs to be deplored. On the contrary, *Crash* is propelled by the options opened up by a technology that proliferates new experiences, and its narrative is driven by the creative–destructive energy that technology harnesses. Thus Vaughan's photographs of diverse sexual acts performed in conjunction with the car encapsulate 'the possibilities of a new logic created by these multiplying artefacts, the codes of a new marriage of sensation and possibility' (*C* 106); Gabrielle, who has been 'turned into a creature of free and perverse sexuality' (*C* 99) by her crushed car, is imagined 'developing a sexual expertise that would be an exact analogue of the other skills created by the multiplying technologies of the twentieth century' (*C* 100); and ultimately the 'deviant technology of the car-crash' is seen to provide 'the sanction for any perverse act' in the belief that the promise of 'a benevolent psychopathology' may thereby be fulfilled (*C* 138).

The search for an ostensibly charitable psychopathology takes place within a libidinal economy that is well beyond the pleasure principle. The fetishisation of car-crash wounds, exhaustively researched and photographically catalogued, project the interaction of body with machine as a self-sustaining circuit. The 'unions of torn genitalia and sections of car body and instrument panel' celebrated in Vaughan's photographs form 'a series of disturbing modules, units in a new currency of pain and desire' (*C* 134) that, once put into service, will be difficult to recall, as is hinted at by Vaughan's scars – 'the marking areas of a future generation of wounds' (*C* 135). Perverse products of the car-crash, these wounds are the markers of a sexuality fixated on trauma – the more extreme, the more desired – a fixation that in Freud's terms may be described as a kind of mourning, 'which actually involves the most complete alienation from the present and the future', a point to which I will return.[49] The terminal nature of these fantasies is already alluded to in the 'Crash' chapter of *The Atrocity Exhibition* where the 'severe genital wounds of an obscene character' are seen to reflect 'polyperverse obsessions of an extreme form' (*AE* 155). The only end-point for this particular trajectory of desire is 'the abattoir of sexual mutilation' (*C* 135) envisioned for famous screen actresses, or the imagined conjunction of vehicle and body in which cars 'become devices for exploiting every pornographic and erotic possibility, every conceivable sex-death and mutilation' (*C* 137), desperate fantasies that disclose a drive to dissolution, which suggests that sex is no longer operative here but rather an instinct for death.

That said, *Crash* also exhibits a kind of counter-narrative that tries to conceive the wound as the source of redemption, tries to imagine how, out of this disaster, the world might be recreated, and nowhere is the text more ambivalent than here. For if the wound is troped as a rent that opens the way to a vision of hell (*C* 192), then it is also figured as a beacon signposting the path to paradise (*C* 53). And these opposed readings of the car-crash co-exist uneasily all the way through the book, as though the writer is searching for some means by which technology can make reparation for all this pain. Glimpses of this restitutive longing are seen, for example, in a haunting vision of death as a release, which recalls the imagery of *The Crystal World*: 'Seagrave's slim and exhausted face was covered with shattered safety glass, as if his body were already crystallizing, at last escaping out of this uneasy set of dimensions into a more beautiful universe' (*C* 185). The narrator, in turn, tries to move to a position in which his initial 'horror and disgust at the sight of … appalling injuries' gives way 'to a lucid acceptance that the translation of these injuries in terms of our fantasies and sexual behaviour was the only means of re-invigorating these wounded and dying victims' (*C* 190). In a world that during the course of this narrative begins 'to flower into wounds' (*C* 146) the only way of conceiving how the blood might be staunched, the trauma annealed, and the cataclysmic future redeemed seems to lie along the path of shared suffering: 'In our wounds we celebrated the re-birth of those we had seen dying by the roadside and the imaginary wounds and postures of the millions yet to die' (*C* 203).

A language in search of objects

The grotesque, like the abject with which it is in close contiguity, testifies to the anomalous and the ambiguous, to that which, in Geoffrey

Galt Harpham's words, acts as an 'affront' to classificatory systems, signalling the invasion of what is conventionally familiar by something that is foreign and disturbing to it.[50] *Crash* deploys both these modes to create a shocking textuality that is traversed by an abject grotesque, which strips away the smooth surfaces of the fetishised commodity in order to expose its inherent destructiveness. The logic it establishes is that of an inverted commodity fetishism; the beguiling promise of a commodified socius is turned inside out to reveal its putrescent innards. The crash is figured here as the purpose for which the car was built: this is its bizarre *raison d'être* and its logical terminus. Advertised as a finely tuned mechanism, an object of sleek functionality and gleaming surfaces, the car is a battered, broken-down engine of destruction, marked everywhere by the scratches, dents, smashed components and leaking fluids that signify its grotesque abjection. The novel's emphasis on a fused machine–body complex works to destabilise received conceptions of both entities, forging a new hybridised organism that is betwixt and between the technological and the human. The car is an inherently unstable object: it *moves* through the spaces of modernity, participating in flows it does not control while at the same time creating patterns and translocations of its own. Providing a stiff carapace for the individuals it encases, it promises a protection it fails to deliver, the crash functioning as the violent, haphazard event that destroys the seemingly bounded identities of its occupants. Thus the supposedly durable car, no less than the more fragile human, is in this text figured as an infirm organism, pock-marked and dented, bruised and battered, leaking fluids (oil, petrol, engine coolant) from its various orifices.

The car is in this sense depicted in anthropomorphic terms, just as the human is seen as a machine, and because both can be wounded, both can fall into abjection. *Crash* is near obsessed with the soft innards of bodies and machines, the signs of their vulnerability to damage, pain, and mutability, and, finally, of their inevitable end in death. Consider the narrator's response to his first car accident:

> Catherine vomited over my seat. This pool of vomit with its clots of blood like liquid rubies, as viscous and discreet as everything produced by Catherine, still contains for me the essence of the erotic delirium of the car-crash, more exciting than her own rectal and vaginal mucus, as refined as the excrement of a fairy queen, or the miniscule globes of liquid that formed beside the bubbles of her contact lenses. In this magical pool, lifting from her throat like a rare discharge of fluid from the

mouth of a remote and mysterious shrine, I saw my own reflection, a
mirror of blood, semen and vomit, distilled from a mouth whose contours only a few minutes before had drawn steadily against my penis.
(C 16–17)

Catherine is associated throughout the text with a scrupulous cleanliness, a desire to control and to wash away all signs of her corporeality, whereas the narrator is fascinated by her pristine orifices, seeking
to discover some sign of effluvium in them out of a contrary desire to
expose the body as a physical, not machine-like, entity (C 112). In this
passage her loss of control over the mechanism of her body discloses
it as at once corporeal and productive, but what the body produces
here is *waste*. This melange of viscosities contrasts sharply with the
metallic body of the car and the bounded identity of the woman,
releasing a line of desire so powerful and transformative that it is
troped as a mystical, thaumaturgic experience. This release is doubtless to be read in terms of an infantile repression of desire, especially
in the anal phase, as the narrator's later reference to the nurses clean-
ing up his leaking body makes clear: 'these starched women in all
their roles reminded me of those who attended my childhood, com-
missionaires guarding my orifices' (C 33). But equally importantly, it
points to the novel's concern with the abject nature of the techno-sex-
uality that is 'liberated' by the crash. The bare, affectless sex-act
between Helen and 'Ballard' concludes with a resonant image in this
context: 'The brief avalanche of dissolving talc that fell across her eyes
as I moved my lips across their lids contained all the melancholy of
this derelict vehicle, its leaking engine oil and radiator coolant' (C 79).
And by the end of the novel Vaughan's car, emblem of his thrusting,
aggressive sexuality, is a virtual wreck marked by 'dents and impacts,
like the self-inflicted wounds of a distressed child (C 217–18). In its
last act prior to his death, 'its engine sound[s] a cry of pain' (C 219).

The abject is typically read as that which the human seeks at all
costs to avoid and to evade; as Žižek pithily observes: 'when our inner-
most self is directly externalized, the result is disgusting.'[51] There is of
course a tradition of writing (de Sade, Bataille, Miller, Burroughs) that
takes abjection as one of its most central concerns, and Ballard's
Crash clearly belongs to it. It has been suggested, however, that abjection cannot be lived through ritual, 'except in the case of something
like "obsessive-compulsive disorder"' and that the idea of transgression, a concept seen as 'parallel to abjection', may provide a viable

alternative.[52] The notion of obsessive–compulsive behaviour certainly offers one way of thinking about the inexorable logic traced in *Crash*, but to what extent can the novel be read as a valorisation of transgression? Scott Bukatman, for example, argues that it 'simultaneously mocks and evokes the "drive" toward transcendence and continuity' and he claims that few literary works 'have been so transgressive'.[53] But before addressing this issue, I want to consider the text's depiction of narcissistic and cerebralised desire.

Dissociation from affects and from the meaning of events is a predominant feature of *Crash*. It is there in the ubiquity of the instrumental approach to human life, in the treatment of body-parts as replicable objects of exchange, and in the reduction of sex to use-value. It is visible in the persistent emphasis on voyeurism, which manifests itself in the behaviour of the crowds who gather at crash-sites, responding to fatal accidents with detachment, observing 'the scene with the calm and studied interest of intelligent buyers at a leading bloodstock sale' (*C* 155). But voyeurism also testifies to a triangulation of desire (ubiquitous in this text) in which the third figure is not a mediating *rival* – as in the Girardian model – but rather a welcome spectator who participates actively in the production of ever more desire. The presence of the third is required here not because desire is *mimetic* in this text but because it is spectacularised and can scarcely function at all without an observer to heighten sensation and provide meaning, as in this sex-act between Helen and 'Ballard': 'Without Vaughan watching us, recording our postures and skin areas with his camera, my orgasm had seemed empty and sterile, a jerking away of waste tissue' (*C* 120). The sexual behaviour that is induced and exacerbated by the observing figure is entirely abstract. Devoid of emotion and lacking reference to other human beings, it becomes a form of self-excitation that recalls Lawrence's vituperations against 'sex in the head' in *Women in Love*. This then follows two trajectories: either as a movement away from the physical expression of desire, erotic interest being 'an interest as much in the idea of making love ... as in the physical pleasures of the sex act itself' (*C* 34), or as a detachment from the human other, which strips sex of intersubjective meaning, so that a possible infidelity no longer has 'any reference to anything but a few square inches of vaginal mucosa, fingernails and bruised lips and nipples' (*C* 35).

These sexual dispositions are fundamentally narcissistic in orientation, producing an auto-eroticism in which humans and machines alike are nothing more than objects for use rather than objects for love. A shared narcissism is the bond that draws all the novel's characters together, and Vaughan, the figure who articulates and channels their desires, is merely the most obvious narcissist, a man trying to re-assemble his shattered identity by equating it with the vehicles that disfigured him. For Vaughan, the car is the site and sign of all his libidinal investments, and his fierce sexuality is directed principally at this object, which it aims to penetrate and possess. He is so closely identified with the car that when detached from it, he 'cease[s] to hold any interest' (C 117). The narrator's homo-erotic attachment to Vaughan is a doubled phenomenon, at once a form of male bonding in which the car functions as the object *par excellence* through which homo-sociality is mediated, and an expression of desire for the object itself, a displacement of libidinal energy from the human to the machine. Just as Vaughan wants to penetrate and thus merge with the car (in the process asserting his phallic masculinity) so 'Ballard' in wanting to penetrate Vaughan is unsure what exactly is his real object of desire. When he first imagines having sex with Vaughan he does so in terms which suggest that a passion for technology is in play more than a longing for the human other: 'I visualized these sections of radiator grilles and instrument panels coalescing around Vaughan and myself, embracing us as I pulled the belt from its buckle and eased down his jeans, celebrating in the penetration of his rectum the most beautiful contours of a rear-fender assembly, a marriage of my penis with all the possibilities of a benevolent technology' (C 148). The act of sex with which their relationship culminates, just before Vaughan's death, exemplifies this confusion of the body and the machine in still more detail, and this confusion, the sign of a gener-alised dehumanisation is visible in the turning away from people to material objects that characterises the behaviour of all the novel's characters.

Crash depicts a relentlessly over-cerebralised world in which affect has been so etiolated that the narrator's experience of techno-sex leaves him thinking about his wife's 'death in a more calculated way, trying to devise in my mind an even richer exit than the death which Vaughan had designed for Elizabeth Taylor' (C 181). A disturbingly extreme form of dissociation is at work here, which points to a psy-chological interiority in which affect has been entirely displaced by abstracted fantasies that derive, as I suggested earlier, from a world dominated by the image. The mechanisation of desire produces a depersonalised view of the self and a derealised view of the world, phenomena that Freud in 'A Disturbance of Memory on the Acropolis' (1936) describes as 'models of psychological disorder', declaring them to be 'abnormal structures.'[54] In *Crash* the attenuation of reality that results from this excessively cerebral view of experience gives rise to 'a language in search of objects' (*C* 35), an extraordinarily resonant phrase, which foregrounds the disconnection of this technologised Volapuk from the phenomena it attempts to describe. The text's proliferation of detached 'acts and emotions' are just 'ciphers searching for their meaning among the hard, chromium furniture of our minds' (*C* 180).

And so we return to the vexed question of transgression. The novel stresses throughout that it is not principally concerned with *sex* at all but rather with *technology*. Its central *leitmotiv* is the inescapable pressure exerted on human beings by the technological force-field, the narrator eventually grasping that all his relationships are 'mediated by the automobile and its technological landscape' (*C* 101). Sex is an epiphenomenon here, the outward sign of the social processes and logics that are expressed through it and that colonise it so effectively: it is the ruse by which technology gives the illusion that desire has been liberated. Thus de Certeau's optimistic view that although the subject's autonomy 'diminishes in proportion to the technocratic expansion' of dominating social systems, 'the individual detaches himself from them without being able to escape them and can henceforth only try to outwit them, to pull tricks on them', is in this text revealed as a fantasy to which Foucault provides the necessary riposte: 'Where there is desire, the power relation is already present: an illusion, then, to denounce this relation for a repression exerted after the event; but vanity as well, to go questing after a desire that is beyond the reach of power.'[55] In *Crash* the thorough permeation of the social life-world by technological power invites us to ask if we can properly speak of 'desire' at all in this context. Baudrillard's view that the novel depicts a 'violently sexed world, but one without desire, full of violated and violent bodies, as if neutralized' is pertinent here, as is Parveen Adams's suggestion that *Crash* is 'not dominated by desire' but rather 'by the death drive'.[56]

Sex without desire: this appears to capture the inexorably unfolding processes of depersonalisation and derealisation tracked in this text, in which the body is estranged from itself and the psyche is separated from the other. Desire is not 'repressed' here but directed into a 'line of flight' expressive of a will-to-destruction whose terminus must be death.[57] The novel's entire narrative trajectory moves to this single goal. It is proleptically announced in its opening line – 'Vaughan died yesterday in his last car crash' (C 7) – an act that already predicts the path that 'Ballard' will necessarily follow at the end of the book: 'Already I knew that I was designing the elements of my own car-crash' (C 224). These individual acts, moreover, are the templates for an all-encompassing annihilation that combines the perverse allure of the atom-bomb Armageddon that figures so prominently in *The Atrocity Exhibition* with the roadway autogeddon that is in *Crash* depicted as a dream 'of metallized death' (C 36). Metaphor and its literal meaning come together here in a celebration of technologised sexuality as world apocalypse. This is why Ballard can laud the book as a narrative of psychic fulfilment: 'The whole dynamic of that book, I suppose, leads toward the ultimate car crash, which we all celebrate.'[58] By insisting so remorselessly on the colonisation of the sexual instinct by the death instinct, in which aggressiveness is turned inwards, *Crash* not only mocks sanitised bourgeois norms and expectations but also spurns the gratifications supposedly provided by the renunciations that underpin civilisation.[59] But the novel is transgressive in another sense, too. Its delineation of a world given over to techno-sexual destructiveness reveals it to be the expression of the logics of power that predominate in the social order that produces it, which, to adapt Marx, 'must nestle everywhere, settle everywhere, establish connections everywhere.'[60] But at the same time – and this, I think, is what makes the book so morally ambiguous – *Crash* suggests that this destructiveness cannot be explained by reference to these logics alone because in some sense it answers to and simply exacerbates a human desire that is always already in place.

Notes

1 R. Luckhurst, *'The Angle Between Two Walls': The Fiction of J. G. Ballard* (Liverpool: Liverpool University Press, 1997), pp. 92–3.
2 S. Dalí, *The Collected Writings of Salvador Dalí*, trans. H. Finkelstein (Cambridge: Cambridge University Press, 1998), pp. 254, 267.
3 A. Burns and C. Sugnet, 'J. G. Ballard', in A. Burns and C. Sugnet (eds), *The Imagination on Trial: British and American Writers Discuss their Working Methods* (London: Allison and Busby, 1981), pp. 16–30, p. 27.

4   F. Guattari, *The Guattari Reader* (ed. G. Genosko (Oxford: Blackwell, 1996), pp. 197–8.
5   G. Deleuze and F. Guattari, *A Thousand Plateaus: Capitalism and Schizophrenia*, trans. B. Massumi (Minneapolis and London: University of Minnesota Press, 1996), pp. 7, 12.
6   J. G. Ballard, 'J. G. Ballard's Comments on His Own Fiction', *Interzone* (April 1996): pp. 19–25, p. 22.
7   Luckhurst, *'The Angle Between Two Walls'*, p. 85.
8   U. Apollonio (ed.), *Futurist Manifestoes* (London: Thames and Hudson, 1973), p. 22.
9   W. Self, 'Conversations: J. G. Ballard', in *Junk Mail* (London: Penguin, 1996), pp. 329–71, p. 339.
10 Deleuze and Guattari, *A Thousand Plateaus*, p. 12.
11 G. Deleuze, *The Logic of Sense*, trans. M. Lester with C. Stivale, ed. C. V. Boundas (London: Athlone Press, 1990), pp. 304, 320.
12 G. Debord, *The Society of the Spectacle*, trans. D. Nicholson-Smith (New York: Zone, 1995), pp. 12, 13.
13 Debord, *The Society of the Spectacle*, p. 14.
14 For more on this point, see Luckhurst, *'The Angle Between Two Walls'*, p. 94.
15 This is the case made by A. Mahon, 'Hans Bellmer's Libidinal Politics', in R. Spiteri and D. LaCoss (eds), *Surrealism, Politics and Culture* (Aldershot: Ashgate, 2003): pp. 246–66. For a view of Bellmer's work as misogynistic see M. A. Caws, *The Surrealist Look: An Erotics of Encounter* (Cambridge MA: MIT Press, 1997).
16 Debord, *The Society of the Spectacle*, pp. 17, 140.
17 A. Jouffroy, *Bellmer*, trans. B. Frechtman (William and Norma Copley Foundation, n.d.), no pagination.
18 S. Sontag, 'The Pornographic Imagination', in *A Susan Sontag Reader* (Harmondsworth: Penguin, 1982), pp. 205–34, p. 224.
19 For a reading that sees this gender problematic in terms of the book's avant-garde lineage, see Luckhurst, *'The Angle Between Two Walls'*, p. 108.
20 R. Barthes, *Sade Fourier Loyola*, trans. R. Miller (London: Jonathan Cape, 1977), p. 123; Marquis de Sade, *Justine, Philosophy in the Bedroom and Other Writings*, trans. R. Seaver and A. Wainhouse (New York: Grove Press, 1966), p. 604.
21 I. McEwan, *The Comfort of Strangers* (London: Picador, 1981), p. 81.
22 E. Adamowicz, *Surrealist Collage in Text and Image: Dissecting the Exquisite Corpse* (Cambridge: Cambridge University Press, 1998), p. 181.
23 J. Baudrillard, *The Consumer Society: Myths and Structures*, trans. C. Turner (London: Sage, 2003), pp. 133, 150.
24 Burns and Sugnet, 'J. G. Ballard', p. 24.

25 S. Bukatman, *Terminal Identity: The Virtual Subject in Postmodern Science Fiction* (Durham and London: Duke University Press, 1993), p. 44.

26 Guattari, *The Guattari Reader*, p. 198.

27 I. Ehrenburg, *The Life of the Automobile*, trans. J. Neugroschel (London: Serpent's Tail, 1999), p. 6.

28 Ehrenburg, *The Life of the Automobile*, p. 168.

29 U. Apollonio, *Futurist Manifestoes* (London: Thames and Hudson, 1973), p. 21.

30 F. T. Marinetti, *Mafarka the Futurist: An African Novel*, trans. C. Diethe and S. Cox (London: Middlesex University Press, 1998), p. 143.

31 Apollonio, *Futurist Manifestoes*, p. 22.

32 Marinetti, *Mafarka the Futurist*, p. 148.

33 J. Ellul, *The Technological Society*, trans. J. Wilkinson (London: Jonathan Cape, 1965), p. 12.

34 G. Benko, 'Introduction: Modernity, Postmodernity and the Social Sciences', in G. Benko and U. Strohmeyer (eds), *Space and Social Theory: Interpreting Modernity and Postmodernity* (Oxford: Blackwell, 1997), pp. 1–44, p. 18.

35 Burns and Sugnet, 'J. G. Ballard', p. 23. He reiterated this point in his 'Introduction' to the 1995 reprint of the novel. See Ballard, *C*, p. 6.

36 J. Baudrillard, *Simulations*, trans. P. Foss, P. Patton and P. Beitchman (New York: Semiotext[e], 1983), p. 2; J. Baudrillard, 'Two Essays', *Science Fiction Studies* 55. 18: 3 (November 1991): 309–20, pp. 312, 315.

37 V. Sobchak, 'Baudrillard's Obscenity', *Science Fiction Studies* 55. 18: 3 (November 1991): 327–9. For other readings that focus on the text's representation of the death-drive, without quite the same moral fervour as that displayed by Sobchak, see N. Ruddick, 'Ballard/*Crash*/Baudrillard', *Science Fiction Studies* 58. 19: 3 (November 1992): 354–60, and, for a subtle Lacanian reading of the film, P. Adams, 'Death Drive', in M. Grant (ed.), *The Modern Fantastic: The Films of David Cronenberg* (Westport CT: Praeger, 2000): pp. 102–22.

38 C. Bresson, 'J. G. Ballard at Home', *Metaphores* 7 (March 1982): 5–29, p. 24.

39 Self, 'Conversations', p. 348.

40 Quoted in J. Donald, *Imagining the Modern City* (London: Athlone, 1999), p. 55.

41 For a different reading of the novel's use of photographic and cinematic imagery, see Baudrillard, 'Two Essays', pp. 317–18.

42 M. Seltzer, *Bodies and Machines* (New York and London: Routledge, 1992), pp. 7–12.

43 Seltzer, *Bodies and Machines*, pp. 12–13.

44 G. Deleuze and C. Parnet, *Dialogues II*, trans. H. Tomlinson and B. Habberjam (London and New York: Continuum, 1987), pp. 98, 97.

45 Deleuze and Parnet, *Dialogues II*, p. 103.
46 W. Burroughs, *Naked Lunch* (London: Flamingo, 1993), p. 33.
47 Seltzer *Bodies and Machines*, p. 19.
48 For a different reading of the wound, with reference to Cronenberg's *Crash*, see Adams, 'Death Drive', pp. 102–22.
49 S. Freud, *Introductory Lectures on Psychoanalysis*, trans. J. Strachey (Harmondsworth: Penguin, 1974), p. 316.
50 G. Galt Harpham, *On the Grotesque: Strategies of Contradiction in Art and Literature* (Princeton: Princeton University Press, 1982), pp. 4, 11.
51 S. Žižek, *On Belief* (London and New York: Routledge, 2001), p. 60.
52 P. Hegarty, *Georges Bataille: Core Cultural Theorist* (London: Sage, 2000), p. 124.
53 Bukatman, *Terminal Identity*, p. 293.
54 S. Freud, *On Metapsychology: The Theory of Psychoanalysis*, trans. J. Strachey (Harmondsworth, Penguin, 1984), p. 453.
55 M. de Certeau, *The Practice of Everyday Life*, trans. S. Rendall (Berkeley: University of California Press, 1988), pp. xxiii, xxiv; M. Foucault, *The History of Sexuality: Volume One: An Introduction*, trans. R. Hurley (Harmondsworth: Penguin, 1978), pp. 81–2.
56 Baudrillard, 'Two Essays', p. 319; Adams, 'Death Drive', p. 103.
57 For the concept of 'lines of flight' see G. Deleuze, *Negotiations: 1972–1990*, trans. M. Joughin (New York: Columbia University Press, 1995), pp. 171–2.
58 C. Platt, *Dream Makers Science Fiction and Fantasy Writers at Work* (London: Xanadu, 1987), p. 91.
59 The text thus reverses Freud's suggestion that the death instinct can be 'made to serve the purposes of Eros, especially by being turned outwards as aggressiveness'. See S. Freud, *New Introductory Lectures on Psychoanalysis*, trans. J. Strachey (Harmondsworth: Penguin, 1975), p. 141.
60 K. Marx and F. Engels, *Manifesto of the Communist Party*, trans. S. Moore (Moscow: Progress Publishers, 1977 [1848]), p. 39. Marx is speaking about the internal needs of expanding markets under capitalism.

3

Uneasy pleasures

It has often been noted, not least by Ballard himself, that his most abiding concern was with the theme of time. His earliest fictions, he has said, 'were obsessed with time, their real subject matter I suppose is time, the finiteness of life.'[1] Although this is an accurate observation, it distracts one from some of the other significant preoccupations evident in his early work. Of these, a real interest in the nature of urban life, especially how it might look in the future, is readily apparent in a number of stories, perhaps most obviously 'The Concentration City' (1957), 'The Overloaded Man' (1961), 'Billennium' (1961), 'The Subliminal Man' (1963), and 'The Ultimate City' (1976), all of which explore different aspects of the inexorable contraction of space. 'The Concentration City' opens with a series of clipped verbal exchanges, fragments of the sort of quick-fire speech rhythms immortalised in countless street-smart American films:

> Noon talk on Millionth Street.
> 'Sorry, these are the West Millions. You want 9775335th East.'
> 'Dollar five a cubic foot? Sell!'
> 'Take a westbound express to 495th Avenue, cross over to a Redline elevator and go up a thousand levels to Plaza Terminal. Carry on south from there and you'll find it between 568th Avenue and 422nd Street.'
> 'There's a cave-in down at KEN County! Fifty blocks by twenty by thirty levels.'
> 'Listen to this – "PYROMANIACS STAGE MASS BREAKOUT! FIRE POLICE CORDON BAY COUNTY!"'
> 'It's a beautiful counter. Detects up to .0005 per cent monoxide. Cost me three hundred dollars.'
> 'Have you seen those new intercity sleepers? They take only ten minutes to go up 3,000 levels!'
> 'Ninety cents a foot? Buy!' (CS 23)

The entire paragraph pulses with energy, the city's illimitable scale blazoned by its preposterously large street and district numbers, its dynamism evident in the breathless speech patterns of its citizens and in the snapshot glimpses they offer of urban arson and falling buildings, its haste communicated by the repeated exclamation marks and the emphasis on super-fast travel, and its subordination to the values of the real estate market proclaimed by the urgent injunctions to buy and sell. An enormous metropolis that extends in all directions, the concentration city is a futurist nightmare, a cell-like concrete termitary which traps its residents economically, spatially and psychologically.

In such an environment it is above all physical space that is at a premium. Space to breathe, space to live, space to imagine. In 'The Concentration City', which posits an infinitely extended metropolis, space is subject to the economic laws of urban development and the price mechanism. 'Billennium', in contrast, focuses on the implications for human life of an extreme contraction of space. It depicts the city of the future as the site of a brain-scrambling sensory overload in which all-night movies boom out their dialogue and music for miles around, buildings constructed out of wafer-thin materials permit no privacy, streets are jammed with pedestrians forced to endure ear-splitting levels of noise and subjected to non-stop visual advertising, and the unstoppable growth of the urban population threatens total civic paralysis. The city is in both stories troped as a malignant, self-replicating cancerous growth that destroys the natural world and subordinates human life to the strictures of a command economy. Thus in 'Billennium' the creation of over-populated urban ghettos has led to the colonisation of the rural world by industrial imperatives: 'The countryside, as such, no longer existed. Every single square foot of ground sprouted a crop of one type or other. The one-time fields and meadows of the world were now, in effect, factory floors, as highly mechanized and closed to the public as any industrial area' (CS 271).

This process of colonisation is revealed in both texts to have enslaved the colonisers. The main figure in 'Billennium' has surrendered 'to the dynamics of the city' (CS 271), while the central protagonist in the earlier story is defeated in his quest to discover the city's boundaries. Dreams of escape once again lie at the heart of both tales, but whereas in one the goal is freedom from the hell of other people, in the other it is liberation from a disciplinary regime which enforces the notion that space is solely functional and thus the site of a necessary productivity. In 'The Concentration City' Franz's desire to build a flying machine stems from his dream of floating in empty, unbounded space, a symbol of freedom from the restrictions of mensuration and the imperatives of labour alike. The aspiration to escape from all-enveloping urban space is thus inseparable from a critique of the political interests served by the colonisation of the city, for its functionaries consider the notion of 'non-functional' space, which serves no instrumental purpose, as an absurdity. Interrogated by the police after he is caught trying to reach the city limits, Franz is eventually sent to see a psychiatrist when it becomes clear that he is guilty of a kind of Orwellian thought-crime. He is informed that the search for free space is as doomed as the quest for an existence outside of temporality, but the twist comes when he realises that the date on the calendar is the same as when he embarked on his journey three weeks earlier, a fact which suggests that if time can be reversed then non-functional space might also exist. Equally significantly, the reversal of time exposes the bureaucratic lies he has been told as the means by which social control is exercised, and this points up the connections between governance of space and political power. The story thus offers a nightmare scenario of complete determinism in which the human being is regarded as a pure economic unit, and agency is expunged.

'Billennium' offers a different take on the question of urban overdevelopment and massive population increase. It depicts a situation in which the 'intensive cultivation' of agriculture on a world scale has just about kept pace with population growth but 'has meant that 95 per cent of the population' is 'permanently trapped in vast urban conurbations' (CS 271). Here all living quarters – in some parody of Corbusian modernist design – are conceived as housing batteries that have been reduced to four square metres per head. Human beings are thus forced to endure chicken-coop living conditions that once again disclose their reduced status. When two characters find a large hidden room they are stunned by 'the sensation of absolute spatial freedom' (CS 275) it induces. But having discovered a node of emptiness that resembles the non-functional space for which the protagonist of 'The Concentration City' was looking, they immediately offer to share it with others. After two girlfriends and their parents have moved in, the room is progressively sub-divided until each individual's living space has been reduced to exactly four square metres, and the new arrivals start to hint that the room's original occupants should leave. An unsettling question remains unanswered: was the decision to share the room an act of altruism or a sign of enslavement to existing living conditions? For if the two men were in fact unable to cope with the spatial freedom they thought they had wanted then it might be that the determinism from which Ballard's protagonists typically seek to escape actually characterises the kind of world they secretly desire and need after all. And this would suggest that it is not autonomy and freedom which are really the dreamed of objectives but rather a mechanised existence in which the subject conforms to the demands of necessity.

An atmosphere of almost unbearable sensory overload pervades these stories. The future of urban space is troped here under the sign of exorbitance. Cities are conceived on an almost incalculable scale in terms of sheer size but they are also imagined as sites of broiling activity, zones of turmoil in which impersonal forces and agencies clash and combine. A relentless proliferation of stimuli characterises these metropolitan terrains: booming soundtracks to publicly aired films, large advertising billboards, incessantly churned out housing prices, huge building projects that devastate entire precincts, and the constant movement of people and traffic. Exaggeration, extravagance, excess: these are the markers of a runaway hyper-modernity. Unsurprising, then, that the theme of escape that is problematised in these stories in relation to the question of agency is then linked to a desire to avoid the life of the city altogether. For if one option is the willing subservience of the subject to urban functionalism and economic control then the only other option appears to be a withdrawal from the external environment so complete that it propels the subject into the empty spaces of the solitary mind. In 'Billennium' the open space provided by the discovered room seems to offer just this possibility: 'Sitting there in the evenings, surrounded by his books and albums, Ward steadily forgot the city outside ... Rossiter and himself began to seem the only real inhabitants of the world, everyone else a meaningless by-product of their own existence, a random replication of identity which had run out of control' (CS 275). Here urban exorbitance is so intolerable that the only viable response to it appears to lie in its negation. If this negation betokens a drift towards solipsism then the rejection of the external world should be read as a reaction to the fear that subjectivity *tout court* is under threat; the meaninglessness attributed to the replicable lives led by others derives from the hive-like existence they are forced to lead. Nor should we ignore the fact that it is only the fortuitous discovery of a private space which has permitted

Ward and Rossiter to withstand this etiolation of identity; their alienation from those replicable others who are interchangeable entities in
a cell-like structure signals their horror at their own recent past and
their anxiety about their immediate future. A room of one's own in
this case provides scant protection from the controlling world outside
its defensive walls.

An awareness of this conundrum motivates the narrative logic of
stories such as 'The Overloaded Man' (1961) and 'The Enormous
Space' (1989). The earlier of these texts begins with an arresting sen-
tence: 'Faulkner was slowly going insane' (CS 244). But as is often the
case in Ballard's work this affirmation cannot be taken at face value:
its truth is what the story calls into question. On the surface of it, there
can be no dispute. A deranged recluse shuts himself off from contact
with the world in an effort to free himself from the constraints of
physical reality, and in the course of this experiment murders his wife
without even realising that he has done so. The story could thus seem
to be a classic cautionary tale, a sly parody of idealist philosophies,
which warns against the dangers of trying to blot out the material
realm in order to enter a domain of pure ideation. But not so fast. For
the world against which Faulkner has set his face is a carefully partic-
ularised one, and his revolt against its limits represents an assault on
a rigorously enforced conception of normality. As in *The Stepford
Wives* the suburban setting and its domestic regime produce docile
puppets rather than purposive individuals. Faulkner lives in a
modern, up-to-date village, but the contraction of urban space is again
an issue, for the problem of 'compressing a great number of small
houses into a four-acre site' has not been solved and living there is
'hell on earth' (CS 245). Looking ahead to the modernist design of the
tower-block in *High-Rise*, the text depicts this village as follows: 'The
whole development was a sprawl of interlocking frosted glass, white
rectangles and curves, at first glance exciting and abstract ... but to the
people within formless and visually exhausting' (CS 245–6). Unable
to orientate themselves within this hyper-architecture, its residents
either leave or become automata. Faulkner's super-efficient wife, 'the
standard executive product', is a programmed cyborg perfectly
attuned to the various machines that govern her daily existence: 'In
the same strict sequence she stacked the cups and plates in the dish-
washer, slid the pot roast for that evening's dinner into the auto-
cooker and selected the alarm, lowered the air-conditioner,
refrigerator and immersion heater settings, switched open the oil

storage manifolds for the delivery tanker that afternoon, and retracted her section of the garage door' (CS 244). When she bids Faulkner farewell, her kiss is 'quick and functional, like the automatic peck of some huge bottle-topping machine' (CS 245).

Faulkner's wife has surrendered her autonomy and her sense of identity to the logics of a machine-tooled world with its over-riding economic imperatives. Subordinated to a series of fixed movements, her daily routine follows a planned sequence that has been programmed into her. For Faulkner, the behaviour induced by this automation of the self is connected with the rationalisation of economic processes, and he envisages his wife spending her days 'in the same whirl of efficiency, stabbing buttons marked "Jones", "Smith", and "Brown", shunting paraplegics to the left, paranoids to the right' (CS 244). His response to this bureaucratic productivity is a strategy of negation, initially marked by a refusal of work and eventually by withdrawal from life itself. Everything about his environment, from the exhausting architecture to the frenzied activity of his wife, betokens acquiescence to the socio-economic relations from which he wants to escape, which leads him to fragment and then disintegrate the objects that dominate his mental space by turning them into disembodied geometric forms. It is significant that this strategy is especially effective in respect of over-associated consumer goods: 'Stripped of their accretions of sales slogans and status imperatives, their real claim to reality was so tenuous that it needed little mental effort to obliterate them altogether' (CS 246). What is at stake here is nothing less than the question of the whole consumer culture. Once released from their habitual associations, and from the desires promoted by these associations, these now defamiliarised consumer products are emptied of meaning.

But if Faulkner is alienated from a world of consumer durables then his alienation also signals a wider phenomenological crisis, a theme already developed in *The Atrocity Exhibition*. For inasmuch as he rejects the values that sustain a capitalist economy he also turns his face away from human existence altogether, an existential choice which seems to suggest that outside this dominative economy there is, quite simply, *nothing*. Faulkner's derealisation of the material world is thus a means for escaping time, which effectively marks the end of life itself. The overwhelming desire to escape phenomenal reality, especially that of one's own corporeality, described here in Sartrean terms as 'the nausea of the external world' (CS 253), proves to be no less destructive a force than the social processes from which Faulkner wants to liberate himself. Faulkner's attempt to overcome this nausea stems from a sense of social alienation that is as much a creation of the society he detests as is his wife's automation. Both fig ures are then *products* of the same system, and both are in different ways its devalued objects. Faulkner's wife may appear to be a dena- tured cyborg but his own dehumanisation is so extreme that it not only renders him capable of murdering her while denying him the presence of mind to grasp the meaning of this act but also leaves him with no alternative to the material world from which he is estranged except the fantasy of disembodiment – 'an absolute continuum of existence uncontaminated by material excrescences' (*CS* 254).

Abject modernity

The dystopian novels that Ballard wrote in the 1960s and 1970s mark a shift from the possibilities inherent in science fiction toward the power of contemporary fabulation. These tightly constructed and rigidly controlled myths of the near future depart from devastatingly simple starting points and then unfold with a relentless logic. A man crashes his car onto a decaying, refuse-strewn traffic island situated between several intersecting carriageways and finds himself unable to escape this abjected industrial waste land; the residents of a brand new tower block – supposed emblem of social planning and designed living – prove to be incapable of creating a community and gradually embark on full-scale clan warfare. The two novels in which these sit- uations are dramatised – *Concrete Island* (1973) and *High-Rise* (1975) – belong to a particular socio-cultural period, the interregnum between the end of the 'old Labour' project begun in 1945 and the beginning of the Thatcher era in 1979. An air of stasis hangs over these works. By isolating their protagonists physically, thereby cutting them off from their social world, the novels psychologise their dilem- mas while depriving them of the possibility of external action. The effect this has is striking. The anger and frustration depicted in these texts are offered no meaningful way of breaking out of a self-willed paralysis and reconnecting with a wider collective reality. Social prob- lems are evoked but solutions to them are blocked at source, and a brooding sense of failure, despair and rage predominates.

    Concrete Island and *High-Rise* belong to the fag-end of post-war wel- fare statism, offering bleak commentaries on Harold Macmillan's claim that the British 'had never had it so good' and Harold Wilson's conviction that the 'white heat of technology' would help to bring about prosperity for all. They also write *finis* to the modernist dream of rational planning and urban design, which drew on technology in order to shape the environment aesthetically and to provide a blue-print for future life. The two novels focus on opposed ends of this utopian project, one taking place on a site that is a non-place, an unin-tended byproduct of a road-building programme, the other situated in a skyscraper expressly built to facilitate a new mode of self-sustaining, high-tech communal life. The concrete island on which Maitland crashes is not just a metaphor for his mind but also a symbol of the waste and destruction modernity leaves in its wake. It is a non-place in precise ways: it exists solely as the space left over and in between a series of interlocking highways, which define and isolate it; it is a for-gotten patch of waste ground shaped by the discarded remnants of urban life; it is a habitus for the city's rejects, who are forced to live on its margins. This non-place functions as an abject, alienated micro-cosm, the dark other to the mundane reality from which Maitland is so suddenly removed. *High-Rise* takes a different tack. Its fashionable tower block is an exemplary product of modernist architectural design. An edifice in the tradition of Le Corbusier and Mies van der Rohe – and probably modelled on Erno Goldfinger's once infamous Trellick Tower – it derives from a machine-age aesthetic, being com-posed of rigid lines, rectilinear shapes, and austere materials. It is the exact opposite of the disjected island, because it is a consciously planned, carefully structured environment intended to solve the prob-lems of urban life. But like the island it too hints at the shadowy sides of modernity, its dehumanising and alienating aspects. The 'concrete landscape' in which the tower block's inhabitants live seems like 'an environment built, not for man, but for man's absence' (*HR* 25).

Foucault's suggestion that a 'whole history remains to be written of *spaces* – which would at the same time be the history of *powers* (both these terms in the plural) – from the great strategies of geo-politics to the little tactics of the habitat, institutional architecture from the class-room to the design of hospitals, passing via economic and political installations' is pertinent to the representation of spaces in *Concrete Island* and *High-Rise*.[2] But whereas Foucault envisaged a project by way of which one would study the interrelation of spaces and powers in time, tracing their historical formations and transformations, Ballard focuses attention on what Marc Augé describes as an ethnography of the near. He isolates a particular conjuncture and then, rather than tracing it back, projects it forward, trying to imagine how it might develop. This approach might be read as emblematic of a *fin-de-siècle* postmodern sensibility, which refuses the consolations of the historical narrative, even in the elliptical modes cherished by Foucault. Augé sees a correlation between a loss of faith in teleological conceptions of human life and recently influential spatial mappings of contemporaneity. The age he designates 'supermodern' exists under the sign of *excess*, but, as in Lutz Niethammer's account of *post-histoire*, the over-abundance of events and the over-loading of the mind has little meaning – it is just so much more *stuff*.[3]

This is a familiar analysis, principally associated with a loss of faith in totalising frameworks, explanatory metanarratives, and teleological conceptions of human life. History is reduced to a mere succession of events (one damn thing after another) that have been evacuated of meaning, and the *idea* of the future – understood as the horizon toward which one looks for the fulfilment of present-day hopes, the culminating point of purposeful human activity – ceases to compel belief. And whereas an earlier generation of modernists mostly experienced this loss of faith as a great disillusionment, late-twentieth-century writers are more likely to assume it as a simple datum, as the ground of their knowing irony. There is a world of difference between these respective positions and their cultural significance: the first is defined in relation to the disappointment of utopian aspirations; the second has always already seen through these aspirations, and thus accepts from the outset the truth of dystopian premonitions. When a modernist such as Wyndham Lewis described himself and his fellow avant-gardists as 'not only "the last men of an epoch"' but also '*the first men of a Future that has not materialized*', concluding that they belonged 'to a "great age" that has not "come off"', he caught that earlier sense of dashed hopes.[4] For a writer such as Ballard this future is a dead zone already destroyed by the relentless drive to reduce everything to the present moment and thus to collapse all the time that has passed and is still to come into the tyrannic embrace of the ever-same now, hence his claim that 'the future is ceasing to exist, devoured by the all-voracious present' (*C* 4).

Ballard's conviction that we inhabit a period in which the future is felt to be already exhausted before it has even arrived is powerfully expressed in novels such as *Concrete Island* and *High-Rise* with their claustrophobic atmospheres and their trapped protagonists. Drained of time, these characters and the worlds they inhabit exist in a permanent present that stretches out towards an eventless horizon. Augé's contention that the question of space has come to the fore because it is 'difficult to make time into a principle of intelligibility, let alone a principle of identity', fits well with Ballard's concerns in these texts.[5] And Augé's account of a particular aspect of this question is suggestive in the context of a discussion of Ballard's work in the 1970s. By refining de Certeau's analysis of space and place, Augé makes a conceptual distinction between place and non-place: 'If a place can be defined as relational, historical and concerned with identity, then a space which cannot be defined as relational, or historical, or concerned with identity will be a non-place'.[6] Supermodernity proliferates non-places (airports, service stations, supermarkets) which erode human interaction and enforce solitude. Non-places are never straightforwardly demarcated from places, nor do they exist in some pure state, but they offer a useful way of thinking about how the contemporary organization of space may create or exacerbate social alienation.[7]

Concrete Island and High-Rise offer markedly different depictions of space – one clearly a 'non-place', the other a 'place' – both of which exist at opposite ends of urban life. If the first symbolises the unintended, forgotten, abjected corners of town planning, then the second emblematises its highest aesthetic and communal aspirations. Yet both sites isolate their inhabitants, promote violent conflict, and destroy belief in the possibility that viable community life might be sustained. The traffic island and the high-rise are worlds within a world. Both are cut off from the rest of the city, one by accident, the other by design. But whereas the island is principally associated with waste products, and is figured as an abandoned site that is horizontally cut off from the wider world by the motorways surrounding it, the high-rise produces a feeling of vertigo and gives rise to the kind of spatial disorientation Jameson has described in his accounts of postmodern architecture. As a kind of waste-land created out of the detritus modernity leaves behind, the island is an *already* alienated terrain, characterised by an absence of meaning and social relations. The high-rise, in contrast, is a designed place, a building created within the framework of town planning and urban regeneration, yet its geometrical structure and its separation from its environment make it a space that *becomes* alienating. It is a self-contained world that cannot sustain the community life it was intended to facilitate, since it is

effectively 'a huge machine designed to serve, not the collective body
of tenants, but the individual resident in isolation' (*HR* 10).

Multiplying fragments

'The Subliminal Man' (1963) offers an early critique of subliminal
advertising, which is presented as a government-led conspiracy with
the aim of pressurising people to keep buying consumer goods. But
this is controlled capitalism, not a free market in which firms com-
pete for customers; everything is bought (and replaced) within the
terms of a bewildering range of loyalty schemes, long-term leases,
bonus points and discount plans. In a world in thrall to the power of
consumerism, all activity revolves around the accumulation of objects
and the maintenance of social status guaranteed by their ownership,
resulting in a situation in which the story's protagonist feels trapped
within a self-perpetuating logic: 'What freedom Franklin possessed
was peripheral, sharply demarked by the manifold responsibilities in
the centre of his life – the three mortgages on his home, the manda-
tory rounds of cocktail parties, the private consultancy occupying
most of Saturday which paid the instalments on the multitude of
household gadgets, clothes and past holidays' (*CS* 414). Because obsolescence has been built in to these products a feverish whirl of buying
and selling gives rise to extensive wastelands, 'continuous junkyards
filled with cars and trucks, washing machines and refrigerators, all
perfectly workable but jettisoned by the economic pressure of the succeeding waves of discount models' (*CS* 419). Huge signs line the
expressways, pulsating with subliminal injunctions to buy specific
products, a strategy adopted by the government to enable them to
introduce a seven-day working week to supplement the 24-hour shopping day. The story's central protagonist dies while trying to expose
the signs, and the story ends with a chilling coda in which another
character, having forgotten the truth about their subliminal messages, embarks with his wife on yet another shopping expedition:
'They walked out into the trim drive, the shadows of the signs swing-
ing across the quiet neighbourhood as the day progressed, sweeping
over the heads of the people on their way to the supermarket like the
blades of enormous scythes' (*CS* 425).

   This is the world from which *Concrete Island*'s Maitland is a would-
be escapee. A fascinating text, the novel works on a number of levels.
The two issues that are most closely intertwined in the novel are its

depiction of technology and its treatment of urban space. The ordinary, normally unexamined world of the everyday is defamiliarised and shown to be the source of threats to personal and social existence. These threats stem from the technologies that make modern life possible, not only because they have destructive and unintended consequences but also because they create human beings who are utterly reliant on them. The long description in which Maitland initially tries to get off the island is revealing in this regard. It focuses on the remorseless flow of streaming cars that continually flash past him, their speed of movement ensuring that he remains unnoticed. The vehicles are a source of danger, almost knocking him off his feet, but they are also symbols of a technological modernity sustained by anonymous forces, which subjects the vehicles' drivers to its imperatives as much as it isolates the stranded crash victim, a fact that Maitland recognises: 'Besides, it would be almost impossible to slow down here and stop. The pressure of the following traffic, free at last from the long tail-backs that always blocked the Westway interchange during the rush-hour, forced them on relentlessly' (*CI* 17).

It is not just that the cars are insensible machines caught up in the pretzel logic of uncontrollable traffic flows, but that their nominal drivers are cut off from the world outside their armoured metal shells. Maitland indulges himself with the language of urban paranoia when he imagines 'that every vehicle in London had passed and re-passed him a dozen times, the drivers and passengers deliberately ignoring him in a vast spontaneous conspiracy' (*CI* 19). In fact, the vehicles' drivers are locked into a privatised reality that is enforced on them by the technology they use, and they are no more in control of the situation than Maitland. The resultant stand-off between the trapped individual and the unstoppable cars discloses the truth of this nightmare dynamic, which is portrayed in the novel as extending far beyond this particular situation, to take in an anonymous world in which people lead parallel lives in arbitrary proximity to one another, while remaining oblivious to each other's needs. A subliminal fear of this dynamic, and of the disastrous consequences of technology failure, pervades the text; by investing the island with a brooding, sinister life, the novel turns it into a quasi-animate presence. Fear informs Maitland's conviction that these 'days one needed a full-scale emergency kit built into one's brain, plus a crash course in disaster survival, real and imagined' (*CI* 37), and the physical realisation of this fear when he crashes onto the island destroys his passive view of reality, forcing him to accept that his assumptions are 'completely false, part of that whole system of comfortable expectations he had carried with him' (*CI* 43) and that he must now discard.

In Augé's terms non-places are characterised by their deadness, their inability to foster social relations and to anchor human identity in a specific form of life. Augé defines them in relation to places that are imbued with the residues of a lived past that testifies to the reality of communal practices. The point here is not to romanticise the past but to distinguish between different orderings of space: non-places discourage the forging of social relations (of whatever kind) because they isolate individuals and disconnect the present from the past. The island initially appears as a place of desolation, a dumping-ground for the abandoned remnants of a no longer functional technology. This zone of dereliction is not of the same ilk as the non-places discussed by Augé, but it produces a similar kind of isolation, creates an environment in which the forging of social life is an unlikely enterprise, and shows little respect for the past. But this is a first impression that is refined as the novel unfolds, Maitland gradually realising that the island is a physical palimpsest – beneath the discarded refuse and the broken-down machinery littering its surface the lineaments of an earlier form of life can be discerned. The motorways have been built over a ruined neighbourhood that survives here and there in the waste land they have created. It is visible in deserted gravestones, derelict ledges and parapets, concealed basements, old air-raid shelters, and in the ghostly streets and avenues. These traces suggest that an older urban geography has not quite been erased. What initially appears as a non-place eventually stands revealed as a historical site that testifies to a former way of life and also undermines the vaunting pretensions of the modernity that has superseded it.

Maitland's realisation that the island is a historical site marks the beginning of a more perceptive mapping of the terrain on which he is ostensibly trapped and leads him to relate the sedimentation of history disclosed by the island's topography to his own past. His spatial mapping of the island is thus also a temporal mapping; the journey across physical space is at the same time a journey over the time of the island. What complicates Maitland's response to the island is that it is also the projection of a disordered mind slipping into delirium. A positive way of reading Maitland's confrontation with this hostile terrain would see it as offering him the chance to free himself from the residues of a corrupt civilisation and thus to overcome his social and psychological alienation. In an updating of a well-worn 'primitivist' move the individual could be seen as discovering a deeper, more authentic self through his interaction with a violent acultural domain. In his preface to *Concrete Island* Ballard offers support for such a reading when he refers to 'the challenge of returning to our more primitive natures, stripped of the self-respect and the mental support systems with which civilisation has equipped us'.[8] On this view, Maitland's refusal to be cowed by the island and his attempt to identify himself with it hints at the possibility of a non-instrumental, holistic interaction with the world. But the novel offers an alternative possibility, since figuring the island as a subjective projection also draws attention to the individual's longing to subjugate the environment and make it serve his inner needs. Ballard's preface countenances this reading too, stressing the character's 'need to dominate the island, and transform its anonymous terrain into an extension of our minds.'[9]

There are two aspects to this recovery of self. On the one hand, the island becomes an extension of Maitland's psyche, the external manifestation of the unresolved inner conflicts he projects onto it, and on the other hand, it represents the physical challenge of survival. Ballard seems interested in both processes, portraying them as interlinked. Drawing on 'primitivist' tropes, he depicts the struggle with an inhospitable environment as the means by which the individual encounters an earlier form of subjectivity. Stranded on a terrain that must be confronted on its own terms, the isolated individual is forced to slough off the habitual, unexamined accoutrements of social life and is thrown onto his own inner resources. The dissolution of the civilised self is depicted as a reversion to an earlier time on the evolutionary scale; the primitive, as so often in discourses inflected by anthropology, is defined in opposition to the civilised along the axis of time. Writers who deploy this trope typically do so in order to suggest that the psychic journey back in time will enable the individual to discover some authentic – and often negative – truths about modern subjectivity, which can then disturb formerly complacent prejudices about its alleged superiority to earlier notions of self and/or society. But *Concrete Island* complicates this narrative schema in interesting ways. If the various features of this terrain represent aspects of the psyche then its topography may do little more than pander to a solipsism in which the external world exists primarily to service the demands of desire. The encounter between the individual and the environment may strip the self of socially programmed assumptions but this does not mean that psychic bedrock will necessarily be reached; what may be revealed is not a tragic knowledge – such as Kurtz's 'the horror! The horror!' – that is potentially redemptive but rather the ruses by which socially induced psycho-pathologies cover their tracks.

Maitland's responses to the island are illuminating in this respect. He initially sees it as a threatening non-place, a twilight zone in which he has been mistakenly confined and from which there is no escape. With the passing of the days he looks more carefully at the island and gradually sees it in different terms. He realises that it is built on the ruins of a once functioning urban site, grasps that it can sustain human life, and starts to adapt to a terrain that at first seemed to be unremittingly hostile. More importantly, he accepts that he longs above all to remain on the island and may unconsciously have willed the crash because he was seeking to escape from a host of unacknowledged problems. The island thus becomes an emblem of his mind in two related ways – as the sign of a profound personal and social alienation and as the site on which a desired self-immolation can be achieved. Maitland's adjustment to an inhospitable environment entails a regression to childhood and a sympathetic identification with the island, which enables him ostensibly to exorcise the demons haunting his mind.

Far from being a site of desolation, the island becomes the source of buried longings that are part of an elaborate fantasy structure. Thus to Maitland's eyes the island appears to be reverting to a primeval terrain in sympathy with his own regression. As this process continues apace, the distinction between his mind and the environment outside it breaks down: 'Moving across it, he seemed to be following a contour line inside his head' (*CI* 131). This identification of the self with the island goes back to an earlier moment at which he tries to heal his physical injuries by making a 'eucharist of his own body' (*CI* 71), leaving various parts of himself in different places, each ritual signifying 'the transfer of obligation from himself to the island' (*CI* 71). By the end of the novel, he has turned this process of self-healing into a full psychological recovery by bequeathing to the island the damaged 'sections of his mind, shucking off those memories of pain, hunger and humiliation' (*CI* 156). Enacting a form of 'splitting' by way of which the 'bad' parts of the personality are cast out of the mind and projected onto someone or something else, this process supposedly permits a purer, less contaminated individual to emerge.

But Maitland's view of what has taken place on the island hardly squares with the novel's ambiguous depiction of events. The environment in which he finds himself releases his most aggressive tendencies, as though the fantasised displacement of parts of the self onto the island gives rise to a reverse process, the disjected, alienated terrain bequeathing its hostility to the unwary intruder. The more Maitland perceives the island as a beneficent place, the more aggressive he himself becomes. Convinced that the only way he can survive is by dominating the physical landscape and those who would share it with him, he systematically sets about psychologically and physically controlling the tramp (Proctor) and the young woman (Jane) who live on it. And although he tells himself that this is necessary because they threaten his safety, it is revealing that he enjoys not only his power over them but also the process of humiliation by which he gains it. There is little evidence that Jane and Proctor are a threat; both help him and whereas they countenance the possibility that human relationships might be re-made on the island, Maitland retreats further into solitude, thereby maintaining long established patterns of repetition compulsion.

This compulsion to repeat has its origins in a childhood predilection for isolation, itself born of unassuaged emotional needs, and it is bound up with the happiness Maitland derives from creating perverse relationships. Perverse not because they revolve around the pleasures of domination and subjection but because these pleasures depend on the establishment of an unbreachable *distance* between individuals – a distance that precisely measures the extent of his alienation from others. There is a connection between Maitland's instrumental view of human relations and his means–end approach to the island: preservation of self is predicated on a need to dominate. Thus his violent confrontation with Proctor and Jane parallels his aggressive response to his external environment. This need to control things (people, environments) outside the self discloses a desire to make that self an inviolable entity. Taken to its logical conclusion, the search for contractual relationships results in a solitude so complete that external reality is dissolved in the self. This desire for freedom from contact with others signifies an alienation so extreme that even an instrumental conception of human relations is eventually deemed surplus to requirements. Cities are of course communal places that evolve out of the exigencies of social life and that are in part shaped through the numerous criss-crossing relationships and associations they facilitate. The notion of the city as an evacuated and internalised space in which the solitary individual can roam at will, free at last from potentially contaminating or threatening contact with all others, parodies the very idea of community, yet Maitland seeks nothing more than to be 'freed from his past, from his childhood, his wife and friends, with all their affections and demands, and to rove for ever within the empty city of his own mind' (*CI* 142).

Like the island, the tramp Proctor is emblematised as the product of social waste: physically injured, beaten and humiliated by the police, propertyless, and illiterate, he is a parodic version of Man Friday. The island is his appropriate habitat not only because it mirrors his abject state but also because it permits him to hide from the social order that has created and then discharged him. Maitland is an interloper from the world that has abused Proctor, appearing as a threat to the latter's hard-won security in that he is a potential rival for control of the land and a representative of the kind of professional success to which the tramp could never aspire. His aggressive confidence and his status in the social world that has all but crushed Proctor ensures that theirs quickly becomes a master–slave relationship, but whereas in *Robinson Crusoe* the hierarchy between Crusoe and Friday is never disturbed, Maitland gradually finds himself taking over Proctor's identity and role. His displacement of Proctor parallels his reversion to childhood and his rejection of his former life. The novel's progressive dissolution of the various sign-systems through which society encodes meaning, symbolically structuring human intercourse and exchange, is central to this process.

The collapse of Maitland's subjectivity is figured above all through the breakdown in his mind of the semiotic codes by means of which he has made sense of his own experience. From the route indicators on the motorways that seem to flicker blankly to the letters of the roman alphabet itself, all the conventional markers that enable modern subjects to conceptualise their identities and to orientate themselves in social space appear to have lost meaning. Proctor's scrambling of the English language and the mixed-up verbal counters he scatters across the island in the mistaken belief that they spell his name and assert his identity are in fact 'the straggling fragments of Maitland's name' (*CI* 153) – signs of the latter's all-devouring ego and social power. This linguistic confusion blurs the distinction between the two men, suggesting that for Maitland Proctor is little more than a plaything or an extension of himself; it also points to the fading of

Maitland's own socially formed identity glimpsed in his memory of 'the multiplying fragments of his own name that had seemed to taunt and confuse him' (*CI* 162). By the end of the novel he has become a version of Proctor but instead of imposing the values of an allegedly superior and beneficent society (as in the Crusoe–Friday couple) has taken on key aspects of the superseded figure's character and has regressed in sympathy with the island's detritus-ridden terrain.

There is, however, another aspect to Maitland's 'primitivist' descent into primordiality, which suggests that the notion that one can slough off layers of the personality like so many sets of clothes in order to uncover some untarnished core of self is a delusion. Maitland's desire to participate in this fantasy is the product of a sense of alienation that has its origins in his personal past, but it is also suggested that this alienation has been exacerbated by the hostile conditions of an urban, technological modernity. There is no possibility here of redeeming the past by way of regression because the formation and maintenance of his subjectivity owe so much to the structures and conditions of the *present*. In other words, his response to the island cannot be explained in archaeological terms alone, for it is equally determined by contemporary realities. It is not only the case that his subjectivity is a product of the society from which he wants to escape, but, more importantly, that the way in which he expresses his hostility to certain of its norms unconsciously reproduces them. Maitland's imbrication in modernity is made clear from the outset, and it is focused primarily on the interpenetration of technology and subjectivity, a theme sounded at the beginning of the novel in the description of the accident: 'His forehead was covered with flecks of dirt and oil carried into the car by the breaking windshield. Maitland squeezed his face, trying to massage some expression into the pallid skin and musculature. His heavy jaw and hard cheeks were drained of all blood. The eyes staring back at him from the mirror were blank and unresponsive, as if he were looking at a psychotic twin brother' (*CI* 9).

The impact of modern technology on human existence is in *Concrete Island* primarily depicted through persistent references to the fusion of the body with the machines that surround it and that mediate its spatio-temporal passage through life. Immediately after his accident Maitland is seen lying 'across his steering wheel, his jacket and trousers studded with windshield fragments like a suit of lights' (*CI* 7). In another passage, this mechanisation of the body is reversed, and the machine is anthropomorphised, as in this view of the car:

'The front end had been punched into itself like a collapsed face' (*CI* 10). Technology and humanity appear in such descriptions to be locked together in an unbreakable embrace, a fusion of disparate realms that is also neatly encapsulated in the novel's title. The destructive power of technological modernity is symbolised through the nightmarish image of the old man wheeling a motorcycle along the edge of the motorway: 'Maitland was certain that this machine he was wheeling was not in fact a light motorcycle, but an horrific device of torture that the old man brought with him on his endless journey around the world, and against whose chain-driven wheels Maitland's already broken body would be applied in a grim judgement by ordeal' (*CI* 60). This dark premonition of torture and suffering is ultimately realised not on Maitland's body but on Proctor's when he is accidentally garrotted by (of all things) a motorway repair vehicle.

But if the island represents the grimy underside of the technological dream, revealing the price paid for its vaunting ambition in human and environmental damage, it is also, as in *The Drought*, the starting point from which any alternative form of life must be built. The possibility of combating the negative effects of technology resides not in some fantasised 'elsewhere' that bypasses it altogether (as in Morris's *News from Nowhere*, say) but in the world it has helped to forge. It is not just that technology is ubiquitous in the bits and pieces of equipment that one might take or leave, use or choose not to use, as Proctor and Maitland do in their reassembly of various discarded machines. The novel portrays a world that has been entirely remade by technology and that now exists, in a self-perpetuating cycle that has spun out of control, to service that technology. Human beings are not simply dwarfed or isolated by it but are penetrated by its logics in ways they hardly comprehend. The island and the characters who inhabit it are all the waste-products of the society that has disjected them. Maitland's desire to recover an original kernel of identity that has escaped these logics is foredoomed because both the terrain on which he tries to achieve this self-exorcism and the identity he seeks to re-establish have been made out of the materials he proposes to discard.

Maitland's account of his own experience must then be treated with scepticism. His desire at the end of the novel to remain on the island, even as he continues to delude himself that he is looking for a way to escape it, reveals a protagonist who has scarcely begun to grasp what has taken place. His obsessive longing for physical isolation from the rest of the world is an external manifestation of his need for mental solitude – his solipsistic desire to be free to people the empty city of his mind with his own thoughts and nothing else. And his callous behaviour to Jane and to Proctor is characteristic of an instrumental conception of human relationships, which shows how profoundly in thrall he is to a means–end view of rationality. In his former incarnation as an architect, Maitland had a predilection for modernism, specifically name-checking La Grande Motte, a futurist resort complex characterised by 'hard, affectless architecture' marked by 'stylized concrete surfaces' (*CI* 65). The resort's lack of affect makes it a place as hostile to the forging of human relations as the island – it represents a kind of dead end for life. Far from overcoming the problem of alienation, Maitland's strategies merely sidestep it, fantasising the transfer of a near pathological psychic structure to an external environment while permitting it to remain intact. His chosen existence is at once the revenge of the cold concrete world symbolised by La Grande Motte on those who see it as the design for a future life and the secret fulfilment of their most hidden desires. It is because Maitland *wants* to live in a state of isolation and alienation that he retreats to the island, cutting himself off from social relations and erasing his own personal history. The island that appeared at the outset of the novel to be a desolate non-place has in fact turned out to be a historical and social site, which has offered the possibility of re-making human relationships but this offer has been spurned, the dystopian view of life predominating over the utopian.

Vertical zoo

Concrete Island focuses on the forgotten and unacknowledged spaces of urban modernity; *High-Rise* mocks its over-weening ambition to create a self-sustaining environment. The two texts are situated at opposite ends of the civic spectrum: one exposes the hidden byproducts of contemporary life, while the other concentrates on its dreams of rational design. *High-Rise* conceives the metropolitan tower-block as the emblem of a modernist architecture that aimed to solve the problems of high-density housing by creating self-contained mini-cities. These functionalist vertical structures were in principle designed to respond to their inhabitants' every need but were in practice beset by numerous practical problems and rarely worked in the ways that their architects had intended. Ballard's novel performs a *tour-de-force* demolition job on these Promethean sky-houses by creating a grotesque fictional world in which the tensions generated by high-rise living are pushed to an extreme. What perverse logics might unfold within these isolated edifices if they ceased to function? How might social breakdown manifest itself if the modernist dream of a rationalist architecture failed to deliver on its promise?

Attempts to improve city housing have a long history in England. Efforts to re-make the urban environment go back at least as far as the Dwellings Improvement Act of 1875, which sought to replace slums with low-cost housing, a strategy that continued in the 1920s and 1930s, accompanied by the Labour slogan 'A Healthy London: Up with the Houses, Down with the Slums'. Housing was still a major problem after World War Two, not least because of the large-scale destruction that had been caused by the bombing of cities. A huge building programme ensued, and tower-blocks were a central feature of post-war urban regeneration. Designed to provide cheap housing and to address the question of transportation across cities, tower-blocks were supposed to be the affordable, practical, egalitarian and *modern* answer to the problem of high-density urban living. The 1956 Housing Act gave impetus to this programme by providing financial incentives for all buildings over five floors, and several thousand high-rises were launched skywards between the 1950s and 1990s. But the high-rise project was always beset by tensions between economic imperatives and social planning. The pressure to keep costs low militated against the desire of architects to create decent living conditions for large numbers of people. Add to this dubious quality control, property speculation and shoddy building practices, and the result was the erection of tower-blocks that were in some cases so poorly constructed that they started to malfunction as soon as their tenants moved in. In the 1960s and 1970s the problems associated with high-rises became a regular feature of the national press, and despite the hysteria that accompanied this reportage, the problems were genuine and have been thoroughly documented: lack of security made tower-blocks vulnerable to burglaries and vandalism; shared utilities were prone to break down and were frequently out of order; rectilinear architectural design produced uncontainable down-drafts of wind, which led to rubbish-strewn environments; insufficient green spaces and communal areas made life difficult for families with children, isolated people in their flats, and impeded the development of social ties; high maintenance costs made tower-blocks expensive to run and to refurbish, with the result that they often fell into neglect; and many tenants were alienated by the uncompromising architecture of buildings that had been envisaged as machines in which they were to live.

The influence of early twentieth-century modernism was prevalent in the whole conception and ethos of high-rise architecture. Most tower-blocks were designed by architects who looked to radical predecessors such as Le Corbusier, van Doesberg and Mies van der Rohe, seeing themselves as the inheritors of a modernist aesthetic that was to help usher in a new socialist Britain. Many of them were aesthetic idealists and political reformists who could remember the pre-war depression and the slums in which much of the population had lived. The drive to build tower-blocks was inseparable from the emergence of the post-1945 welfare state – alongside a national health service and education system, good cheap housing was central to Labour's reformist agenda. High-rises aroused controversy from the outset: for some they represented the arrogance of a theory-driven conception of architecture, which failed to consider the needs of those who would live in them, whereas others argued that there was nothing wrong with tower-blocks, which functioned perfectly well when they were properly designed and built.

In the 1960s and 1970s tower-blocks seemed to be compromised by dehumanised architectural forms and inadequate workmanship. The Brutalist movement was influential in the design of many high-rises, for which it suffered much opprobrium. Brutalism evolved from the austere architecture of Le Corbusier, seeing itself as the continuation of a still emergent modernist tradition, but to its critics it seemed the epitome of a bleak machine-made world. Reyner Banham gave the movement its name when he labelled the work of architects such as Peter and Alison Smithson – who had designed the controversial Hunstanton School in Norfolk (1954) – as the 'New Brutalism', claiming of the school that it sought a kind of modernist architectural purity.[10] Brutalist architecture was based on rigid lines, austere forms, and the geometrisation of living space, following Le Corbusier's dictum that the 'great problems of modern construction must have a geometrical solution.'[11] It advocated 'truth to materials', which gave rise to a paradoxical aesthetic whose *point d'appui* was an anti-aesthetic commitment to transparency: the mode of construction and the functions of buildings were to be left exposed, even flaunted, in a bid for design honesty. Its critics lambasted the New Brutalism for what they saw as its abstract conception of architecture and its stark remodelling of the urban environment, accusing it of producing housing that was ugly, alienating and uninhabitable.

Criticisms of tower-blocks followed two lines of attack. In one variant, the entire vision of high-rise housing was assaulted on *a priori* grounds; the idea of tall vertical buildings housing large numbers of people was thought to be misguided. A second line of argument was practical; resistance to tower-blocks mobilised around the reality of how badly they had been built and not around reservations as to their theoretical viability. Ballard's *High-Rise* conflates both criticisms in its morbid depiction of one such estate's collapse into tribal warfare. Just as La Grande Motte in *Concrete Island* symbolises a cold architecture that seems never to have been intended for human habitation, existing rather as a hubristic paean to the gods of abstract design, so the tower-block in *High-Rise* exemplifies 'an environment built, not for man, but for man's absence' (*HR* 25). This environment contributes to the disorientation felt by the novel's characters, but, typically for a Ballard text, it is suggested that it may simply be exacerbating a sense of alienation which is already theirs and which has led them to select the high-rise as the habitat that expresses their detachment and ennui. There is ambiguity as to causality here, for in a variation on the old nurture/nature theme *High-Rise* envisages a symbiosis between the building and its inhabitants, figuring the edifice as a living mechanism tenanted by standardised cybernetic organisms. Through a series of anthropomorphising images, the tower-block is portrayed as conscious, whereas the people it houses are depicted as replicable automata incapable of communal life. Anonymous but gargantuan, the building enforces its reality by dominating the environment and severing itself and its inhabitants from external social life. The high-rise has been constructed by its Luciferian architect as an experiment in urban living, an attempt to make an alternative world, but in typically gothic fashion the creation becomes monstrous, turning on those whom it was supposed to benefit and destroying the creator in his penthouse lair. When one of the novel's characters anxiously refers to it 'as if it were some kind of huge animate presence, brooding over them and keeping a magisterial eye on the events taking place' (*HR* 40), the observation tellingly captures the text's urban gothic atmosphere and its indebtedness to the dystopian traditions of science fiction: 'There was something in this feeling – the elevators pumping up and down the long shafts resembled pistons in the chamber of a heart. The residents moving along the corridors were the cells in a network of arteries, the lights in their apartments the neurones of a brain' (*HR* 40).

The bleak functionalism and sheer anonymity of the high-rise make it a cell-like hive in which certain kinds of individual can thrive. The aggressive Wilder is out of place, whereas figures such as the detached Laing and the implacable Steele are its hideous progeny: 'A new social type was being created by the apartment building, a cool, unemotional personality impervious to the psychological pressures of high-rise life, with minimal needs for privacy, who thrived like an advanced species of machine in the neutral atmosphere' (*HR* 35). In a contemporary version of Golding's inheritors, these mechanised, robotic figures, who are effectively programmed by the building itself, exemplify the logic of a technologised world that the high-rise represents on a miniature scale. Within this microcosm, those who belong to an older tribe will always be defeated:

> Sadly, they had little chance of success, precisely because their opponents were people who were content with their lives in the high-rise, who felt no particular objection to an impersonal steel and concrete landscape, no qualms about the invasion of their privacy by government agencies and data-processing organizations, and if anything welcomed these invisible intrusions, using them for their own purposes. These people were the first to master a new kind of late twentieth-century life. (*HR* 36)

In the course of a discussion of the panopticon Foucault makes a brief allusion to eighteenth-century gothic fiction. The obverse of dreams of enlightenment, gothic writing developed 'a whole fantasy-world of stone walls, darkness, hideouts and dungeons', and 'these imaginary spaces are like the negative of the transparency and visibility which it is aimed to establish'.[12] In gothic literature anxieties about the over-dominance of an excessive rationalism manifest themselves in portrayals of secretive, sinister characters and in depictions of old, brooding buildings. Harking back to the past, to historical sites of human habitation that have fallen into desuetude, gothic projects inner anxiety onto physical space and spells the doom of enlightenment in the rubble of ancient ruins. *High-Rise* draws on this tradition but reverses its trajectory: it is the contemporary tower-block, the symbol of a rationally planned existence and the blueprint for a self-sufficient communal life, that harbours the gothic nightmare. As in Kubrick's *The Shining*, which reverses the horror genre's traditional reliance on shadows and darkness, the destructive mini-history that unfolds within its clean-cut steel and concrete walls takes place in the light, marking a return of the repressed that is called forth by the building itself, which is 'a model of all that technology had done to make possible the expression of a truly "free" psychopathology' (*HR* 36). In a grotesque deformation of enlightenment philosophy, this far from beneficent technology releases human beings from sociality only to make them slaves to their most destructive inner tendencies. The blankness of the building creates a dead space in which anything is possible and nothing is forbidden.

But *High-Rise* sits somewhat uneasily with any repressive thesis, for the psychopathologies unleashed in the text are not traced to early infancy but are shown to be generated by the tower-block itself. The novel has it both ways. If the impersonal nature of the high-rise seems to be responsible for a death of affect that enables repressed desires to emerge, then at the same time this impersonality is the external manifestation of pathologies that are already in place. There is a precise homology between the high-rise and its residents so that its failure to function properly results in a corresponding breakdown in the behaviour of its inhabitants, who are caught up in sympathetic mimicry, the deviant strains in their personalities being created and shaped by the id-like building itself. In keeping with Freud's spatial model of the psyche, the degeneration of the tower-block is mapped in spatial terms. Frustration at the building's failures is not directed at its designer or its builders but is deflected onto others by way of a predictable scapegoating reflex, and residents are then classified into groups according to where they are located in the high-rise. The block's physical structure imposes a vertical social hierarchy on its inhabitants – the higher up the apartment, the more elevated the class position – establishing a 'system of precedences entirely based on floor-height' (*HR* 14). Initially the anonymity of the building leads to a carnivalesque atmosphere of revelry characterised by an easy promiscuity and a slackening of proprietorial instinct, but when anarchy descends the differences between individuals harden and groups are formed around 'neighbourhoods', which promote a sense of tribal belonging based on the defence of territory and raids on adjacent 'turfs'. A crude politics asserts itself, and the high-rise becomes progressively Balkanised.

Unusually for a Ballard novel, *High-Rise* is focalised through the perspectives of several protagonists, principally those of Laing,

Wilder and Royal. The book begins and ends with Laing calmly dining off a roasted Alsatian while he blithely concludes that 'normality' has been restored. Laing's sense of detachment from the events he has witnessed mark him as a brother to *Concrete Island*'s Maitland; a cool observer who remains untouched by the carnage occurring around him, he is blind to his own involvement in the building's social dissolution. But Laing is the block's exemplary resident precisely *because* of his detachment – his lack of affect, solitariness, and defensive irony are the psychological counterparts to its brutalist minimalism. Although he is able to acknowledge the callous nature of his involvement in the 'uncertain materials' of 'the erotic and perverse' (*HR* 38), his insight is cast in the form of an abstract mental exercise. An extreme form of psychological dissociation enables him to convince himself that 'it no longer mattered how he behaved, what wayward impulses he gave way to, or which perverse pathways he chose to follow' (*HR* 172) and to feel grateful to Royal 'for having helped to design the high-rise and make all this possible' (*HR* 172–3). From the vantage-point of this benumbed sensibility only the desiring self has a palpable reality: all else is a droll spectacle staged for the observer's amusement. In contrast to Laing, Wilder is the hugger-mugger male whose behaviour is governed by instinctual aggressiveness. His hostility to those who are spatially above him is motivated by *ressentiment*, and his determination to ascend the high-rise in order to confront Royal represents a literal bid for upward social mobility. This strategy is part of an outmoded masculinist mythos, and his conquest of the block's summit – a parody of male prowess – is accompanied by a regression to painted savagery and blood-bolstered violence. Gradually losing the power of speech, he ends by being able to communicate solely in grunts; exhibiting an infantile wonderment at behaviour he cannot decode, he kills Royal and embraces his own death at the hands of a new matriarchate without even realising what is taking place. David Punter acutely observes (with reference to *Concrete Island* and *High-Rise*) that the narratives of the escape and the slow climb 'represent two points of entry into systematic delusion, two ways of beginning to satisfy needs, but needs which have themselves been shaped through the narratives: the story-lines *are* the reduction and adjustment of needs, a twinned recognition also of the inappropriateness of masculine aspiration in worlds where the strength of the subject is demonstrably superseded.'[13]

Depicted as acting out trajectories that have been set in motion by the building itself, Laing and Wilder are behaviourist puppets, futile dolls whose actions are determined by the impersonal technological forces that surround and permeate them. Imbued with the belief that by rejecting civilised values they are uncovering an authentic mode of existence and a true sense of identity, they merely externalise the logics that impel them into action. The text does not dispute that a bestial repressed 'nature' may lurk beneath a socialised veneer but it concentrates on the ways in which human subjects can be moulded, manipulated and coerced into forms of behaviour that they consider to be normal and unobjectionable. *High-Rise* is chilling because it traces a logic that connects an initial disorientation in *physical* space to the loss of bearings in *moral* space. The isolation of the building from the world is crucial to the process by which those who live in it are brought to think of its pathological micro-society as a safe and beneficent reality. In truth, the freedom and authenticity that Laing and Wilder imagine they have discovered are culturally, socially and technologically mediated. Given contemporary culture's obsession with 'reality television', the novel is prescient in the way it isolates the high-rise from the rest of the world (in an uncanny premonition of a giant Big Brother house), depicting its tenants as participants in a bizarre survival programme. Like *The Truman Show*'s shadowy creator, Christof, Royal is the aloof director of ceremonies who appears as 'an eccentric camp-commander or zoo-keeper' (*HR* 66). Initially convinced that only an immovable social structure could provide order and stability within the tower-block, Royal eventually concludes that the breakdown he is witnessing represents an escape 'into a new life, and a pattern of social organization that would become the paradigm of all future high-rise blocks' (*HR* 70).

Some paradigm, this. Large-scale vandalism, total collapse of social ties and any sense of community, casual sexual abuse, and indiscriminate violence leading to murder. Unable to confront this reality, Royal mystifies it in order to explain it as an inadvertent success: 'Without knowing it, he had constructed a gigantic vertical zoo, its hundreds of cages stacked above each other. All the events of the past few months made sense if one realized that these brilliant and exotic creatures had learned to open the doors' (*HR* 134). But the brilliance of this uncaged menagerie has already been better described: 'They were now moving into a realm of no social organization at all. The clans had broken down into small groups of killers, solitary hunters who built man-traps in empty apartments or preyed on the unwary in deserted elevator lobbies' (*HR* 133). This account perceives the release of desire as a source of truth about the self, but such desire is not the expression of some fabled core identity that finally guarantees the subject's authenticity – it is a mediated phantasm, a simulacrum of a simulacrum. The entire text is staged as a spectacle, functioning as a hybrid mix of reality TV, game-show and docu-drama all rolled into one. The protagonists are 'characters' in a televised show; with no valid life when off-camera, they play out pre-arranged roles and script their actions in terms of televisual genres; they are ciphers, fictive representations constructed out of the synthetic images of the culture they think they are casting off but that has manufactured them as its typical products, freezing them 'together like mannequins in a museum tableau – "late twentieth-century high-rise dweller"' (*HR* 102). And in a neat doubling of this spectacularisation, most of them are also busy with their ciné-cameras, voyeuristically filming the violence and sex around them so that they can replay it later, a practice that foregrounds the endless recursivity of mediation in this textual world. The building is thus a vast set, a huge artificial prop for the staging and acting out of life as a perverse pageant: 'The true light of the high-rise was the metallic flash of the Polaroid camera, that intermittent radiation which recorded a moment of hoped-for violence for some later voyeuristic pleasure' (*HR* 109). The novel's characters are the mass-produced exemplars of technological modernity – all their tastes, attitudes and values, right down to their belief in the liberatory power of transgressive behaviour, have been programmed into them.

In *Concrete Island* Maitland chooses the derelict terrain on which he is stranded as the habitat that mirrors his alienation from society. A detritus-ridden, post-industrial scrap of waste land, the island embodies an inner state of mind. In *High-Rise*, a different kind of (perverse) unity is forged out of the disparate materials of buildings and bodies. Here, the synergy between form and function lies in the way the tower-block's rebarbative architecture interpellates those who inhabit it as dehumanised subjects – a fit species for a machine-made world. The real psycho-pathology at work in the high-rise manifests itself in the production of a certain kind of subjectivity; the numerous examples of deviant behaviour catalogued in the novel are the epiphenomena of an affectless, detached, and morally neutral state of mind. The tower-block's smashed machines, graffiti-covered walls and dismembered bodies are the visible markers of a mentality produced by a determinate socio-cultural history. Texts such as *Lord of the Flies* and *Heart of Darkness* stalk the wings of *High-Rise*, and a key passage in the novel alludes to Conrad's 'grove of death' scene: 'In the yellow light reflected off the greasy tiles, the long tank of the bone-pit stretched in front of them. The water had long since drained away, but the sloping floor was covered with the skulls, bones and dismembered limbs of dozens of corpses. Tangled together where they had been flung, they lay about like the tenants of a crowded beach visited by a sudden holocaust' (*HR* 170). The hidden, dystopian logic of the high-rise suggests that it exists to facilitate death, extirpating those who inhabit it but for whom it was never really built. The most sinister and cold-hearted of the 'new men' hatched by this charnel-house imagines re-peopling it with artificially bedecked corpses masquerading as living beings, just as Jim in *Empire of the Sun* imagines resurrecting the dead so that they can retake their places in the theatre of war and thus perpetuate the cycle of violence and death. It is absolutely the correct conclusion to draw and a compellingly macabre tribute to the unchained replicants still roaming about inside the building:

> His imagination ... came alive particularly when he was playing with the dead. The previous day Laing had blundered into an apartment and found him painting a bizarre cosmetic mask on the face of a dead account-executive, dressing the body like an over-blown drag-queen in a voluminous silk nightdress. Given time, and a continuing supply of subjects, the dentist would repopulate the entire high-rise. (*HR* 150)

Ultimate city

If these texts seem unremittingly pessimistic then they should be read in relation to Ballard's longest story: 'The Ultimate City' (1976). This complex work is an *hommage* to the vaunting ambition and irrepressible energy of metropolitan life. An act of memorialisation, the text recuperates the heady aspirations of urban existence in language that recalls the utopianism of early modernist technophiles. That said, 'The Ultimate City' is also a cautionary fable. It recapitulates the history of a city's life from its formation to its descent into civic corruption, social conflict, violence, crime and chaos, mapping this trajectory onto the narrative of *The Tempest*. But the brave new world imagined by Miranda at the sight of Ferdinand is here that of a rebuilt city which is revealed as an ambiguous place, the site not of a utopian commonwealth but of dystopian lawlessness. All this notwithstanding, 'The Ultimate City' remains loyal to the confusion, unpredictability, and anarchic joy of city life, recalling the young Jim's passion for Shanghai in *Empire of the Sun*, or Ballard's description of *Vermilion Sands* as a celebration of 'the neglected virtues of the glossy, lurid and bizarre' (*VS* 7). Ballard's 'Preface' to *Vermilion Sands* pinpoints the ambiguities dramatised in 'The Ultimate City' in its reference to the resort's 'dreams and illusions, fears and fantasies' (*VS* 7). The defining contrast here is between the ecologically responsible Garden City, which is puritanical and lifeless, and the untamed petroleum-driven metropolis, which sings with energy and passion. Well before he discovers the city, the story's protagonist is driven by an inner compulsion that connects him 'with the metal relics, the superchargers embedded in lucite, the fuel pumps and speedometers that lay around the studio like the ornaments of a shrine dedicated to the vanished spirit of the Otto Cycle' (*CS* 875). When Halloway does find the city it immediately appears to him as 'an abandoned dream waiting to be re-occupied' (*CS* 876).

This is a dream of power and excitation, a harnessing of dammed up energies depicted as a libidinal release from repression and constraint. The seemingly beneficent polity that Halloway leaves behind is a curiously sexless zone, its putatively civilised values masking discontents of an explicitly sexual nature. Halloway's return to a city of skyscrapers and wide-laned carriageways is a homecoming that traces a path from technological passion to sexual awakening. His memory of 'the overwhelming energy' and 'the power and excitement beyond anything else' (*CS* 879) of the engine in his father's workshop is the spur to a voyage of self-discovery within a metropolis in which Miranda acts as the sign of sexual-urban ambivalence: 'That ambiguity she showed, that moody combination of challenge and allure, was exactly what the city was about' (*CS* 899). The city is a zone of possibilities, a site upon which the game of self-fashioning may be played with impunity, while the erotic trajectories opened up admit of hitherto undreamt of permutations. Thus Halloway can turn himself into the city's new czar with the goal of re-animating urban space all over again, and his electrification of its districts provides the *frisson* of excitement that his sexual pursuit of Miranda requires. But violence is from the outset inseparable from both Halloway's re-invention and the city's rebirth. His arrival there coincides with a scene of mindless destruction in which the text's Caliban figure, Stillman, rampages through the streets in a revved-up car, smashing up shopfronts and strewing mannequins all over the streets. As in *Crash*, the car is the embodiment of unconscious drives, a deadly projectile harnessed to an instinct for aggression. And although the will to destruction is associated with Stillman, Halloway is also in thrall to the thrill of violence and is before long engaged in motorised duels all over the city centre. Stillman is a projection from Halloway's psyche, the cool, stylised avatar of a death-instinct that finds in the metropolis the perfect domain in which it can manifest and express itself. The city seems to welcome, perhaps even to encourage, the inscription of violence on its topography in the form of smashed cars, shattered glass and looted shops.

A conflict between life-and death-instincts is played out here. It calls to mind Freud's conclusion to *Civilisation and its Discontents*, which pondered the 'fateful question' of the conflict between these two 'Heavenly Powers'.[14] Freud situated this conflict, on the eve of war, in a technological context, since he grasped that technology had the power to bring about total global destruction. His evocation of the struggle between Eros and Thanatos is in Ballard's story associated not with war but with the internal contradictions of technology itself. What is at stake in Halloway's re-animation of the city is the legacy of the twentieth century. Buckmaster, the story's Prospero-figure, a parodic version of the mad scientist with benevolent intentions, has invested technology with the power to transform human life, attributing a messianic potential to technology itself. But he has abandoned this view as an unworkable hubristic dream, declaring that the project of scientific transformation must be shut down. Attentive to the negative consequences of the technological revolution (pollution, exploitation of materials, depletion of resources), Buckmaster has bid farewell to the technophilic vision of social improvement and has abjured its rough magic, but Halloway, the thrusting young Ferdinand-figure, insists that technology can still forge a brave new world. By bringing the metropolis back to life he sets out to re-write history, not as farce but as utopia: 'There's so much that should have happened here that never did ... I want to bring everything alive again, and give back to the city all that lost time' (*CS* 905).

The *Tempest* narrative woven in to the story establishes a schematic opposition between a Calibanesque aggressive modernity and a beneficent technology associated with the character Olds, the Ariel-figure who dreams incessantly of flight, and this opposition puts

Halloway in the position of having to make a choice. The text's rich-
est ambiguities are located in the tension between these two conceptions of an industrial modernity, partly because Halloway's idealism
is inseparable from his libidinal investment in technology's rapacious
tendencies and partly because Olds, a creature of the air, is a utopian
dreamer whereas the earthy Stillman, Halloway's other, is the city's
true representative. Halloway seeks to create a city characterised by
energy, and he is convinced that aggression is its necessary counterpart. No less than a Marinetti, with his exaltation of violence as a
means of social renewal, Halloway believes in metropolitan
dynamism; in his mind he keeps contrasting 'Buckmaster's limitless
appetite for steel, power, concrete and raw materials with the self-
denying, defeatist lives of the engineers and architects at Garden City'
(CS 897), and he is energised by the fact that the city operates 'an
exciting knife-edge away from total collapse' (CS 915). For Halloway,
violence can be dished out in controlled homeopathic doses for the
greater health of the social organism. It is only when death comes to
the city, Olds implacably rejects his attempts to manipulate the citi-
zenry, and urban dissolution results in outward migration that Halloway accepts the flaws in his conception of metropolitan life and
grasps that Stillman, for all his potent attractiveness, is a creature of
death who needs 'a dying city, not a living one, a warm cadaver that
he could infest like a maggot' (CS 920).

Yet the whole story still turns on the dream of flight, from Halloway's love of gliders and powered aeroplanes to Olds's symbolic
voyage into the skies at the end of the text. Halloway's final recognition that he must make peace with Miranda seems to look towards
some sort of integration of technology with ecological concerns, as
Ballard's choice of metaphor implies: 'Somehow he would come to
terms with Miranda, and help her to re-forest the cities' (CS 924). But
at the same time, there is no hint here that the original aspiration has
been abandoned; on the contrary, although Halloway looks to Olds to
teach him to fly, he is still planning fantastic constructions 'larger
than anything of which Buckmaster and the Twentieth Century had
ever dreamed' (CS 924). The very idea of the twentieth century, with
all its romantic longings and utopian hopes, is still alive, and the text's
haunting evocation of its failures bespeaks a refusal to foreclose on its
ambitions, as Halloway's response to an industrial wasteland makes
clear: 'Far from disfiguring the landscape, these discarded products
of Twentieth-Century industry had a fierce and wayward beauty.

Halloway was fascinated by the glimmering sheen of the metal-scummed canals, by the strange submarine melancholy of drowned cars looming up at him from abandoned lakes, by the brilliant colours of the garbage hills, by the glitter of a million cans embedded in a matrix of detergent packs and tinfoil ... He gazed raptly at the chalky whiteness of old china-clay tips, vivid as powdered ice, abandoned rai-lyards with their moss-covered locomotives, the undimmed beauty of industrial wastes produced by skills and imaginations far richer than nature's, more splendid than any Arcadian meadow. Unlike nature, here there was no death' (*CS* 915). A utopian reworking of industrial disaster is here envisaged as a distinct possibility. The dream of a technological renewal of a degraded present is in ultimate cities rarely far from the margins of the urban text.

Paradisal gardens?

The Unlimited Dream Company (1979) offers an ambiguous riposte to the gloomy prognostications of *Concrete Island* and *High-Rise*. An intensely visionary work, the novel abandons the grim urban reality evoked in the two earlier texts in order to envisage the transformation of suburban existence. Set in Shepperton, on the outskirts of London, it tells the fantastic tale of a half-crazed loner who imagines that he has magically been imbued with the power to transfigure the world. The novel's none too subtly named central protagonist, Blake, crashes a light aircraft in the suburb and, apparently passing through death back to a renewed life, emerges from the wrecked fuselage as a meta-morphosing god. Shepperton is recast as a lush jungle paradise, a land of impossibly tropical vegetation, joyfully sportive creatures, and strangely reinvigorated human beings. In a return to the preoccupa-tions of *The Crystal World*, the novel dreams a new life in which the sicknesses of a post-lapsarian realm are purged away through a rap-turous fusion of all elements of the creation into a delirious unity. By metaphorically flying into the empyrean, *The Unlimited Dream Com-pany* appears to set its face against the sordid realities of prosaic daily life anatomised in earlier works, thereby acknowledging the limits of the attempt to re-make that life through the strategy of *bricolage*.

But as so often in Ballard's writing, the status of this extravaganza is unclear. How to read it? As a narration of the inner fantasy life of a sick individual? As a dream of a dying man in the moments before his extinction? As a mystical insight into the realm of truth that glimmers behind the veil of unhallowed life? As an allegory of the transfiguring but dangerous power of the artistic imagination? These are all possible accounts of the novel. The narrator is a classically 'unreliable' central protagonist: there are reasons to believe that he is a deluded, possibly psychotic, charlatan with a narcissistic god-complex, or that he never survives the crash at all. *The Unlimited Dream Company* is a clear example of 'fantastic hesitation', wherein the membrane between the fictive and the real is permeable, its textual world situated in that liminal space between waking life and insubstantial dream. When Blake emerges from the aircraft he thinks he is 'looking at an enormous illuminated painting, lit both by the unsettled water and by a deep light transmitted through the body of the canvas' (*UD* 17), and this evocative novel, with its montage of overlapping realities, might best be read as a tribute to the 'naïve' vision of the Douanier Rousseau and the Surrealist imagination that celebrated the *madness* presupposed by its grand project of worldly re-enchantment.

The close connection between madness and imagination (a staple of post-Romantic thought) is also a marked feature of *The Day of Creation* (1987) and *Rushing to Paradise* (1994), two later works whose concerns are related to those of *The Unlimited Dream Company*. In these novels it is the dangers of the unfettered imagination that come to the fore in the shape of the all-devouring ego. If *Concrete Island* and *High Rise* concentrate on protagonists whose lack of affect causes them to withdraw from the world, then *The Day of Creation* and *Rushing to Paradise* focus on characters whose detachment from reality leads to phantasmatic attempts to remake the world in their own bloated image. These figures body forth the potential *monstrousness* of the creative imagination when it is unleashed upon others. In *The Day of Creation*, an allegory of the deluded self-exculpations of the colonialist enterprise, the central protagonist's vision of irrigating Africa originates in an emancipatory impulse that is quickly over-run by his self-aggrandising dreams of power and glory: 'already I imagined the Mallory irrigating the Sahara and saw myself as the third world's greatest benefactor' (*DC* 112). That this is a fantasy is evident from the monomania with which Mallory pursues this chimerical vision and from the ironic commentary provided on it by the educational tapes that are busily constructing a new post-colonial subject, in the form of the young girl Noon: 'tourism and bourgeois hegemony ... the natural park as neo-colonialist folk-lore ... African wild-life and the exploitation of racist stereotypes' (*DC* 118). The entire narrative,

moreover, is from the outset subjected not only to the fevered imagination of its main protagonist but also to the controlling influence of
the television documentary, a new form of colonisation, which divides
the African continent up in accordance with a new logic: 'The prime
sites – Ethiopia, Chad, the Sudan – had been allocated to the most
powerful television interests, the huge American networks and the
British record companies' (*DC* 35). Mallory's desire, on the surface of
it a laudable dream of topographic transformation that is intended to
be beneficial, is in fact a viral sickness that spreads out from an ego-
istic identification of self and world, with the result that what presents
itself as an emancipatory project ends by mapping 'the profiles of a
nightmare slumbering inside [his] head' (*DC* 17).

Rushing to Paradise is in turn more pessimistic still. Whereas the
hesitations and ambiguities that mark *The Day of Creation* blur the
boundary between fantasy and reality, *Rushing to Paradise* offers a
bleak depiction of the rampant ego at work. Ostensibly a satire of eco-
feminism, this aspect of the novel is neither especially persuasive nor
very interesting. Its real subject is power, specifically the power that
may be wielded by personalities whose grasp on reality is so attenu-
ated that this reality is equated with the desiring mind itself. All the
novel's characters want to remake the world in accordance with their
private fantasies, but only Dr Barbara has the force of will to carry
through a project of extermination through which the male members
of her new tribe are progressively wiped out once their procreative
function has been fulfilled. This character's headlong rush to a self-
willed, self-created paradise, in which a recalcitrant reality is subordinated to the law of desire, draws on the millenarian rhetoric of
restoration – 'we'll hand to the next Millennium a small part of this
terrible century that we've redeemed and brought back to life' (*RP* 42)
– while in practice it plays out its apocalyptic fantasies of negation,
disclosing 'a dream of death more real than any fantasies of nuclear
war' (*RP* 238). Here the profane world will never be enough
and will always need to be destroyed and remade in a cycle of creation–destruction that will know no end because it is referred not to
external reality but to the insatiable demands of a self-defeating desire
whose only terminus is the cessation of all life. Dr Barbara's religion
is then that of a 'sheer magnetic egoism' (*RP* 94) desperately in
search of the peace of inanimate matter: 'Death, for Dr Barbara, was
a secret door through which the threatened and the weary could slip
to safety' (*RP* 237).

The Day of Creation and *Rushing to Paradise* (especially the latter)
take some of the themes raised in *The Unlimited Dream Company* to
extreme conclusions. They are of relevance to a discussion of that text
because it is all too easy to be beguiled by its vision of a re-enchanted
world, whereas its depiction of the process of transfiguration is not
solely a laudatory one. The novel depicts Shepperton as an ersatz
world, a vacuous domain of wafer-thin façades and stupefied lives –
'the everywhere of suburbia, the paradigm of nowhere' (*UD* 35). This
generalised symbol of urban sprawl lacks any reason to exist, hence
the torpor of its inhabitants. This parody of a genuine 'place' is presented as a film-set peopled by individuals who are merely lip-synch-
ing to scripted parts and who resent Blake's disturbance of the
charade since they are little more than 'actors recruited from the film
studios to play their roles in an elaborate conspiracy' (*UD* 26). A powerful anti-Platonic strain runs through *The Unlimited Dream Company*. Portraying Shepperton as a pale copy of the world, an empty
simulacrum of the real, the novel alludes to Plato's myth of the cave
in the sense that the suburb's inhabitants are depicted as living out an
existence that is a shadowy imitation of true life. Blake's assault on
this illusory 'knowledge' is figured as a stripping away of the veil; his
task is to offer 'a sudden glimpse into that real world' which he is
unfolding as he draws back 'the curtains that muffle Shepperton and
the rest of this substitute realm' (*UD* 90). But the reality he uncovers
is not one of Platonic Forms that are unreachable by the senses. On
the contrary, this reality, which is not so much uncovered as co-cre-
ated by the imagination, is corporeal and non-rational. A mutable
ever-moving flux, it is a Dionysian fount of energy that flows in and
through the whole of creation.

The reference point for this line of thought is Nietzsche's critique
of Platonism and Christianity. In *The Birth of Tragedy* (1871) the figure
of Dionysus is the sign under which Nietzsche exalted a vigour that
could destroy sterile modes of thought and preside over the unification of self and world.[15] Dionysus was a shorthand epithet for the Anti-
Christ, his representative of 'an affirmative instinct for life, turned
against morality', which in contrast to idealist thought creates 'a fundamentally opposite doctrine and valuation of life, purely artistic and
anti-Christian'.[16] Nietzsche's assault on Christianity and Platonism
depended   on   *inversion*:   these   traditions   were   the   sources
of error and sickness.[17] The 'deviant' makes an unblushing return in
Nietzsche's thought, in the shape of the instinctual, desiring, drive-

based body; a thorough-going naturalism locates value in corporeal life and the senses. Dionysus symbolises an affirmative philosophy that refuses what Nietzsche takes to be the renunciative ethos of Christianity. Instead of setting out to extirpate passion, it asks: 'How can one spiritualize, beautify, deify a desire?'[18] A dream of transformation lies behind this question: reality is to be redeemed through the acceptance of its materiality and the life-force that courses through it. The key to a unification of self and world lay in the transforming power of art, and in this conception of art reality is not reflected but is transfigured. Humanity is sick because it has severed itself from the instinctive sources of life, vainly imagining that the enlightenment provided by reason leads to truth and authenticity.

The Unlimited Dream Company's Blake is the unheralded avatar of pantheism, a pagan god come to fecundate this pale copy of an animate world with his phallic power. Setting out to invert the false values that hold sway in suburbia, he is a Dionysian lord of misrule bent on unleashing the divine *energeia* that Shepperton has dammed up behind the walls of social convention, sexual repression and horticultural order. The transformation of Shepperton, the visible sign of changes that must also take place within the minds of its residents, acts as a prelude to Blake's passage through the four elements of air, water, earth and fire, a process through which the god Zagreus (a manifestation of Dionysus in dismembered form) must also pass, and which Nietzsche sees as presaging the end of individuation – in other words, the schism between humanity and the rest of creation – and offering 'a presentiment of a restored oneness'.[19] Blake passes through similar stages of dismemberment before re-emerging with the power to heal and renew, a power, in turn, that is indissociable from a drive to unify all living things by conjoining them with himself, and this process of fusion creates a new order of life marked by the interpenetration of bodies. Drawing on cannibalistic imagery, Blake sees himself incorporating the townspeople 'into the host of my flesh ... merging with all creatures until I had taken into myself every living being, every fish and bird, every parent and child, a single chimeric god uniting all life within me' (*UD* 182–3), a vision that calls to mind Nietzsche's descriptions of the Dionysian man as one who 'transforms things until they mirror his power' and who 'enters into every skin, into every emotion ... continually transforming himself.'[20]

This transformation of the external world, a dream of belonging and togetherness, functions as a critique of a whole way of life. The

4 W. Lewis, *Blasting and Bombardiering: An Autobiography* (London: John Calder, 1982), p. 256.
5 M. Augé, *Non-Places: Introduction to an Anthropology of Supermodernity*, trans. J. Howe (London: Verso, 1995), p. 25.
6 Augé, *Non-Places*, pp. 77–8.
7 Augé, *Non-Places*, pp. 78–9.
8 Ballard, *CI*, unpaginated 'Introduction'.
9 Ballard, *CI*, unpaginated 'Introduction'.
10 R. Banham, *The New Brutalism: Ethic or Aesthetic?* (London: The Architectural Press, 1966), p. 19.
11 Le Corbusier, *Towards a New Architecture*, trans. F. Etchells (London: The Architectural Press, 1948), p. 8.
12 Foucault, *Power/Knowledge*, p. 154.
13 D. Punter, *The Hidden Script: Writing and the Unconscious* (London: Routledge and Kegan Paul, 1985), p. 18.
14 S. Freud, *Civilization, Society and Religion: Group Psychology, Civilization and its Discontents, and Other Works*, trans. J. Strachey, ed. A. Dickson (Harmondsworth: Penguin, 1991), pp. 330–40.
15 F. Nietzsche, *The Birth of Tragedy*, trans. S. Whiteside, ed. M. Tanner (Harmondsworth: Penguin, 1993), p. 18.
16 Nietzsche, *The Birth of Tragedy*, p. 9.
17 F. Nietzsche, *Twilight of the Idols/The Anti-Christ*, trans. R. J. Hollingdale (Harmondsworth: Penguin, 1990), pp. 196–7.
18 Nietzsche, *Twilight of the Idols*, p. 52.
19 Nietzsche, *The Birth of Tragedy*, p. 52. For a general account of this symbolism in Ballard's work see D. Pringle, *Earth is the Alien Planet: J. G. Ballard's Four-Dimensional Nightmare* (San Bernardino CA: Borgo Press, 1979).
20 Nietzsche, *Twilight of the Idols*, pp. 82, 83.
21 Nietzsche, *Twilight of the Idols*, p. 119.
22 W. Self, 'Conversations: J. G. Ballard', in *Junk Mail* (London: Penguin, 1996), pp. 329–71, p. 344.

4

The destructive element

Empire of the Sun (*ES*; 1984) is a very funny book. Granted, most of the novel's humour is dark in tone: levity scarcely seems an appropriate response to the grim experiences recorded in its pages. But comic it is, the comic, always following its own paths, having a tendency to crop up in unpredictable places and at unexpected times. Towards the end of the Second World War the internees of the Lunghua Civilian Assembly Centre realise that the prison-camp's rations have run out, and they prepare to depart for Nantao in the hope that there they will find food. The novel's central protagonist – the young boy Jim – begins to laugh manically at the thought that the Japanese guards do not need to kill the escaping prisoners because they are all in fact spiritually dead. Mr Maxted suppresses Jim's rising hysteria by cuffing him gently and enjoining him to remember that he is British. When Jim informs Mrs Vincent that he will soon be reunited with his parents, the woman with whose family he has shared a cell, but who has refused to help him, asks him if he thinks they will give her a reward. Jim's reaction to this ironic question is telling:

> Embarrassed, Jim lowered his head. During his illness he had mistakenly tried to bribe Mrs Vincent with the promise of a reward, but it intrigued him that she could see the humour in her refusal to raise a finger to help him. Jim hesitated before leaving the room. He had spent nearly three years with Mrs Vincent, and still found himself liking her. She was one of the few people in Lunghua Camp who appreciated the humour of it all.
>
> Trying to match her, he said: 'A reward? Mrs Vincent, remember you're British.' (*ES* 240)

The novel's multiple ironies and ambiguities are compressed into this amusing vignette. Neither of the two combatants in this playful verbal joust has behaved in the way the 'British' like to think of themselves as behaving; Mrs Vincent has studiously ignored the temporarily orphaned boy, while Jim has tried to buy her support, in an obvious parody of the dictum that virtue should be its own reward. Jim, moreover, may be 'British' by birth, but his personality has been formed by a childhood spent in Shanghai, and this character formation makes him an outsider among the expatriates in Lunghua, not least because of his ability to adapt in response to the conditions imposed by war. The British in Lunghua are the source of his greatest contempt; unable to adapt to prison-camp life, they are paralysed by a self-defeating nostalgia that prevents them from confronting the realities of the situation and a duplicitous ethical code that enables them to conceal their hypocrisy from themselves. Jim sees through the façade of a national identity that is based on an imaginary heritage, on spurious distinctions between 'us' and 'them', and on naïve conceptions of 'right' and 'wrong'. He not only grasps that this 'imaginary community' is an arbitrary construct but also realises that it belongs to a way of life, and upholds a scheme of values, that have little purchase on reality. The unspoken bond between Jim and Mrs Vincent lies here: both know that the humour of it all lies in the gap between convention and truth.

At its simplest, the comic is associated with reversal and inversion, where what is known or anticipated is suddenly transformed into its opposite and made to look ridiculous in the process. Such situations can be casually funny, as in the banana-skin pratfall, but they can also be premonitions of darker insights into human life. But in a century marked by intimations of the absurd a sense of nothingness has often been attributed to existence *in toto*. Bergson located humour in the fissure between the body's mechanised corporeality and the mind's idealisation of human life, a discrepancy that mocks all pretension to meaning: 'The attitudes, gestures and movements of the human body are laughable in exact proportion as that body reminds us of a mere machine.'[1] Wyndham Lewis, contemplating William James's claim that 'from nothing to being there is no logical bridge', wrote as follows of the absurdity inherent in the physical dimension of life: 'It is the chasm lying between non-being, over which it is impossible for logic to throw any bridge, that, in certain forms of laughter, we leap. We land plumb in the centre of Nothing.'[2] In the writing of Camus, the absurd emerges out of 'the confrontation of the irrational and the wild longing for clarity' experienced by human beings, and this confrontation between an unyielding world and an aspiring humanity binds them to each other 'as only hatred can weld two creatures together.'[3]

But it is from the perspective of Pirandello's subtle theory of humour that the best approach to *Empire of the Sun* can be made. Pirandello distinguished between the merely 'comic' and 'humour' proper, arguing that the latter is a doubled phenomenon in which the object of ridicule is both laughed at and understood *at the same time*. What he called 'the feeling of the opposite' – which ensures that the way the comic object is represented will induce reflective understanding and not just provoke ridicule – was central to a theory that distanced itself from the Hobbesian view that in comedy the laugher feels superior to those being laughed at. For Pirandello, because 'the comic and its opposite are both present in the humoristic disposition itself and are inherent in the process which results from it', genuine humour implicates the laugher in the risible scene and in the course of doing so induces feelings of perplexity: 'I feel as if I was suspended between two forces: I feel like laughing, and I do laugh, but my laughter is troubled and obstructed by something that stems from the representation itself.'[4] This laughter disturbs because it is disintegrative, unstitching the illusions by which life attempts to sustain itself: 'We shall see that all fictions of the spirit, all the creations of feeling are the basic material of humor; that is, we shall see that reflection becomes something resembling a diabolical imp that takes apart the mechanism of each image, of each phantasm produced by the emotions; it takes it apart in order to see how it is made; it releases the mainspring, and the whole mechanism squeaks convulsively'.[5]

Empire of the Sun is reflective in this way. Inasmuch as the novel presents aspects of the war in a comic light, it does so with a pathos born of understanding and sympathy. Consider this blackly comic description of the internees' departure from Lunghua, in which a swathe of apparently pointless possessions suddenly rematerialises, as though from nowhere:

> Recreation had clearly come high on the prisoners' list of priorities while they packed their suitcases before being interned. Having spent the years of peace on the tennis courts and cricket fields of the Far East, they confidently expected to pass the years of war in the same way. Dozens of tennis racquets hung from the suitcase handles; there were cricket bats and fishing rods, and even a set of golf clubs tied to the bundles of pierrot costumes carried by Mr and Mrs Wentworth. Ragged and

under-nourished, the prisoners shuffled along the road on their wooden clogs ... Already the effort of carrying the baggage had begun to tell, and one of the Chinese peasant women seated outside the gates now clutched a white tennis racquet. (*ES* 241)

The passage works by heaping incongruity upon incongruity, ending with the farcical image of a starving peasant brandishing a racquet. It exposes the discrepancy between these characters' expectations that the war would be a recreational break (those suitcases, that sports equipment) and the experiences they were subsequently forced to endure. At the same time, it plays on the bizarre contrast between these malnourished spectres and their totems of physical prowess. What makes this scene doubly, if almost cruelly, funny is that three years of internment seem to have taught the prisoners nothing – having initially taken items that could never have been of any earthly use, they now insist on taking them back, even though they can scarcely carry them. Yet there is also a 'feeling of the opposite' here, a kind of bemused sympathy for such misguided choices, which manifests itself in the recognition that what is elsewhere described as 'the fifty-year-long party that had been Shanghai' (*ES* 82) had left these people utterly unprepared for what was to come.

The voice that articulates this perspective is not Jim's. It belongs to an older, wiser figure who has had time to process the experiences that are in this text filtered through Jim's youthful consciousness. This unnamed figure functions as an anonymous narrator who occasionally gives information that Jim would not have known at the time or who hints at an understanding of events that would have been beyond Jim's comprehension. Thus, inasmuch as the book is narrated from Jim's standpoint, it permits other perspectives to emerge, 'voicing' them either through an implied author or through an often implicit clash of viewpoints. Jim's limited understanding is revealed in inventive ways, as in his muddled reconstruction of events in the family house:

> In the talcum on the floor around him he could see the imprints of his mother's feet. She had moved from side to side, propelled by an over-eager partner, perhaps one of the Japanese officers to whom she was teaching the tango. Jim tried out the dance steps himself, which seemed far more violent than any tango he had ever seen, and managed to fall and cut his hand on the broken mirror. (*ES* 64–5)

And still other perspectives are provided by the characters (such as Basie, Ransome and Maxted) whose remarks and observations Jim faithfully reports, even though his grasp of their meanings is tenuous. In his preface to *What Maisie Knew* (1897), the *locus classicus* of this mode of narration, Henry James reflected on the challenge it presented:

> Small children have many more perceptions than they have terms to translate them; their vision is at any moment much richer, their apprehension even constantly stronger, than their prompt, their at all producible, vocabulary. Amusing therefore as it might at the first blush have seemed to restrict myself in this case to the terms as well as to the experience, it became at once plain that such an attempt would fail. Maisie's terms accordingly play their part – since her simpler conclusions quite depend on them; but our own commentary constantly attends and amplifies.[6]

Empire of the Sun is in Bakhtinian terms an example of double-voiced discourse, neatly defined by Simon Dentith as one in which the reader can 'recognise that there are two distinct consciousnesses operating in a single utterance, and that their evaluative attitudes are not the same.'[7] The text's humour derives from the gap between these discrepant attitudes; the implied author's mature perspective is comically juxtaposed with Jim's misunderstandings of what people are saying and with his wild, frenetic imaginings. Jim, in short, is often muddled, and this muddle produces most of the text's laugh-out-loud moments. But the novel's humour, just as in James's *Maisie*, has a more serious role to play; it strips away illusions like so many layers of gleaming lacquer. Jim is Pirandello's diabolical imp, an ambiguous revealer of uncomfortable truths and a sly debunker of social conventions. This perverse role is hinted at in an early chapter when he solemnly considers informing Mr Maxted that he has not only left the cubs and become an atheist but has also become that dread thing, a communist: 'The communists had an intriguing ability to unsettle everyone, a talent Jim greatly respected' (*ES* 27). It is a talent he possesses himself, in spades. *Empire of the Sun* depicts the effects of war on an unformed mind at the same time as it uses that mind to unsettle naïve assumptions about how the war might be expected to affect a young boy and to undermine spurious accounts of how adults coped with it.

A doubled figure who uncannily combines innocence and experience in one personality, Jim is the locus of the novel's ambivalent exploration of these troubling issues. His imagination is the source both of his penetrating insights and of his wayward fantasies, enabling him to be alternately in touch with realities that others wish to ignore and detached from the world outside his own mind. At the same time, his unpredictable behaviour reveals the pragmatism that is needed to survive but which most of the prisoners are unwilling to contemplate. The scene that best exemplifies Jim in a subversive role occurs when he approaches some Japanese soldiers for water and ostentatiously drinks the entire bottle himself, a 'selfish' act that only he and the soldiers find amusing: 'The Japanese burst into laughter, chortling to each other with great amusement. Jim laughed with them, well aware that only he, among the British prisoners, appreci-ated the joke. Basie ventured a wary smile, but Dr Ransome seemed baffled' (*ES* 135). As well he might be. Jim's dark trick is funny because it overturns expectations with such finality. That a boy would have the nerve to face possible death and the cheek to keep the reward all to himself is beyond the other prisoners' comprehension. Jim laughs with the Japanese because like them he understands not only that he has committed an incongruous act but also that he has dis-closed a shocking truth about the reality of war, which only he and the soldiers have grasped. His action is a calculated attempt to undeceive the British, to expose the values to which they adhere as defunct, and to awaken them from somnolence. By taking care of his own bodily needs and ignoring those of his fellow prisoners, Jim demonstrates that the war has already over-ridden the moral imperatives and social considerations to which they still cling. It is a sickening joke, nonethe-less, and the disturbing corollary of Jim's disassociation from the weak prisoners is his identification with the powerful oppressor.

The pivot on which *Empire of the Sun* turns is the attack on Pearl Harbour and the destruction of Jim's pre-war life. The early chapters portray an almost adolescent boy gifted with intelligence, curiosity, energy and imaginative sensitivity. Shanghai is the electrifyingly exotic space in which his febrile mind is most at home – it licences his passion for *flânerie* and nourishes his dreams. When the world of Shanghai in which he feels so safe is turned upside down, his identity is destroyed along with it. The book will go on to show how the 'small exploding boy' (*ES* 63) sets about re-assembling himself out of the broken shards of his pre-war identity during his time in the camp at Lunghua. This identity can never be recovered: it can only be re-made. The novel tracks the history of that process in a cool, crystalline prose, its detached tone reflecting the disconnection from reality that the boy is forced into so that he can survive. A relentless logic drives this history, revealing that Jim's adaptability comes at a heavy price: it depends on the power of a saving imagination, which enables him to fill his mind with evasive dreams, but it relies on a numbing of affect, which permits him to accept the inverted values of camp life as normal. These two psychological strategies are polar opposites: one relishes the phantasms of the mind and excites them to an ever more lurid life, while the other closes the brain off and prevents it from confronting the meaning of events. But both deflect or block out the pain of experience. Jim survives because he is able to escape into the world of his over-active imagination, while at the same time treating life in the camp with a casual disregard, as though it were an utterly unobjectionable form of existence.

This acceptance of the conditions imposed by war leads Jim to embrace an entirely different set of codes and conventions in which preservation of the self is the first priority. Within this asocial realm there is little room for altruism or moral scruples of any kind; a closed, self-perpetuating circuit links physical survival, emotional deadness and ethical silence. The process by which Jim learns how to steer by these new co-ordinates is explored in detail, from his early realisation 'that kindness, which his parents and teachers had always urged upon him, counted for nothing' (*ES* 86) right through to his dehumanisation, perhaps best exemplified in the scene in which the Japanese guards kill a Chinese coolie. The scene is shocking not so much because it depicts the passivity of the prisoners but because it shows Jim's disconnection from what is taking place. The juxtaposition of the slow killing with Jim's idle desire to read a cherished magazine emphasises the boy's inability to respond emotionally to an act of murder:

> Jim smoothed the pages of the *Reader's Digest*, wondering whether to read an article about Winston Churchill. He would have liked to leave, but all around him the prisoners were motionless as they watched the parade ground … Jim thought about his algebra prep … Later that evening, when he had finished Basie's potato skin, Jim lay on his bunk and at last opened the magazine. There were no advertisements in the *Reader's Digest*, which was a shame, but Jim looked at the reassuring picture of the Packard limousine pinned to the wall of his cubicle. (*ES* 227–9)

The prisoners' helplessness is harrowing enough, but Jim's capacity to consider the implications of what is happening in a detached manner, with half a mind on his journal and his homework, is more disturbing still, for what is revealed here is a loss of affect and of moral bearings that puts the killing of another on the same plane as the question of whether or not to glance at a magazine. The 'shame' Jim feels at the lack of advertisements in the magazine provides a painful commentary on the lack of real shame at the deed perpetrated before his indifferent eyes.

Fictional footprints

In this flattening out of emotional sensitivity and moral empathy we see *in nuce* the preoccupations of Ballard's work in the 1960s and 1970s, and before completing my account of *Empire of the Sun* I want to offer some observations on another semi-autobiographical reading of these preoccupations, namely that provided by *The Kindness of Women* (1991). In *Empire of the Sun* the closing down of one set of imaginative possibilities and the ethical vocabulary they sustain opens up the path to various forms of psychopathology. By showing from the outset that Jim is endowed with a compulsive imagination, the novel portrays him as a figure who requires a rich interior life. In a text that returns again and again to the prisoners' hunger and to their daily struggle for extra rations, what stands out in Jim's case is his need for mental nourishment. He is hungry above all for stimulation, for inspiration, for excitement – anything that might fill up his emaciated mind and, temporarily satiating it, give it momentary succour. This over-heated imagination leads him to fantasise that 'he himself had probably started the war, with his confused semaphores from the window that the Japanese officers in the motor launch had misinterpreted' (*ES* 43), and to dream that he can conjure aeroplanes out of thin air, when he fancies that 'the B-29s would appear without warning in the sky above his head, as if summoned by [his] starving brain' (*ES* 233). Whereas before the war Jim's imaginative needs are sustained by his immersion in the phantasmagoric life of Shanghai and the fantasy-laden world of film, far more ambiguous influences come into play during and after it.

   The Kindness of Women offers another perspective on the events of the war, mainly by focusing on its consequences for the adult protagonist's life in the post-war period. Switching from a third-person to a first-person narration, it ostensibly provides a more 'personal' and therefore more 'truthful' account than that vouchsafed by *Empire of the Sun*, which relies so heavily on distancing techniques. But the later text is no less artfully constructed, and its reflections on the experiences of a character named 'James Ballard' are neither straight-forwardly autobiographical nor unproblematically veridical. *The Kindness of Women* is like *Empire of the Sun* preoccupied with the question of identity and the ambiguous role played by the imagina-tion in its formation. The first part of the book briefly replays the nar-rative of *Empire of the Sun*, giving a summary of the story recounted in that text but altering certain events and presenting them from a different angle of vision. The truth-telling status of both narratives is thereby called into question – both are to be read as *versions* of the past, not as definitive reconstructions. And this narrative self-reflex-ivity is in turn closely linked to both texts' problematisation of the imagination, which is shown to recast experience in a variety of deflecting, defensive, and possibly delusional ways. The narrator's acknowledgement that his 'entire world had been shaped by the camp' and that instead of 'wanting to escape from it' he had sought 'to burrow ever more deeply into its heart' (*KW* 48), suggests that unusual experiences have shaped his identity and that his perception of reality will be coloured by them to no small degree. The emotional dissociation from his own experience – and from wider events more generally – depicted in *Empire of the Sun* is here linked to the failure to work through personal trauma, leaving the protagonist in an unre-solved psychological limbo: 'So much had happened that I had not yet been able to remember or forget ... My sense of myself had changed, and I had mislaid part of my mind somewhere between Lunghua and Shanghai' (*KW* 65).

The Kindness of Women thus occupies a Ballardian interzone: inas-much as it is a quest narrative, its central character trying to retrieve a sense of self that has been mislaid, it does not follow a linear psy-chological trajectory but circles around the question of identity, prod-ding and probing it from a variety of perspectives. It does follow a historical chronology (from childhood in Shanghai to the adult return to the same place nearly half a century later) but this chronology is tra-versed and interrupted by all the fictions Ballard has written in between, so ensuring that throughout the text there is an ongoing dia-logue between different texts. Thus although the book is cast as a nar-rative of redemption in which psychological death (symbolised by the murder of a young Chinese prisoner) is eventually undone by a life-saving rebirth, almost the entire action takes place in the limbo between these two defining events, and this means that the narrator's perspective on those events is itself a shadowy, uncertain one. This perspective vies with other, equally plausible ones: Ballard's alter ego David sees him as a classic case of repression and denial, as a man unable to face up to the 'true' character of his deviant nature, whereas his substitute-mother Peggy considers that through a process of sympathetic identification he has taken upon himself the destructive violence of the war, becoming a human embodiment of the death-instinct. Neither viewpoint is granted decisive explanatory power (they are perhaps two sides of the same coin), but the first of these two perspectives refers in the main to Ballard's retreat into the comforting womb of domesticity, while the second refers primarily to the ambivalent power of his lurid imagination.

Empire of the Sun has already opened up the possibility that Jim's survival has depended on a mimicry that has enabled him to identify with, and thus to deflect, the aggression that has been directed against him, but *The Kindness of Women* draws out the implications of this viewpoint in greater detail. Peggy recalls that immediately after the war all Ballard 'wanted to do was sit in the dark and watch ... suicide pilots crashing into American ships' (*KW* 269). Her conclusion is that what he has always needed is 'glamourised violence', and by tracing this need back to the murder of the Chinese prisoner she links it to his vicarious experience of his own death, an experience he has been replaying ever since: 'A part of it actually happened to you. All those car crashes and pornographic movies, Kennedy's death, they're your way of turning it into a film, something violent and glamorous. You want to Americanise death' (*KW* 270). For Peggy, Ballard's identification with this violence is so total that his mind is 'up there, moulded against the screen' (*KW* 269). This powerful image suggests not only that he is transforming his experience of violence into a representation but also that he is thereby rendering it safe (displacing it into the realm of the imaginary), while the price paid for this defensive strategy is the colonisation of his psyche by the glamorised allure this violence subsequently represents. It is a compelling view, and although Ballard mildly resists this interpretation, he later acknowledges its partial truth when, having through his own children rediscovered and relived the childhood taken away from him by war, he claims that the 'time of desperate stratagems was over, the car crashes and hallucinogens, the deviant sex ransacked like a library of extreme metaphors' (*KW* 347). But this is in turn a desperate stratagem, a way of resolving profound dilemmas and of imposing closure on a psychological narrative that cannot be tidied up quite so easily.

For if anything is clear in this multi-layered text it is that the particular literary imagination forged by the experiences recounted here is driven by enormously powerful obsessions that cannot simply be cast off like so much unwanted psychological bric-a-brac. It is significant that the description which shows Ballard to be so mesmerised by the screen that he is virtually inhabiting it emphasises his identification with a representation: it is the *spectacle* of violence that haunts his mind and compels his imagination. The fictive worlds produced by that imagination are then expressions of a particular psychology, which creates its pictures of reality from a specific angle of vision. The question of how far this vision may be regarded as reliable is a key issue in the book. Thus when Ballard's future wife, struck by his collection of Surrealist prints, enjoins him to hold on 'to his imagination, even if it is a bit lurid', his retort is that the 'world *is* lurid' and that she is lucky she has 'never had to rely on [her] imagination' (*KW* 90). This ambiguous response seems to imply both a reflectionist and a productivist model of the imagination: the Surrealist view of reality with which his perspective is aligned is said to reflect the real truth about the world (it *is* lurid), but at the same time this view is associated with psychological defensiveness (the world is *perceived* as lurid in order that it may be coped with). There is a persistent slippage between these two possibilities in *The Kindness of Women*. The reliability of the author's view of the world remains uncertain, not least because it is so intimately bound up with fantasies of atomic devastation that he himself finds deeply dubious: 'The sight of these immense explosions at Eniwetok stirred and enthralled me ... The mysterious mushroom clouds, rising above the Pacific atolls from which the B-29s had brought to Nagasaki the second day of apocalypse, were a powerful incitement to the psychotic imagination, sanctioning everything. Fantasies of nuclear war fused forever with my memories of Shanghai' (*KW* 102–3).

Apocalyptic dreams are in this passage yoked together with childhood recollections in imagery which insists that 'the psychotic imagination' is indissociable from the experiences that have contributed to its formation. Various intertextual resonances are in play here, for Ballard is going over ground that has already been covered in *The

Atrocity Exhibition – even using the exact same phrase in both books
– but this time attributing to himself a psychosis that is in the earlier text mapped onto 1960s culture.[8] This blurring of the public and
the private is another feature of *The Kindness of Women*, which inves-
tigates the sources of the imagination that produced works like *The
Atrocity Exhibition* and *Crash*, and in the course of doing so ponders
to what extent they are purely subjective projections rather than genuine social diagnoses. *The Kindness of Women* comes close to suggesting that the former view is the more accurate of the two. Or, to
put it another way, it is as though the two narrative trajectories I
described in the 'Introduction' to this book (Ballard's life on the one
hand, and the unfolding events of the 1960s on the other) are here
figured as being on a bizarre collision course from the outset. Peggy
suggests that the 'Viet Nam war, the Kennedy assassinations, the
Congo, those ghastly *ratissages* ... might have been invented for you'
(*KW* 269), while the narrator considers that in 'many ways the
media landscape of the 1960s was a laboratory designed specifically
to cure me of all my obsessions' (*KW* 190). The book thus stages a
narrative of uncanny recognition in which the truth that must be
confronted is not embodied in an alter ego but in a historical epoch.
This doubling of individual subjectivity and the culture at large pervades the entire book, so that descriptions of social pathology may
also be read as thinly disguised self-diagnoses, as in this account of
a group's response to a car accident: 'Born out of an ecology of violence, acts of numbing brutality now ruled the imaginative spaces of
their lives, leaching away all feeling and emotion. Perhaps, in their
thoughtful communion with the crashed car, they were trying to
come to terms with the televised disasters and assassinations that
enfolded their minds, and doing what they could to restore a lost
compassion' (*KW* 221).

Recognition takes place when the trajectory of the narrator's life
coincides with that of the 1960s, and from that point on the nightmare visions that have haunted his waking life are gradually dispersed. The domestic idyll that David has previously mocked as the
fragile product of repression now returns as the site of a solid psychological reality that has been 'worked through', and the narrator's
rebirth into a transfigured world is experienced as an emancipation
from the burden of the past. In *Empire of the Sun* the newly cynical Jim
'knows' that kindness 'count[s] for nothing' (*ES* 86), but in the later
book it is numerous kindnesses, principally those associated with the

women and children he has loved, that 'rescue' him (*KW* 161). But in
a book that is uncompromisingly self-questioning it would be too
much to expect so tidy a resolution. Its closing scenes enact the final
stage in a journey of self-discovery and exorcism that involves a fictional return to Shanghai by way of one last representation of the narrator's life: the film of *Empire of the Sun*, which is seen as 'the last act
in a profound catharsis that had taken many decades to draw to a
close' (*KW* 345). It is a powerful ending to a moving book. But it
cannot quite achieve the finality that is here imputed to it, not least
because it is so obviously just one more fictional account, one more
version of events, in a multi-perspectival text that has foregrounded
the questionable status of the shaping imagination from start to
finish. Ballard describes the book as 'an autobiographical novel written with the full awareness of the fiction that that life generated
during its three or four decades of adulthood', and he emphasises its
doubled character when he sums it up as 'the life reconstituted from
the fictional footprints that I left behind me'.[9] And this returns us to
the novels and stories themselves, perhaps especially those – such as
The Atrocity Exhibition – that resonate most directly with this book's
concerns. In *The Kindness of Women* the issues that had seemed so
pressing appear as superseded personal obsessions and historically
obsolete memories: 'Now only the graffiti endured, like the bird-drop-
pings on the statues of Victorian generals and statesmen in the
squares of London' (*KW* 325).

Laughter from the abyss

In *Empire of the Sun* the preoccupations that obsess the older narrator
of *The Kindness of Women* are traced back to the life of the camp at
Lunghua and to the absence of adequate role models at a key stage in
the formation of Jim's identity. Two opposed father figures vie with
each other for influence over Jim: Ransome, the pattern of stiff-
necked British public-school values, and Basie, the epitome of a casually amoral instinct for survival. Jim's relationship with Ransome is
awkward because the doctor, vainly trying to instil an altruistic code
of behaviour in Jim, is so uneasy about his acceptance of camp life
and his lack of moral scruple: 'He had formed his only close bond in
Lunghua with Dr Ransome, though he knew that in many ways the
physician disapproved of him. He resented Jim for revealing an obvious truth about the war, that people were only too able to adapt to it'

(*ES* 208). There is an irony here, which Jim cannot see. Not only is the 'truth' he asserts so glibly less obvious than he thinks, since most of the prisoners have in contrast to himself adapted poorly, but also Ransome is aware that the boy is being damaged by his breezy assent to the conditions imposed on him by Lunghua. Jim's enjoyment of life in the camp, which he finds such a reassuring place, is inseparable from a slackening of all constraints on his behaviour. But in escaping from various kinds of repression he exposes the terrain of his mind to a different kind of colonisation, which is quickly effected by the brutalities of daily existence and Basie's cunning tutelage. He is 'free' in that he can roam the camp at will and can allow his mind to explore hitherto undreamt-of possibilities, but he is unaware of the extent to which this exploration is moulded by the war and blind to the fact that the competing claims made on him by Ransome and Basie contribute to his split identity. The reconstructed boy, whose starveling mind is avid for nourishment of any kind, feeds on the meagre diet afforded him and becomes the unwitting creation of the camp itself. Thus his impatience with the British, which is directed mainly at their inability to cope with altered circumstances, needs to be looked at from another angle: he, it seems, has adjusted all too easily, but this apparent adjustment cannot hide the extent to which it has required him to introject the baleful world surrounding him.

I suggested earlier that the novel's cool, dispassionate tone registers Jim's detachment from his experiences. This detachment is the product of denial. Reflecting on the implications for the literary imagination of an earlier cataclysm – the First World War – Virginia Woolf wrote: 'In the vast catastrophe of the European war our emotions had to be broken up for us, and put at an angle from us, before we could allow ourselves to feel them properly in poetry or fiction. The only poets who spoke to the purpose spoke in [a] sidelong, satiric manner.'[10] For Woolf, the distress of the war was so immediately overwhelming that it was unassimilable, requiring an obliquity of approach. As her metaphor of 'breaking up' implies, this obliquity was seen as the product of a trauma that affected both body and mind, physical dismemberment acting as an analogue to mental collapse. In his work on neurosis Freud suggested that war trauma originated in a fear of external danger that has been introjected and subsequently threatens to destroy the ego from within.[11] Psychoanalytical work on trauma focused from the outset on the difficulties its sufferers have in processing their experiences, which may prove to be unthinkable and hence unrepresentable.[12] Commenting on the possible effects of trauma in infancy, 'before a coherent ego (and its defences) is formed', Donald Kalsched refers to the emergence of *'a second line of defenses'* that 'comes into play to prevent the "unthinkable" from being experienced.'[13] For Kalsched, in its response to trauma 'we see the psyche operating not to link but to de-link – to split or to dissociate',[14] a kind of fracturing that, in John Steiner's words, gives rise to 'the appearance of a *rent* in the relationship between the ego and reality.'[15] Debates have raged over the extent to which dissociation from trauma entails a seemingly paradoxical identification with what caused it, such that the trauma itself cannot be known. As Ruth Leys puts it: 'In short, from the beginning trauma was understood as an experience that immersed the victim in the traumatic scene so profoundly that it precluded the kind of specular distance necessary for cognitive knowledge of what had happened.'[16]

Empire of the Sun complicates this contentious scenario. There can be little doubt that dissociation and identification figure in its portrayal of Jim. The splitting process is referred to on a number of occasions, with Jim experiencing a separation of mind from body and a division of the self in which detachment from experience is a marked feature: 'A strange doubling of reality had taken place, as if everything that had happened to him since the war was occurring within a mirror. It was his mirror self who felt faint and hungry, and who thought about food all the time. He no longer felt sorry for this other self' (*ES* 103). However, Jim is also portrayed as someone who is aware of a good deal of what is happening to him, even though he cannot adequately process it. His understanding of the effect of trauma on his psyche is limited and incomplete, but it is not *absent*. And although the novel is written by the adult Ballard, who has the benefit of temporal distance from the events depicted, it is revealing that in filtering these events through Jim's consciousness, he elects to grant his character a fair degree of insight at the time in which these events are occurring. Two passages are particularly significant in this respect. In the first one, Jim reflects on the significance of his manic activity during his time in the camp and the fantasies of omnipotence that have sustained him, making explicit reference to the repression this has entailed:

> The activity screened his mind from certain fears that he had tried to repress, that the years in Lunghua would come to an end, and he would find himself building the runway again. The light that emerged from

the burning body of the Mustang pilot had been a warning to him. As long as he ran his errands for Basie and Demarest and Cohen, to and from the kitchens, carrying water and playing chess, Jim could sustain the illusion that the war would last forever. (*ES* 225–6)

The second passage occurs at a time when he is in a state of almost complete mental collapse during which he deliriously imagines that he can raise the dead. In a moment of lucidity, faced with the corpse of a Japanese pilot, he considers the implications of the airman's death for his own desperately conceived survival strategies:

> For so long he had invested all his hopes in this young pilot, in that futile dream that they would fly away together, leaving Lunghua, Shanghai and the war forever behind them. He had needed the pilot to help him survive the war, this imaginary twin he had invented, a replica of himself whom he watched through the barbed wire. If the Japanese was dead, part of himself had died. (*ES* 337)

It may be that there is an unintended slippage here between the two voices out of which *Empire of the Sun* is woven, and that an implausible degree of insight is being granted to its central character, but I would suggest that Ballard is in control of his material and that Jim's perceptions serve to show that although parts of his mind have been colonised in ways he cannot grasp, he is also able to access and begin to process much of what he has experienced. In most accounts of trauma, precisely this capacity to reflect on its impact is denied, on the grounds that the shock of trauma has been so great that it cannot be permitted to penetrate to consciousness. Leys sees this view as hypothesising that 'the traumatic scene was never present to the hypnotized subject and hence was constitutively unavailable for subsequent representation and recall'.[17] This is clearly not true of Jim. If in one sense the novel traces the path by which he dissociates from events and severs his emotional links with external reality, in another sense it reveals his unfettered imagination as at once a protective shield and the source of his potential regeneration. The trauma of war is not just recalled and represented some forty years later, but is depicted as already a scene of 'working through' some forty years earlier.

But to put it like this is to risk disregarding the novel's equally powerful account of the price that has been paid. Writing about the formation of human identity, Christopher Bollas describes the feeling that one has a 'self' as follows: 'It may be unknowable, but when one senses that it is there, it gives a person a sense of being the author of his existence.'[18] What meaning might such an assertion have for the text's representation of Jim? If he is to be seen as little more than a victim of trauma then it is hard to imagine how agency of this sort could be attributed to him. But the novel treats this question with the complexity it deserves, portraying Jim as inescapably bound to the environment in which a decisive stage in his development has taken place but also as an immensely resourceful interpreter and transmuter of the world into which he finds himself thrown. The space within which he can enact choices contracts further and further as the novel's bitter trajectory unfolds, and it is also made clear that life in the camp depends on chance, whether it be the arbitrary behaviour of the guards or the unpredictable progress of the war. But Jim refuses to be trapped by these confines and contingencies: he goes to extraordinary lengths to author his own existence and thereby to forge a viable sense of self. He creates the persona of 'Shanghai Jim', a sceptical outsider-figure who mocks British pretensions while acting as a resourceful gopher for Ransome and Basie; he carries out the tasks that are expected of him while secretly seeing them as a game; and he fantasises that he alone can keep the prisoners going. In his own mind, these different responses are part of a survival strategy that depends on meeting reality on its own terms.

But Jim's manic restlessness and hyper-vigilance tell another story. His inability to slow down, to take pause, or even to be temporarily calm reveal someone trying to hold himself together through a ceaseless activity that must fill up every waking moment. The novel suggests that he has not been able to face the present in quite the way he imagines. His confusion is disclosed through a preoccupation with cognitive mapping – an attempt to find some way of orientating himself within a situation he is not equipped to understand. Borrowing from James, one could say that Jim's apprehension of events is stronger than his producible vocabulary and that the text depicts him struggling to discover a vocabulary adequate to his experiences. A self-conscious fascination with words plays a large part in his development, and is often the source of textual ironies that elude him:

> 'You did your schoolwork today, Jim? You learned all your words?'
>
> 'I did, Basie. A lot of Latin words.' Basie was intrigued by Jim's command of Latin, but easily bored, so he decided not to recite the whole passive tense of *Amo*. 'And some new English words. "Pragmatist",' he suggested, which Basie greeted with gloom, 'and "survivor".'

'"Survivor"?' Basie chuckled at this. 'That's a useful word. Are you a survivor, Jim?'

'Well ...' Dr Ransome had not meant the term as a compliment. (*ES* 218)

These words are, of course, carefully chosen. Alluding to scenes such as the one in which Jim drinks all the water before thinking of his fellow prisoners, they name him in deliberately ambiguous terms. Jim, in turn, is obsessed with appellations, seeing them as keys to an unfamiliar world, tools by which its secrets can be unlocked.

Jim's hunger for names remains unsatiated not just because his mind is so voracious but because he learns that languages are arbitrary systems that cannot map reality with any completeness. When the British prisoners mark out the camp's main pathways with the names of London streets, Jim is both intrigued by this attempt to translate one reality into the terms of another through the use of sign-systems and irritated by what is to him a mismatching of sign and referent: 'He remembered a line from one of the poems that Dr Ransome had made him memorize – "a foreign field that is for ever England ..." But this was Lunghua, not England. Naming the sewage-stained paths between the rotting huts after a vaguely remembered London allowed too many of the British prisoners to shut out the reality of the camp' (*ES* 167). For Jim, this is a process that falsifies. And the different ways in which a terrain or a state of mind can be mapped give rise to doubts about the validity of the entire project, which comes to seem little more than the means of providing delusive comfort. Struck by the sheer multitude of things in Basie's cubicle, Jim reflects on their significance: 'The abundance of objects, even if they were useless, was reassuring, like the abundance of words around Dr Ransome. The Latin vocabulary and the algebraic terms were useless too, but they helped to make up a world' (*ES* 221). His own attempts to find a vocabulary in which to couch his experience of war are perhaps not useless, but so hedged about with uncertainties that the broken-backed sentences he forms scarcely enable him to construct a coherent account of the world. When towards the end of the novel he encounters another terminology through which to view the war, which depicts it as a 'heroic adventure' (*ES* 287), he grasps that his ambivalence about the war is inseparable from his linguistic scepticism.

Jim's inability to decide what he thinks about the war alludes to the ambiguous mimetic identifications he has stumbled into. In

psychoanalytical accounts of trauma both dissociation and identification are seen as typical responses to shock. The process of identification leads the traumatised subject to take over into itself an image of
the aggressor in order to assimilate the shock. Jim dissociates from
his experiences but he also identifies with the aggression that has
occasioned them. His passion for machines of destruction is matched
by the respect, at times bordering on adulation, that he feels for the
Japanese soldiers, which leads in turn to the desire to become one of
them and to join forces with their army. Thus his isolation within his
ostensible community turns into a fully fledged fantasy of belonging
to his captors and participating in their conquest of his own people.
This identification with the aggressor is inseparable from his contempt for the British, who have been comprehensively routed but
behave as though nothing were further from the truth. Yet his contempt is equally inseparable from a thinly disguised self-loathing,
since despite his attempts to disassociate himself from the British he
is one of them and has been subdued by the Japanese just as they
have. There is, moreover, the almost unbearable paradox that the
camp is a place of relative safety and that the Japanese soldiers are at
one and the same time captors and protectors. And Jim grasps too
that his awareness of the soldiers' hold over his life or death (symbolised by his life-threatening work on the runway) lies behind his identification with them: 'If the Japanese triumphed, that small part of his
mind that lay forever within the runway would be appeased. But if
they were defeated, all his fears would have been worth nothing' (*ES*
188). Propitiation functions here to create meaning out of enforced
labour and to salvage life from an experience of near death, but this
strategy requires the individual to pay a heavy price – namely, to identify with the source of the threat to that life. Moreover, the coincidence
of the oppressor with the oppressed is merely the outer layer of a
more disturbing identification with the war itself. A mind that has
already been primed for glamorised violence (the point that is developed in *The Kindness of Women*) discovers in the war the most complete expression of a sublime will-to-destruction. Nourishing him
with aggression, violence colonises his imagination so thoroughly
that he is unable to see that his identification with the war is a product of the very trauma he believes he is so pragmatically evading.

In a fine analysis of modern wars, Daniel Pick speaks of war 'as the
unconscious of progress, the driving force which does not recognise
the word "no" and which, ultimately, cannot be fully repressed.'[19]

Empire of the Sun not only supports the truth of this assertion but also discloses the extent to which war may install itself within the unconscious of its traumatised victims. In Jim's case, the image of war in his head is connected above all with a fetishisation of violence and dreams of death. Death stalks the novel's pages from its opening, coffin-laden paragraph to its closing lines, its ubiquity attesting the novel's relentless focus on corporeality. Signs of destruction and decay are visible everywhere – in the rotting corpses, water-bloated torsos, broken bodies, crushed heads, stripped skins, amputated limbs and strangled necks that are put on display on page after page. *Empire of the Sun* insists without flinching on this materiality, portraying the bodies of all those caught up in the war as the substance out of which it is made and which it in turn destroys. War is represented as perversely *productive* – perversely, not only because it transforms existence into its opposite, thereby generating mass upon mass of corpses, but also because it presses life into the service of death, turning humans into killing machines. This reversal gives rise to images of the deceased as more alive in death than they were in life, of corpses being fed in the night, and of extinction as a release into safety. Within this logic of war the individual exists as a small-scale instrument of destruction, a reified object, whose sole purpose is to take his place within this militarised economy. This seemingly unstoppable logic is evoked most chillingly by the phantasmagoric images of a resurrection that brings people back to life solely to enable them to serve death, from the crazed Price, 'the first of the dead to rise from the grave, eager to start the next world war' (*ES* 304) to Jim, who fantasises about participating in this forthcoming conflict: 'He would raise his mother and father, Dr Ransome and Mrs Vincent, and the British prisoners in Lunghua hospital. He would raise the Japanese aircrew lying in the ditches around the airfield, and enough ground staff to rebuild a squadron of aircraft' (*ES* 340). This violent dream of a productivity driven by the desire to halt life in its tracks amply discloses the self-destructiveness that for Freud signalled the presence of a death instinct, which opposed the unifying work of the erotic instinct and 'sought to do away with life once more and to re-establish the inorganic state.'[20]

This view of a life driven by an all-consuming will-to-death points to the global, apocalyptic dimension of the novel's portrayal of abjection. Jim's sense that his entire existence has been reduced to matter alone, and that all meaning has been expunged from it, gradually grows on him as the novel unfolds. It is there in his conviction that he is 'closer now to the ruined battlefields and this fly-infested truck, to the nine sweet potatoes in the sack below the driver's seat, even in a sense to the detention centre, than he would ever be again to his house in Amherst Avenue' (*ES* 153), but it manifests itself most clearly in his equation of the pre-packaged ham he eats with the 'fattened corpses' around him, an equation that depends on his refusal to distinguish between different kinds of matter: 'Each was enveloped in the same mucilage. The living who ate or drank too quickly ... would soon join the overfed dead. Food fed death, the eager and waiting death of their own bodies' (*ES* 304). These bleak visions of an abject humanity recall Ruskin's account of the 'terrible grotesque' in which the individual is sensitised to the 'occult and subtle horror belonging to many aspects of the creation around us' and stunned by 'the continual fading of all beauty into darkness, and of all strength into dust.'[21] They also bring to mind Bataille's reflections on abjection and his attempts to write philosophy from the perspective of pure matter. In his role as outsider, Jim acts as a vehicle for much of the novel's humour, undermining the humanist conventions by which his community lives, and which the war has mockingly destroyed. So inasmuch as the novel is undoubtedly funny, its humour is bleak. *Empire of the Sun* may be read as a dark satire on humanity's refusal to face the nihilism that lies just below the surface of civilised life. The laughter generated by such satire provides no comfort and no hope of redemption. As Mikkel Borch-Jacobsen remarks in his commentary on Bataille, such laughter reconciles humanity to nothing at all. It is, rather, an abyssal laughter that drags us 'into a vertigo where we *are* finally – *other*: being and at the same time not being, laughing and at the same time being dead, laughing at being already dead. Laughing at being.'[22]

The real porn

There is nothing funny about *Running Wild* (*RW*; 1988), the tightly structured fable that offers a coda to *Empire of the Sun*. An elegant but chilling exercise in psychological notation, the novella depicts the grotesque consequences of a supposedly 'enlightened' approach to family life. A massacre has taken place on a luxury housing estate: all the parents have been murdered and the children have disappeared. It is initially thought that they have either been abducted or perhaps also killed and then despatched somewhere else. The novel's narrator, Dr Greville (a forensic psychiatrist), is brought in by the police to see if he can shed any light on what might have happened. Under the prompting of a world-weary sergeant (Payne), it takes Greville half the book to grasp what the reader realises immediately, namely that the children have meticulously planned a programme of assassinations and have killed their parents, before escaping to some carefully chosen hiding place. The text traces the process by which Greville and Payne piece together the sequence of events, concluding with a 'Reconstruction' and a postscript in which Greville speculates about the socio-political implications of the children's acts.

Greville's failure to understand what is before his eyes creates a temporal lag in the reading process; the reader is ahead of the psychiatrist, who is not so much an unreliable narrator as a rather slow-witted one. The discordance between these two perspectives is central to the novella's effect: for the first half of the book the narrator's myopia is part of its wider indictment of society; in the second half, once the penny has dropped, he is a more perceptive figure, although his commentary is never straightforwardly authoritative. In Poe's *The Purloined Letter*, the twist in the tale is that the more obvious the site of concealment, the less likely it is that the object will be found, not only because it blends so well with its environment but also because, *being so obvious*, its real hiding place will be ignored. *Running Wild* extends this trope to the entire set of events (the 32 killings) that it narrates, using it to expose the detective's personal lack of discernment as the sign of a wider social nescience. In this revision of the classic whodunnit, the point of the novella is not to discover the culprits – that is 'obvious' from the start – but to explore the less 'obvious' mystery of why nobody else has grasped the truth, and this is the text's real subject.

Visual metaphors lie at the heart of *Running Wild*, and Greville's language foregrounds this aspect of the text when he ponders the implications of not seeing that which is perfectly visible. This inability to connect what is open to view with its meaning, to link the seen with the known, is the source of the novel's grim social satire. For everything about the Pangbourne Estate, from its ubiquitous surveillance cameras to its over-watchful parents, speaks of lives led under the eyes of others. Nothing is concealed, all is visible, but little is seen. There are numerous ironies here. To begin with, the Pangbourne Estate has been designed as a housing scheme in which the total visibility at all times of its bounded terrain and its inhabitants is a matter of security. It is an early version of the security-obsessed and defensive gated 'communities' of our fast-approaching future. CCTV observation rules this domain day and night, making it a fortress from the outside and a prison from the inside. This system is structured to repel external threats, so it is defenceless against a well-orchestrated attack that comes from within. But the exposure of its daily life to the eye of the camera is as nothing to the over-involvement of the parents in their children's lives, all in the name of an enlightened, liberal approach to child-rearing. Wired up via computer to the rooms of their offspring, the parents are able to plan their days down to the last detail, monitoring their activities, commenting on their achievements, and reminding them of their unfinished tasks. A parody of parental solicitousness, this over-regulation of childhood is a 'surveillance of the heart' (*RW* 37) that enforces compulsory happiness, imposing a rationalised linear logic on human desire and closing off all avenues to spontaneous behaviour or independent thought.

It is hard to avoid thinking of Foucault's panopticon in this context, and Dennis A. Foster, pointing out that its efficacy 'has less to do with the restraint of the body than with the formation of a subject', has invoked it in his discussion of *Running Wild*.[23] But the Foucauldian account of panoptism is useful only up to a point in relation to this text because the latter's account of the formation of subjectivity does not conform to the panoptic theory. During his reflections on the significance of Bentham's panopticon, Foucault describes it as 'a technology of power designed to solve the problems of surveillance', and he stresses both that such surveillance could be decentralised and that it did not only describe an external process but involved an internalisation of the gaze that turned the subject into 'his own overseer, each individual thus exercising this surveillance over, and against, himself'.[24] Panoptism nonetheless implies a unidirectional model in which the State and/or its representatives observe those who fall within the purview of power, while the observed are the constructed objects of its dominative gaze. But Foucault problematised this model, which he found unsatisfactory. He not only argued on empirical grounds that it was inapplicable to twentieth-century life, which was characterised by complex intersecting networks of power that could not be reduced to the principle of visibility, but he also insisted that the repressive thesis was inadequate, since it tended to presuppose an already formed identity that was then subjected to disciplinary regimes. For Foucault, this was to misconceive the overdetermined and multiple ways in which power and subjectivity were intertwined: 'it's my hypothesis that the individual is not a pre-given entity which is seized on by the exercise of power. The individual, with his identity and characteristics, is the product of a relation of power exercised over bodies, multiplicities, movements, desires, forces'.[25]

Pangbourne Village epitomises a disciplinary regime but it is not reducible to an optic system based on the principle of visibility. Visual surveillance plays a key role in the way power is exercised here, but the cybernetic information network is no less important. Power is thus exercised by means of a system of flows and circuits that are multi-directional: it is dispersed and it ramifies. Equally significantly, in Pangbourne the law of prohibition has been lifted from a habitus that is ostensibly structured around acceptance, not repression. There is a subtle shift here from the internalisation of the gaze that Foucault associates with the panopticon, which produces the self-monitoring of the punitive super-ego, to the interiorisation of a spirit of tolerance, which gives rise to the openness of an unbounded subjectivity. This shift is seen by the Pangbourne parents as nothing more than a radicalisation of the principles of Enlightenment – an extension of the historical aspiration to social and psychological transparency – which Foucault connects to the panopticon and which Adorno and Horkheimer see as an attempt to bring about 'the dissolution of myths and the substitution of knowledge for fancy', a process of disenchantment that was to demystify the world and liberate human beings from entrapment in the realm of nature: 'Man imagines himself free from fear when there is no longer anything unknown.'[26] Despite their theoretical and methodological differences, Foucault, Adorno and Horkheimer all draw attention to the Enlightenment's project of bringing to light what has been obscured or hidden.

Thus although the endlessly recording cameras in Pangbourne are important, the 'enlightened' regime that the parents impose on the children is more significant; the cameras monitor physical movement, but the parents control psychological development. Ensuring that scarcely 'a minute of the children's lives' is not 'intelligently planned' (*RW* 32), they preside over a supposedly 'civilised' existence in which everything is at once ordered and made transparent. But if every moment of every day is mapped out, then at the same time all behaviour meets with infinite tolerance and understanding, and it is the tension between these two imperatives that eventually produces the text's explosive denouement. There is a version here of what Foucault describes as 'a new mode of investment which presents itself no longer in the form of control by repression but that of control by stimulation'.[27] Encouraged to develop themselves in any and every direction, in the belief that stimulus is a good in and of itself, the children are subjected not to a law of repression but to a law of transgression: the logic of full enlightenment is here figured as the dissolution of all boundaries and hierarchies of value and the instauration of a socius in which nothing is forbidden and all is permitted. For Greville, this regime results in an attenuation of affect and a loss of moral bearings, which lead the children to withdraw from the world and to secrete themselves in a realm of fantasy. Thus in his view the 'enlightened' society in which they were forced to live actually produced a sensory deprivation that led to the 'same schizophrenic detachment from reality' (RW 84) as that seen in 'the Manson gang, in Mark Chapman and Lee Harvey Oswald, and in the guards at the Nazi death-camps' (RW 84), but in the case of the Pangbourne killers this detachment is the product of their entrapment 'within a perfect universe', for in 'a totally sane society, madness is the only freedom' (RW 84).

The social microcosm depicted in the novella is of course not 'totally sane' at all – it is a parody of the completely open and unrepressive polis. And Greville's view that the children's 'madness' represents a bid for freedom through its reversal of expected norms is a comfortable delusion, which refuses to trace the real logic at work here. As Foster points out, Greville is an adult observer 'whose understanding is simplistic, reductive, and judgmental'.[28] The murders are only in one sense an act of rebellion, a rejection of a social order that has proved to be insufferably constraining; in another, deeper sense, they are this order's most perfect expression. It is not just that the killings are made possible by a deadening of affect that has been induced by the society the children want to negate, but also that the meticulous way in which they are planned and carried out depends on the system (the cameras, the computers, the carefully structured activities) that the parents have put into place. Greville's invocation of 'madness' implies an oppositional strategy, a revolt against an intolerable burden, a sanguinary return of the repressed. But the text suggests that we are in the presence not of an irruption from below but rather of the unfolding logic of the system itself: the instrumental use of technology for destructive purposes and the emotional detachment from the consequences of action derive from the desensitised world that has produced the children as subjects. For the events that are anatomised in this text are not explained with reference to the parents alone but are related to the emergence of contemporary estates designed to facilitate and to promote a certain kind of social life. Pangbourne is a commuter-belt enclave, a self-enclosed and self-contained compound, which is isolated from the environment and disconnected from wider communal relations: 'Pangbourne Village has no connections, social, historical or civic, with Pangbourne itself' (*RW* 11–12). Pangbourne offers a privatised notion of social life in which the estate is externally cut off from all other social groups and internally subdivided into discrete cells. Thus it is emphasised that 'for all their participation in group activities at the recreation club, the parents themselves did not mix socially, never invited each other into their homes, and seem to have known one another only as casual acquaintances' (*RW* 23–4). The design of the estate reflects the logic of an atomised view of life and a contractual conception of human relations in which intimacy plays no part. The estate is a template for a future life in which armoured domains of this kind 'constitute a chain of closed communities whose lifelines run directly along the M4 to the offices and consulting rooms, restaurants and private clinics of central London' (*RW* 12), bypassing all other social structures and networks.

The controlled regime at the estate places its inhabitants in a social straitjacket, giving them no space for self-expression outside carefully structured activities. But estates like Pangbourne are also products of late capitalism: the gated enclave functions as the site of a rigidly formalised rest and recuperation that services individuals in order to enable them to *work*. The 'lifelines' that so tellingly run straight from the estate to the work-place turn the subject into a relay in a circuit. Human life is a programmed code from which emotion, autonomy and spontaneity have been evacuated. A profoundly *asocial* habitus, the estate resembles the tower-block in *High-Rise* in being 'an environment built, not for man, but for man's absence' (*HR* 25). But this negation of the human takes a specific form in *Running Wild*, and to understand it we should consider how it contrasts with *Empire of the Sun*. For the ideal that lies behind Pangbourne Estate is that of absolute order: it exists to expunge all traces of the accidental, the haphazard, the imperfect. Through its architecture (think of the self-contained houses with their large plots of land, which keep the neighbours at a distance), its pristine cleanliness (all those gardeners, cleaners and chauffeurs), its precise time-tabling of activities, and its careful repulsion of outsiders, the estate is a paranoid domain from which the elements that defined Lunghua Camp have been expelled. The camp is a site of mess, grime, disorder, decay and death; it is a confusing, anarchic place marked by the contingent and the abject. The estate is the exact opposite: 'there is an antiseptic quality about Pangbourne Village, as if these company directors, financiers and television tycoons have succeeded in ridding their private Parnassus of every strain of dirt and untidiness. Here, even the drifting leaves look as if they have too much freedom' (RW 7). A zone of clarity and routine characterised by a diminution of affect and a deadening of the senses, the estate presides over the evacuation of chance and choice. Thus the grey colours and soundless images of the police video are a fitting simulation of what is seen as already a simulation of 'life': 'This minimalist style of camera-work exactly suits the subject matter, the shadowless summer sunlight and the almost blank facades of the expensive houses – everything is strangely blanched, drained of all emotion, and one seems to be visiting a set of laboratories in a high-tech science park where no human operatives are employed' (RW 4).

In *Empire of the Sun* the central protagonist is exposed to shocking levels of violence to which he responds mimetically, internalising a complex, wayward structure of feeling that associates aggression with glamour. *Running Wild* addresses a different problematic: what might happen if the child's imagination is exposed to very little? Or, to put it another way, what might be the consequences of reining in the imagination so tightly that it is scarcely permitted to develop at all? The text thus re-works a key theme of Dickens's *Hard Times*. But instead of suggesting that the blighted imagination merely produces a stunted emotional life, *Running Wild* goes for the jugular; whereas Sissy Jupe finds herself unable to relate fully to others, the Pangbourne children embrace a full-scale psychopathology and become mass murderers. Here the imagination has been closed down so completely that the act of murder appears to have no meaning for its perpetrators, at least in the sense that the existence of the other is so derealised that it can have no palpable presence. An extreme form of alienation is at work: the children are depersonalised victims of parents who have themselves been depersonalised by the subordination of their identities to the logics of a late capitalist economy. Greville's reconstruction of the murders (with its unintentionally revealing fetishisation of clock-time) provides a blackly ironic commentary on these logics, since the successful prosecution of the killings is shown to depend on the technology and techniques of the social system that produced both the children and their parents.

The external world *does* appear to have been derealised here, even if Greville's glib commentary is not to be taken at face value. Mid-way through the story Greville is led by Payne to some gun publications lying camouflaged by some soft-core pornography magazines, a stash that elicits the following remark from the hard-bitten sergeant: 'If you want to find the real porn have a look underneath' (*RW* 38). The real porn is discovered in the thrill of a fantasised violence that will eventually be unleashed; the real porn hides coiled beneath the shiny surface of a supposedly enlightened form of life that in actuality operates a coercive model of subject formation and relies on an instrumental conception of human relations. Greville fails to see that the killing of the parents expresses these very logics, since he insists on seeing the murders, like the sexual fantasies discovered in some of the girls' secret journals, as a way of escaping from an 'over-civilised' world 'into a more brutal and more real world of the senses' (*RW* 70), whereas the novella suggests throughout that 'the senses' have been so thoroughly deactivated that such passional language can have no meaning in this context. The book's coda describes the attempted murder of the prime minister (Thatcher is presumably the model), and Greville reads this last act as a sign that 'all authority and parental figures' are now 'the special target' (*RW* 105) of the children. Foster, in turn, reads this in oedipal terms as a sign that 'the children continue to live through denial of the law, restaging the scene that tied them most firmly to the social structure'.[29] Both readings remain caught up in the repressive model that *Running Wild* has systematically called into question. The murders are certainly a revolt against the symbolic law but the futility of this revolt is no less clear since the form it takes is so obviously an expression of this law, whose power continues to traverse them. In Foucault's terms, this text represents power 'as a productive network which runs through the whole social body, much more than as a negative instance whose function is repression', and what the novel shows above all is that the 'individual which power has constituted is at the same time its vehicle'.[30]

Notes

1   H. Bergson, *Laughter: An Essay on the Meaning of the Comic*, trans. C. Brereton and F. Rothwell (London: Macmillan, 1911), p. 29.
2   W. Lewis, *The Wild Body* (London: Chatto and Windus, 1927), p. 244.
3   A. Camus, *The Myth of Sisyphus*, trans. J. O'Brien (Harmondsworth: Penguin, 1980), pp. 26, 39.
4   L. Pirandello, *On Humour*, trans. A. Illiano and D. P. Testa (Chapel Hill NC: University of North Carolina Press, 1960), pp. 124, 118.
5   Pirandello *On Humour*, pp. 124–5.
6   H. James, *What Maisie Knew* (Harmondsworth: Penguin, 1971), pp. 9–10.
7   S. Dentith, *Parody* (London: Routledge, 2000), p. 64.
8   The notes to the earlier work claim that 'the endless newsreel clips of nuclear explosions that we saw on TV in the 1960s (a powerful incitement to the psychotic imagination, sanctioning everything) did have a carnival air' (*AE* 14).
9   W. Self 'Conversations: J. G. Ballard', in *Junk Mail* (London: Penguin, 1996), pp. 329–71, pp. 360, 361.
10 V. Woolf, *The Common Reader* Vol. 1 (New York: Harcourt, Brace and Company, 1953), p. 34.
11 S. Freud, *Introductory Lectures on Psychoanalysis*, trans J. Strachey (Harmondsworth: Penguin, 1974), p. 429.
12 S. Freud, *On Metapsychology: The Theory of Psychoanalysis*, trans. J. Strachey (Harmondsworth: Penguin, 1984), p. 282.
13 D. Kalsched, *The Inner World of Trauma: Archetypal Defenses of the Personal Spirit* (London: Routledge, 1999), p. 2.
14 Kalsched, *The Inner World of Trauma*, p. 66.
15 J. Steiner, *Psychic Retreats: Pathological Organizations in Psychotic, Neurotic and Borderline Patients* (London: Routledge, 1999), p. 64. For a clear account, see 'Splitting of the Ego in the Process of Defence' (1938) in Freud, *On Metapsychology*, pp. 461–2.
16 R. Leys, *Trauma: A Genealogy* (Chicago: University of Chicago Press, 2000), p. 9.
17 Leys, *Trauma*, p. 9.
18 C. Bollas, *Cracking Up: The Work of Unconscious Experience* (London: Routledge, 1997), p. 166.
19 D. Pick, *War Machine: The Rationalisation of Slaughter in the Modern Age* (New Haven: Yale University Press, 1996), p. 189.
20 S. Freud, *New Introductory Lectures on Psychoanalysis*, trans. J. Strachey (Harmondsworth: Penguin, 1975), p. 140.
21 J. Ruskin, *The Stones of Venice* Vol. 3 (London: George Allen, 1898), pp. 136, 137.
22 M. Borch-Jacobsen, 'The Laughter of Being', in F. Botting and S. Wilson (eds), *Bataille: A Critical Reader* (Oxford: Blackwell, 1998), pp. 148, 164.

23 D. A. Foster, J. G. Ballard's Empire of the Senses: Perversion and the
    failure of Authority', Proceedings of the Modern Languages Association
    (May 1993): pp. 519–32, p. 521.
24 Foucault, Power/Knowledge, pp. 148, 155.
25 Foucault, Power/Knowledge, pp. 73–4.
26 T. Adorno and M. Horkheimer, Dialectic of Enlightenment, trans. J. Cum-
    ming (London: Verso, 1973), pp. 3, 16.
27 Foucault, Power/Knowledge, p. 57.
28 Foster, 'J. G. Ballard's Empire of the Senses', p. 520.
29 Foster, 'J. G. Ballard's Empire of the Senses', pp. 520–1.
30 Foucault, Power/Knowledge, pp. 119, 98.

5

Exhausted futures

The three novels I discuss in this chapter belong to the genre of detective fiction, although the centre of interest lies not in identifying the perpetrator of the crime but in grasping its wider ramifications. In *Cocaine Nights* and *Super-Cannes* the culprit is known, and in *Millennium People* it soon becomes obvious who is responsible for the murders that have been committed – the narrator's task is to get at the significance of these crimes. The plots of all three novels follow the same basic pattern. The first-person narrator, a troubled but pliable figure, plays the role of amateur detective who tries to piece together the order of events in order to comprehend them. In the course of doing so, he blends in, chameleon-like, with the subculture he will eventually expose, and this capacity for affiliation not only calls his motives and character into question but also discloses the power and seductiveness of the subculture itself. By the end of each novel, although the narrator has seen through these microcosms, he has also revealed his attraction to them. He announces his complicity with what he finally rejects, an admission of guilt that then implicates the reader, much as the haunted stare which closes Bertolucci's *The Conformist* demands that the film's viewers turn the camera on themselves.

Each novel enacts a process of self-questioning. However, it is not the psychology of the criminal that is primarily at stake in these texts but rather the nature of the society in which he was encouraged to commit his crimes. The detective's work is that of ethnography: a social explorer in the tradition of the reformers who investigated urban slums in the nineteenth century, his job is to articulate a repressed knowledge. It is not the people of the abyss who are under scrutiny, however, but the narrator's own class; thus he is implicated in the scene he depicts and is forced to recognise himself in the events he recounts. The classic technique deployed by novelists to bring such recognition about is of course that of the uncanny double, and doubling is central to these late Ballard works. But they do not just rely on straight one-to-one doubling – which revolves around a self/other dynamic – but establish triangulated relationships in which three figures are locked together, a mediating third presence facilitating the homosocial bond between the original (male) doubles.

Triangular relationships go beyond the dyadic structures in which doubled narratives are trapped. The binary of self and other falls snugly into an ego/alter-ego conception of inner conflict, which relies in one way or another on theories of repression. Triangulation offers a more complex representation of the ambiguities and ambivalences that come into play when desire is modelled on the desires of more than *one* other. René Girard's account of triangular desire emphasises its imitativeness: desire simulates the feelings attributed in fantasy to a rival figure. Desire for another originates in the desire that a rival is thought to have for a loved object, which becomes ever more desirable in proportion to the apparent intensity of the rival's passion.[1] Girard is mainly concerned with passion for a specific other, but his theory has a wider application, and his view of the determining role played by the mediator in this calculus of desire is suggestive for the same-sex identifications that are so prevalent in Ballard's novels. Love of another person is not at stake in works such as *Cocaine Nights*, *Super-Cannes* and *Millennium People*, but love for the mediating figure and the alluring world-view he represents very much is. Girard makes two remarks that are relevant to this process of identification and its consequences. Firstly, that from 'the moment the mediator's influence is felt, the sense of reality is lost and judgment paralysed' and, secondly, that the 'closer the mediator comes, the greater his role becomes and the smaller that of the object'.[2] Because the mediator is the true source of desire, he has the capacity to take over the psyche of the protagonist and to propel him into the world of his own overpowering fantasies. Mimetic desire in such cases moves away from any particular object and toward the mediator himself.

The narrators are in these texts caught in a triangular pattern of relationships in which they are drawn to authority figures who urge them to accept and embrace the twisted social logics they uncover. These relationships are oedipalised (especially in *Super-Cannes* and *Millennium People*), the mediator acting as a representative of the lost father. Thus the journeys of self-discovery narrated in these texts involve a powerful identification with the paternal presence, which is then followed by an oedipal revolt that returns the narrators to the 'normality' of the social realm and permits a new identity to be forged. But there is a reversal here: the paternal figures do not represent the social order, but transgress against it. In contrast to Lacan's reading of Freud's reading of the Oedipal myth as a system in which the 'father, the Name-of-the-father, sustains the structure of desire with the structure of the law', these texts project the father figure not as the symbol of the super-ego, which in Freud's account 'takes over the severity of the father', but rather as the representative of the untrammelled id, which then proposes to reverse all received values.[3] In *Cocaine Nights* Crawford insists that he is 'freeing people ... returning them to their true selves' (*CN* 240); in *Super-Cannes* Penrose urges Sinclair to be 'true to [his] real self, embrace all the possibilities of [his] life' (*SC* 173) and to 'think like a psychopath' (*SC* 266); in *Millennium People* Gould sees the twentieth century as 'a soft-regime prison built by earlier generations of inmates' from which 'we have to break free' (*MP* 139). Thus these figures offer a resolution to the oedipal scenario that refuses to quell desire and to subordinate the subject to the symbolic law, and the narrators' fascination with the freedom they offer may be read as a longing to return to the pleasures of polymorphous perversity. Except that in the late novels these pleasures are associated not with sexual *jouissance* but with unbounded violence, criminal irresponsibility, and nihilistic terrorism, which are in the end shown to be expressions of the very systems against which the oedipal protest is supposedly being made. The evasion of oedipal repressiveness – what Deleuze and Guattari refer to as 'a release from the father's hold on the man', the 'possibility of living *beyond* the father's law, beyond all law' – is shown here to have disastrous consequences, either because this escape subjects the individual to a different possession of its subjectivity, that which is enforced by all-embracing social logics (*Cocaine Nights, Super-Cannes*) or because it opens him up to far more dangerous fantasies.[4] Thus in *Millennium People* Gould replaces Markham's lost father and makes up for his oedipal lack, 'drawing me into his fragmentary personality, almost offering himself as a kit from which I could construct a vital figure missing from my life' (*MP* 178), but both this figure and that which Markham mimetically constructs out of it for himself end up unleashing a violence so total that it threatens to annihilate the social order altogether.

Nonetheless, the narrators of these novels refuse to disown their complicity in the structures of desire they uncover and to which they have all along been covertly drawn. But it also ensures that *Cocaine Nights*, *Super-Cannes*, and *Millennium People* end on a note of uncertainty because there is a strong sense that the narrators' culminating protest (their eventual turn away from the psychopathic visions that have been vouchsafed them) will be ineffectual, and that the social forces ranged against them will prevail. Inasmuch as deterministic systems have always figured prominently in Ballard's texts, in these late works the power of such systems appears to be all-embracing. The belatedly awakened subject becomes aware of the system's criminality but is powerless to do anything about it; this personal knowledge, in short, makes no difference, precisely because the subject is figured as a puny entity whose interventions have no capacity to disturb the flows and exchanges of globalised multinational networks of power. The most chilling ending is to be found in *Super-Cannes* where it is clear that Sinclair's rebellion will fail because he is a figure from a superseded past whose values will be no match for the streamlined supercharged networks of the future: his one-man uprising, a parody of male heroism, will be no match for the corporate world, and the text's last image is of obdurate multinational power.

Looking at the future

From *The Atrocity Exhibition* onwards, Ballard's novels have attended to the warping of the mind and the damage done to human relationships in the last decades of the twentieth century. But *Cocaine Nights*, *Super-Cannes*, and *Millennium People* write *finis* to this socially produced psycho-drama, depicting an alienated world as capitalism's terminal zone. Alienation marks virtually every aspect of communal life in these texts, the saturation of social existence by capitalist logics being so complete that the possibility of experiencing life in a non-alienated form is portrayed as a utopian dream. The Costa del Sol leisure society of *Cocaine Nights*, seemingly offering a life of freedom after decades of work, turns out to be a pre-fabricated fantasy characterised by *anomie*, as evidenced by its isolation from Spanish society, its thraldom to satellite TV, and its retreat from public space. At the other end of the spectrum, *Super-Cannes* depicts a world dominated by the imperatives of the high-tech economy in which individuals exist as producers, their lives outside the work-place dwindling away to nothingness. *Millennium People* portrays a society close to the verge of collapse, its civic sense eroded, its infrastructure falling apart, and its disaffected populace staging destructive 'happenings' under cover of which the real extremists prepare a programme of nihilist terror. The old revolutionary aspiration of changing the system in its entirety has long receded from view. As Crawford informs Prentice: 'Politics is over, Charles, it doesn't touch the public imagination any longer' (*CN* 245). Henceforth, the struggle for freedom will take the form of celebrating criminality and psychopathology, in blithe ignorance of the extent to which these supposedly oppositional practices are the alienated products of the social realm they propose to subvert.

Ballard's late novels insist on this causality. With a compelling logic, they trace the criss-crossing connections between economic structures, social systems and psychological modalities. Estrella de Mar, for example, is characterised by a 'memory-erasing white architecture' and an 'enforced leisure that fossilize[s] the nervous system', which give rise to 'the timelessness of a world beyond boredom, with no past, no future and a diminishing present' (*CN* 35). Stasis and irreality are the signatures of this ersatz world, which seems to have been lifted out of time and space into some phantasmagoric realm half-in and half-out of life. Temporality is locked into an unchanging present, while spatiality is folded into expanses of whiteness and reflecting water. With the impetus to act taken away, everything settles into a blank torpor and passively waits for the world to wind itself down. In contrast, although the gleaming architecture of *Super-Cannes* is equally deadening, the business-park's destruction of social life takes a form that is reminiscent of the gated estate at Pangbourne:

> An invisible infrastructure took the place of traditional civic virtues ... The top-drawer professionals no longer needed to devote a moment's thought to each other, and had dispensed with the checks and balances of community life. There were no town councils or magistrates' courts, no citizens' advice bureaux. Civility and polity were designed into Eden-Olympia ... Representative democracy had been replaced by the surveillance camera and the private police force. (*SC* 38)

Whereas the built environment of Estrella de Mar is soporific, a lotus-eaters' paradise, Eden-Olympia is a streamlined microcosm that arrogates to itself the functions previously allocated to society. The self-contained corporate estate has been designed in accordance with a mechanised view of humans as automata and an instrumental con-

ception of their affectless relations. If community life has been
expunged from Eden-Olympia, this is because the world-view hardwired into it sees individuals as detached monads, considers that civic
responsibilities can be handled by programmed systems, and believes
that the best guarantor of liberty is an armed security force. It is
against the values of this world that the middle-class rebels of *Millennium People* are in revolt, as they grasp that they are part of a ramifying network of power relations that interpellates them as capitalist
subjects, making them the docile dupes of a system that has colonised
their minds.

The early Marx of *The Economic and Philosophic Manuscripts of
1844* argued that estranged labour, external to the producer and
belonging to another not only alienated 'from man his own body, as
well as external nature and his spiritual essence, his *human* being'
but also alienated '*man* from *man*.'[5] Marx's emphasis on species
being is central to his text. He describes the effect of estranged
labour on man thus: 'It changes for him the *life of the species* into a
means of individual life. First it estranges the life of the species and
individual life, and secondly it makes individual life in its abstract
form the purpose of the life of the species, likewise in its abstract
and estranged form'.[6] For Marx, the individual is the *product* of this
alienation. By an uncanny reversal, estranged labour commodifies
the individual, now abstracted from the species, turning him into a
fetish that is an '*alien* being'[7]. These observations belong to the context of nineteenth-century capitalism, and thus to a different stage of
industrial production, but they are suggestive in relation to Ballard's
account of alienation, which has affinities with Marx's conviction
that a consequence of alienation was the severance of the individual
from the species, and the abstract conceptualisation of both. Ballard's late novels trace the path by which this abstraction of the individual leads from alienation of the self from the other to
derealisation of the wider world. They depict in fictional form what
Henri Lefebvre, following Marx, articulates in theoretical terms:
'The ever-unfinished development of the productive forces – in economic terms – has the philosophical implication of a new stage in
human fulfilment, of limitless possibilities. But the corresponding
alienation here is just as all-encompassing. It encompasses life in its
entirety.'[8] Lefebvre's account of daily existence under capitalism
focuses on its permeation by consumerism. Here 'the commodity,
the market, money, with their implacable logic' dominate the social

realm with the result that the 'extension of capitalism goes all the way to the slightest details of everyday life.'[9]

These are familiar themes in critiques of capitalism, but attention has recently turned to the accelerated nature of change within a globalised economy made possible by advanced telecommunications systems. Edward Luttwak distinguishes the more controlled capitalism of the period from the end of the Second World War to the 1980s from the 'turbo-capitalism' of the last twenty years of the century, which is characterised by 'private enterprise liberated from government regulation, unchecked by effective trade unions, unfettered by sentimental concerns over the fate of employees or communities, unrestrained by customs barriers or investment restrictions, and molested as little as possible by taxation.'[10] For Luttwak, global capitalism increases economic efficiency but causes a range of social ills typically ignored by its apologists, such as regional destabilisation, the decline of community values, the erosion of extended and nuclear family life, the creation of a permanently unemployed under-class, and rising levels of crime. Luttwak's view is close to Lefebvre's: 'Turbo-capitalism not only conquers markets and economic relationships, but also extends the reach of the market into every sphere of human activity'.[11] One consequence of this reach is that the individual becomes an adjunct to the system, and Ballard's late novels focus on this displacement of the human organism by the economic networks in which it is imbricated. In *Super-Cannes* Sinclair's wife Jane is gradually folded into the microcosm of Eden-Olympia: 'She stepped from the car, a self-disciplined professional already merging into the corporate space that awaited her' (*SC* 54). Sinclair is aware that this process of merging will eventually erase any sense of selfhood or autonomy, noting that after several months 'she would be as institutionalized as any long-term convict, locked inside a virtual cell she called her office' (*SC* 81), a perception that is later confirmed when Jane informs him that: 'Outside the clinic I hardly exist' (*SC* 270).

Ballard is particularly concerned with the waning of affect in what has often been thought of as the sacrosanct, untarnished space of the private realm in which individuals can truly be themselves. But he suggests that both the private domain and the ideal of intimacy located in it have been transformed: relationships now take the form of contractual liaisons between objects. When Markham's wife acknowledges an infidelity in *Millennium People*, she views it in terms of damage to a physical commodity: 'She always apologized, smiling hopelessly, as if she had dented my car or ruined a new electric razor' (*MP* 144). Anonymity extends to most aspects of daily existence, emerging as a life-style preference; people elect to live in isolation from others without realising how deeply the choice made (to say nothing about the ideology of choice itself) is determined by a marketised economy and the cultural imaginary it has produced. *Super-Cannes* offers the harshest depiction of a world in which all characters use and are used. No less than in Zamyatin's *We*, individuals are units in a technological organism, but in Eden-Olympia they are also the subjects of a laboratory experiment. Presided over by the demented Wilder Penrose, Eden-Olympia is a testing ground for a form of life in which the subordination of the individual to the imperatives of work has been elevated to a principle. Thus it eventually becomes clear that in tracing his predecessor's trajectory through the Alice-world of the corporate estate Sinclair is following a path mapped out for him by an experiment that has been planned in advance. But in a significant twist, he is shown to participate willingly in the experiment because he has internalised the logics according to which it is being run. He too is a researcher in Penrose's mould whose detachment from events enables him to observe with a cool eye his wife's descent into drug addiction and her near collapse. Sinclair is thus a replica of Penrose, his hypocritical *semblable*, as his wife's view of him makes clear: 'You're keeping an eye on me, Paul. I'm your guinea pig. You want to know what happens to people in Eden-Olympia' (*SC* 271). More significantly yet, both Penrose and Sinclair are themselves the guinea pigs of a system that construes human subjectivity in terms of engineering. It is a mark of Sinclair's returning sanity that he finally refuses to 'use' his wife and attempts to 'save' her from Eden-Olympia. His turn away from a socio-economic microcosm that produces and perpetuates alienation is inseparable from his eventual hostility to a system that Penrose celebrates with pride: 'We're breeding a new race of deracinated people, internal exiles without human ties but with enormous power. It's this new class that runs our planet' (*SC* 256).

The waning of emotion *vis-à-vis* others is in these late novels turned inward, giving rise to an affectless view not just of others, but of one's own self, which is accepted as an object of value only insofar as those others wish to make use of it. *Cocaine Nights, Super-Cannes* and *Millennium People* represent this self-alienation through an exploration of the cinematic imaginary. Cinema is a key element in these texts.

References to films abound, plots are taken from well-known movies, cinematic tropes are borrowed and redeployed, and characters frequently orientate themselves in relation to events by invoking particular films. An obvious point to make here is that Ballard shows how far present-day culture has moved away from the written word. He was preoccupied with this issue early on in his writing career, declaring that: 'People have enough fiction in their lives already, they're living the stuff, it's pouring out of the air, it's affecting everything, the ways people furnish their homes, the sorts of friendships they have, their vocabularies. It's quite amazing to see how people's lives are influenced by movies, television and constant advertising'.[12] In Ballard's late fiction the shift from a literate to a visual culture is taken as a simple datum, with the result that it is no longer a question of people's lives being 'influenced' by the mass media but rather one of the extent to which their entire way of conceptualising reality and making sense of their existence has been structured by these media. Nor is this change necessarily presented in a negative light. Markham, for example, is in *Millennium People* something of a reluctant recruit to a middle-class revolt that targets video-stores and the National Film Theatre, since he is a cinephile whose life has been powerfully influenced by the life of the screen. Rejecting the view that cinema in general (though Hollywood is the obvious and predictable target) has 'poisoned a whole century' (*MP* 118), he identifies himself as an integral part of its dreams and passions. From Markham's perspective, the torching of the NFT is a puritanical act that reduces cinema's visionary and metamorphic power to a unitary ideology promoting false consciousness, an act that fails to acknowledge cinema's haunting beauty and blots out the complex role it has played in the history of the twentieth-century imagination.

Notwithstanding this positive reading of cinema's potential, there is also another dimension to Ballard's treatment of the visual media, which presents its blurring of the boundary between the fictive and the real as a contributory factor to the deadening of emotion discussed earlier. In *Cocaine Nights* and *Super-Cannes* especially, characters are depicted as actors inhabiting pre-scripted personalities, as ciphers going through the motions of life. This sense of distance from one's own emotions, a kind of inability to *feel* them, is caught in sporadic reflections such as this: 'I knew we were very happy, but at the same time I felt that we were extras in a tourist film' (*SC* 40). Or this, where inquiry about a character's identity – 'Who is he exactly?' (*CN* 12) –

receives the following response: 'Not even Bobby Crawford knows that. He's three different people before breakfast. Every morning he takes his personality out of the wardrobe and decides which one he'll wear for the day' (*CN* 120). Markham, in turn, is susceptible to Gould's personality at least in part because his own precarious identity is constructed out of little more than props and façades: 'By now you're a stage set, one push and the whole thing could collapse at your feet. At times you feel you're living someone else's life, in a strange house you've rented by accident. The "you" you've become isn't your real self' (138). Emotions are observed here as though they were being experienced by someone else, personae are adopted like interchangeable masks, and 'personalities' are equated with theatrical façades.

In one sense, such figures are presented as knowing, self-ironising subjects picking up on cinematic cues and constructing plausible narratives for themselves around them. But in another sense, they are lost without such signposts, unable to work out who they are or how they should act in the absence of direction. These protagonists are 'others' to themselves, visitors to their own lives, subjects in someone else's dramatic plot. They model themselves on cinematic icons, as in the case of Crawford, or they struggle to work out who they are meant to be by trying to place themselves dramatically, as in the case of Markham. Like all the other figures in these texts, Markham is a role-playing actor requiring someone else to feed him his lines. But in these texts the producer-directors who supposedly play this role are themselves being fed their lines by the systems whose representatives they are. All are caught up in narratives that precede and encompass them. Thus although Ballard draws on a range of narratives from cinema, television and literature, deploying them as metaphors for the formative work done in society by a wide range of ideological systems, such narratives are shown to be less significant in the production of subjectivities than those that are imposed by socio-economic networks of power. *Cocaine Nights* may be indebted in important ways to Hitchcock's *Psycho*, say, but *Super-Cannes* explores the effect on individuals of the pressures exerted by corporate society in a technologically super-charged world. Different kinds of interpellation are at work here, ensuring that subjectivity is constructed in a variety of ways, according to where the pressure points are located, but in each case individuals are co-opted to determinate modes of life by a form of power that, in Foucault's words, 'is employed and exercised through a net-like organisation'.[13]

Both *Cocaine Nights* and *Super-Cannes* stress this point. In the former novel, Crawford's allegedly public-spirited desire to free Estrella de Mar's residents from an anaesthetised life dominated by satellite television by encouraging them to make their own films is not as innocent as it seems. He tells Prentice that

> People have to learn to switch off their TV sets. I want a club where people make their own films, learn how to storyboard a narrative, how to handle close-ups, dollies, pans and tracking shots. Film is the way we see our world ... I want you to be the producer, keep an overview of everything, steer funding to the right places. (*CN* 261–2)

If Prentice is to be the producer, deciding what gets funded and what does not, then Crawford will be the *eminence grise* still further back behind the scenes, but behind him are the criminal cartels that run Estrella de Mar. Power is here dispersed across several intersecting points, none of which is in complete control of its effects. Prentice, for example, both resists and colludes with the role he is expected to play when he grasps that he has been cast in a starring role in the film that Crawford is trying to direct but which Prentice will subvert. Similarly, Sinclair's role in *Super-Cannes* has also been planned, and he is depicted as an intertextual cipher caught up in another narrative, that of *Alice in Wonderland*. But there is a wider issue at stake in both novels, which bears on the colonisation of the mind by the visual media. In being permitted to write scripts, make movies, and act in them, the residents of Estrella de Mar are not just co-opted into the bigger script that the criminal syndicates are trying to write, but are subjected to a view of the world as having meaning only insofar as it is *filmed* and only insofar as they can see themselves on screen. In this hyperreal domain of simulation the camera alone provides the sense of reality required for identity to sustain itself. As Crawford puts it: 'There's a kind of amnesia at work here – an amnesia of self. People literally forget who they are. The camera lens needs to be their memory' (*CN* 262). But in these texts the camera is much more than a memory: it is the device *par excellence* by means of which characters are assured that they exist. The truth they embody is captured in Paul Breines's claim that 'in industrial society, everyone is reduced to the mode of spectator at the show of his own alienated activity.'[14] And this mode has two consequences: on the one hand, subjects experience themselves as anonymous and insignificant in their off-camera lives, which without the glow imparted by celluloid cease to be meaningful, and on the other hand, they view others as cartoon figures in a fantasy realm. Events are characterised by a grey depthlessness that drains away all colour and texture, leaving a dull monochromatic world that needs to be pricked to life in ever more bizarre ways.

It is because of this that spectatordom, or more accurately voyeurism, is such an all-pervasive feature of Ballard's novels. It points to a derealisation of the external world and a depersonalisation of the other so far-reaching that the capacity to grasp the consequences of actions has been destroyed. In all three novels this manifests itself in vicious acts of sexual and physical violence that their perpetrators regard as games, mere recreation for the jaded palate, while in *Cocaine Nights* and *Super-Cannes* there is the added element that the violence is filmed for later viewing pleasure. This, from *Cocaine Nights*, is Prentice's introduction into this perverse imaginary after he has witnessed a near rape: 'I noticed the row of parked cars that faced the Porsche across the access lane. Several of the front seats were occupied by the drivers and their passengers, all in evening dress, faces concealed by the lowered sun vizors. They had watched the rape attempt without intervening, like a gallery audience at an exclusive private view' (*CN* 58). Sinclair is in *Super-Cannes* a passive observer of similar scenes as gangs of executives unwind after work by ravaging houses, firing boats, and beating up immigrants: 'In the rear seats of cars stolen for the evening, I watched as the photographer – a financial analyst with a Japanese bank – recorded the ratissages on his camcorder' (*SC* 279). In this novel in particular, all the violence is recorded on film by amateur camera-men whose disengagement from the scenes taking place signals a desire to undergo the experience of violence vicariously and reveals a failure to distinguish between the imaginary and the real. Penrose, always ready with the demented rationale, glibly tells Sinclair: 'Think of these people as film extras, paid for a few minutes' discomfort' (*SC* 298).

Film, of course, even in its faked-up docu-*verité* modes, is always artificial and stylised. Ballard has long seen the stylisation of human behaviour in the late twentieth century as a parodic reflection of the moving image. Stylisation is a mimetic response to the potency of dream-laden celluloid icons and the fictive realm they inhabit, but although this response depends in some sense on the spectator being drawn into this realm, it is also marked by a curious kind of detachment from both the projected and the real world. It is not enough to say that a kind of ontological confusion takes place here, the world projected onto the screen being mistaken for the world beyond it, and then displacing it. More subtly, a progressive detachment from both worlds takes place so that neither is 'real': both are conceived as fantasy realms for the trying out of roles that have no consequences in either domain. If figures taken from the screen or from contemporary myth are models to be copied (think of Malick's beautifully judged *Badlands*) it is not because they are mistakenly thought of as 'real' but because they release the springs of desire, the desire to be different from, greater than, one's self and more like the fantasised other. Yet this very process of mimetic identification is possible only on condition that both the self and the cinematic presence are unmoored from any anchorage in reality, which would otherwise disturb the illusion that identity can be re-made at will and that it is little more than a series of aestheticised postures. The camera is the machine that permits this kind of distancing to take place. Except in those cinematic traditions that refuse the bait of verisimilitude – deploying a number of estranging techniques and frame-breaking devices – the camera projects a world that seems to be 'real' even as it detaches this filmed world from that of mundane everyday life. At once compelling and dematerialised, this world can in some instances contribute to a confusion of ontological categories. The Delages couple in *Super-Cannes* are an example of aestheticised automatons for whom this confusion results in an inversion of values. The scene in which Sinclair finally sees what has been happening reveals their detachment from events, as does their response, which reverses the relationship between fantasy and reality: 'They seemed disappointed but resigned, accepting that I had committed a modest social gaffe, an investor so caught up by the drama that he had mounted the stage to rescue the leading lady' (*SC* 384).

If an aestheticisation of the psyche's fantasy-life lies at one pole of a denatured society then a remaking of the subject's physical body may be found at its other pole. This has been a major theme of Ballard's – most notably in *Crash* – and it turns up again in *Super-Cannes* and *Millennium People*. In *Millennium People* the damaged body is that of Markham's wife Sally, whose legs have been run over by a tram, enabling her to identify with Frida Kahlo and to play whimsical games in imitation of her illustrious predecessor. For Sally, this is an elective affinity, a role adopted as a protest against a world in which random accidents exact a fearful price. But Markham, despite his physical health, is the product of a deeper alienation, which he figures to himself in terms of his wife's remodelled car: 'In many ways, my life was as deformed as this car, rigged with remote controls, fitted with over-riders and emergency brakes within easy reach. I had warped myself into the narrow cockpit of professional work at the Adler, with its inane rivalries and strained emotional needs' (*MP* 145). Still separable from the retooled machine, Markham nonetheless identifies with it, seeing his own psychological disfigurement as its counterpart and visualising himself as trapped by its design. This imagery approaches a kind of hybridisation of man and machine without quite embracing it. In *Super-Cannes*, as in *Crash*, this logic is taken further, the car becoming a prosthetic extension of the individual, a large-scale auto-mated mannequin pressed into the service of eroticism: 'Her hips pressed against the BMW, and the curvature of its door deflected the lines of her thigh, as if the car was a huge orthopaedic device that expressed a voluptuous mix of geometry and desire' (*SC* 117).

Here the notion of the prosthetic body is connected to a techno-cratic ideology of perfectibility. If the body is vulnerable to technology (Sally's tram accident, Sinclair's aeroplane smash), it is also repairable by it. Moreover, as with the Robocop hybrid, by permitting itself to be mechanised, it can be improved by the very technology that damaged it in the first place but will now make it better, stronger, and less vulnerable. The congress on orthopaedic surgery into which Sin-clair stumbles, and which acts as a high-tech reproach to his out-moded leg-brace, has a key symbolic function in *Super-Cannes*. Sinclair is a temporarily crippled individual, whose own prosthesis is a pre-industrial bit of scrap in comparison with the elaborate accou-trements built by an advanced science:

> Remembering my modest knee-brace, I stopped by a glass cabinet that displayed two lifesize mannequins in full orthopaedic rig. Replicas of a man and a woman, they each wore a cuirass of pink plastic around the torso, and their jaws were supported by moulded collars that encased them from the lower lip to the nape of the neck. Elaborately sculptured corselets and cuisses, like the fantasies of an obsessive armourer, sur-rounded their hips and thighs, discreet apertures provided for whatever natural functions were still left to these hybrid creatures. (*SC* 109)

Two things are apparent here: the emphasis on protection, technology being deployed to shield the body from further (destructive) incur-sions into its physical territory; the stress on an aestheticised sculpt-ing of the body that exceeds any simple notion of replication in order to embrace a promethean dream of technological self-fashioning. The body is little more than inert matter to be remoulded. Hal Foster underscores this point in his account of the ways in which after the First World War the 'mechanization of the modern body' was bound up with the search for 'a new principle of corporal order', which treated the body as though 'it were already dead ... *as if the only way for the body to survive in the military-industrial epoch of capitalism was for it to be already dead, in fact deader than dead.*'[15] Prosthetics offers a way of reanimating the body, but in doing so it objectifies the body further still by progressively stripping away whatever is left of an originally organic entity. Commenting on Kleist, Aura Satz suggests that the 'maimed body is the possible human equivalent of the marionette, where puppet-ness has already developed in a limb, and might gradually advance into the rest of the body, replaced bit by bit by the same craftsman who made the first limb', and she notes a general 'mimesis in the direction of object-hood' here.[16] In *Super-Cannes* the prosthetic subject is more of a bio-robot than a marionette, but it discloses a similar logic.

In sharp contrast to the sleek armoured mannequins, Sinclair hobbles around like some hapless intruder from a superseded world. A 'crippled ex-pilot barely able to pump the clutch pedal of his rebored Jaguar' (*SC* 284), he exemplifies a form of humanity that has been consigned to the past, as Delage makes clear: 'It's the turn of the sciences. Everything is possible again – organisms with radial tyres, dreams equipped with airbags' (*SC* 103). The prosthetic self is figured here as an *improved* human entity, one part of a far wider scientific rationalisation of the whole of society. If Estrella de Mar is the resting ground for a world conceived along these technocratic lines, then Eden-Olympia is the mainframe in which the codes it will follow are being programmed. The hybridised body is part of an economic system and a technological network of power in which it is a function, in real terms little more than a small piece of code. The logical terminus of the prosthetic organism is the fully automated cyborg who lives only to work, and although this is as yet an unachievable dream, the domain of Eden-Olympia is well on the way to reducing its inhabitant–workers to the status of technocratic labourers who neither need nor desire leisure or relationships. With its dream of a planned world in which all activity is subordinated to the demands of the economy, Eden-Olympia, like Estrella de Mar, negates human existence, leaving it to be lived on people's behalf by others. In Villiers de l'Isle-Adam's

Axel the eponymous protagonist's melancholy realisation that he and his lover have already exhausted the future leads him to make a haughty declaration of refusal in which the value of life is derided: 'As for living? our servants will do that for us'; in *Super-Cannes* this trivial task is left to children, while in *Cocaine Nights* it is allotted to the security camera.[17] Zygmunt Bauman's description of the struggle to eliminate *noise* and *randomness* (in other words, autonomy and contingency) in this technological imaginary could have been written with Ballard's Eden-Olympia in mind: 'The ultimate limit of the war against noise is a fully controlled life-world and complete heteronomy of the individual – an individual located unambiguously on the receiving end of information flow and having his choices safely enclosed within a frame strictly defined by the expert authority.'[18]

Towards the end of *Super-Cannes* this administered and eventless world seems to be on the verge of realisation:

> The future was a second Eden-Olympia, almost twice the size of the original, the same mix of multinational companies, research laboratories and financial consultancies ... The site-contractors were already at work, clearing the holm oaks and umbrella pines that had endured since Roman times, surviving forest fires and military invasions. Nature, as the new millennium dictated, was giving way for the last time to the tax shelter and the corporate car park. (*SC* 356)

The colonisation of space described here is the counterpart to its internalisation in the minds of those who live under these conditions, a kind of retreat which mirrors that of nature. If the future has arrived, and human life is at an end-point, Eden-Olympia offering a farcical reminder of Hegel's earlier identification of this terminus with the German nation-state, then a teleological conception of the historical process no longer has warrant. The loss of the future as a horizon toward which human activity might be projected results in an increased sensitivity to the category of *space*, conceived now as all that there is. And in Ballard's late works, there is a shift from a concern with temporality to a preoccupation with spatiality, particularly with a defence of physical space, which is seen to be under threat from external aggression, and a retreat from outside space to psychological interiority.

Both Estrella de Mar and Eden-Olympia are of course classic examples of gated enclaves constructed with fear of a dangerous outside world very much in mind, and both are depicted as templates for the life to come. In *Cocaine Nights* and *Super-Cannes* these estates are the forerunners of bigger and better defended building complexes. With a nod back to *High-Rise*, Crawford describes the new Residencia Costasol thus: 'This is Goldfinger's defensible space raised to an almost planetary intensity – security guards, tele-surveillance, no entrance except through the main gates, the whole complex closed to outsiders. It's a grim thought, but you're looking at the future' (*CN* 210). In answer to the innocent question of whether people ever leave the resort, Crawford replies with an air of puzzlement: 'No, that's the eerie thing about it all. The sea's only two hundred yards away but none of the villas looks out on to the beach. Space is totally internalized' (*CN* 210). What does it mean to internalise space in this way? In *Cocaine Nights* physical space offers a haven from temporality itself. Burrowing further and further inwards, and turning away from everything that lies outside clearly demarcated and defended boundaries, the leisure-resort's inhabitants are trying to escape from the collapse of time itself. A similar kind of abdication characterises *Super-Cannes*, suggesting that modernity's last chapter has now been written and the book can be closed:

> The residents of the high-security complex might have retreated so deeply into their defensible space that they had eliminated the need for food, bread and wine. The advertising displays in the estate office overlooking the roundabout on the RN7 had the look of museum tableaux, and the artist's impression of a concourse as crowded as the Champs-Elysees, lined with boutiques and thronged by high-spending customers, seemed to describe a forgotten twentieth-century world. (*SC* 324)

Estrella de Mar and Eden-Olympia are all-embracing systems devised to cater to the 'needs' they have created and that they plan to control. Giving the illusion of freedom, they are in fact administered systems that produce and maintain a certain form of subjectivity, which they then subordinate to a determinate social and moral economy. Sinclair reads this in the design and style of the buildings themselves. Observing one of the 'security-obsessed compounds that were reshaping the geography and character of the Côte d'Azur', he sees its 'vernacular architecture' as a failed attempt 'to disguise this executive-class prison' and identifies it as the blueprint for a new society: 'Taking their cue from Eden-Olympia and Antibes-les-Pins, the totalitarian systems of the future would be subservient and ingratiating,

but the locks would be just as strong' (SC 133). With respect to the ideology of consumer capitalism that ratifies both Estrella de Mar and
Eden-Olympia, Marx's view that 'the *increasing value* of the world of
things proceeds in direct proportion [to] the *devaluation* of the world
of men' is still pertinent, with the postmodern rider that at the end of
the second millennium this devaluation is accepted as the only reality
there is, and, indeed, the only one worth aspiring to.[19] In *Millennium
People* when Markham is disturbed by the seemingly inexorable
spread of huge identikit conurbations around Heathrow, he shudders
at the thought of an existence lived out 'in the suburb of an airport'
(*MP* 133), but Gould is unruffled by people's choice of this transient,
affectless habitat: 'They like that. They like the alienation ... There's
no past and no future. If they can, they opt for zones without meaning – airports, shopping malls, motorways, car parks. They're in flight
from the real' (*MP* 133). In flight from time or in flight from the real?
It seems to come down to the same thing: the rejection of any perspective from which social totality could be envisaged as different
from what it is. In a period that is portrayed as belonging to post-his-
torical time – an interminable limbo – temporality ceases to have
meaning, while the real appears as a series of endlessly proliferating
simulacra lacking any external referents. In offering his diagnosis,
Gould reverses the trajectory of revolutionary thought, in which liberation from oppression, however differently conceived, has always
been the goal. But here alienation is embraced as deliverance from
troubling thought and destabilising action. In flight from anything
that might disturb the safety of an alienated habitat, Ballard's characters retreat from the beckoning light into the darkness of the cave, and
this retreat sounds the death-knell of all politics.

Nietzsche on the beach

Cut adrift from all transcendental justifications of life, humankind
was for Nietzsche forced to confront the truth that existence lacked
purpose or meaning, and realisation of this truth – a shattering of
external grounds of value – gave rise to forms of despair that suc-
cumbed to nihilism. *On the Genealogy of Morals* (1887) was explicit:
'Here precisely is what has become a fatality for Europe – together
with the fear of man we have also lost our love of him, our reverence
for him, our hopes for him, even the will to him. The sight of man
now makes us weary – what is nihilism today if it is not *that*? – We are

weary *of man.*'[20] For Nietzsche, this weariness originated in a misunderstanding of previously dominant philosophical and religious systems, such as the Judaeo-Christian tradition and all idealist philosophies, which held that a transcendent realm of value lay beyond the material world. The path *through* and *beyond* nihilism lay in rejecting this false dualism in order to accept the world as the sole reality and to affirm it exactly as it is. At the heart of this revaluation, a turning upside-down of all idealist categories, was an uncompromising naturalism, which valorised the will-to-power as a healthy instinct for life. Rejecting ethical conceptions as compromised, because derived from idealisms of one kind or another, Nietzsche offered a diagnosis of human depravity, 'free of any *moralic acid*', that he located in a turning away from instinct: 'I consider life itself instinct for growth, for continuance, for accumulation of forces, for *power*. Where the will to power is lacking there is decline. My assertion is that this will is *lacking* in all the supreme values of mankind – that values of decline, *nihilistic* values hold sway under the holiest names'.[21]

This has been a potent view. Within a world in which meaning has disappeared from the horizon, to say nothing of one that appears to have been colonised by economic demands and subordinated to administrative imperatives, the turn to the instinctual self as a source of value is eminently plausible. Charles Taylor notes that 'the moral energy and excitement attending the naturalist rejection of religion and traditional ethics comes from this sense of empowerment, of releasing nature and desire from a stultifying thraldom, releasing them to a fuller affirmation', even if this entails a recognition that nature may not always be a beneficent force.[22] It is not just external nature but human nature that is part of this affirmation: the self, constituted by drives and instincts, becomes a locus of truth that is discovered through their expression and enactment. Hence Nietzsche's insistence that the psychology he saw as 'once again the road to the fundamental problems' be freed from all moral considerations and be conceived 'as morphology and the *development-theory of the will to power*'.[23] Hence, too, his view that beneath all the vain theories of human psychology 'the terrible basic text *homo natura* must again be discerned' and his assumption of the task 'to translate man back into nature'.[24]

This psychological naturalism is one thing when it is descriptive morphology, but another when it is used as a ground of normative value. And Nietzsche did not hesitate to derive one from the other. Instincts are always described as good, so the more closely man approaches the animal, the more complete he is; equality between humans is a nonsense, because some are innately superior to others; a new, value-conferring nobility is required to rejuvenate society; egoism is to be praised; and pity is to be resisted.[25] Thus interpreted, naturalism may not only uphold a view of the self as a drive-based entity but also valorise a hierarchical conception of social relations. And although Nietzsche's thought is unsystematic, warrant for both conclusions exists, since he regarded free will as a chimera, individuals acting as they do because they *must*, and believed some groups are rightly subordinated to others, with only those societies organised on the basis of rank being healthy.[26] In contrast to Freud's cautious defence of the repressions demanded by the social apparatus for the wider communal good, Nietzsche espouses a naturalism that reverses this order of priorities, advocating the view that society should serve the strong, value-creating individual. Whereas Freud claims that the 'replacement of the power of the individual by the power of a community constitutes the decisive step of civilization', the first requisite of which 'is that of justice ... the assurance that a law once made will not be broken in favour of an individual', a characteristically universalising conception of the socius that connects the Freudian project to that of the Enlightenment, Nietzsche holds that if a state that guaranteed 'a good life for the greatest number' were established, 'it would destroy the earth from which a man of great intellect, or any powerful individual grows.'[27]

This conflict is powerfully portrayed in Ballard's late novels, which deploy key Nietzschean motifs to dramatise the psychological and social dangers of succumbing to this account of subjectivity. The three novels' guru figures – Crawford, Penrose and Gould – all preach quasi-Nietzschean philosophies in justification of their actions, although Gould is perhaps closer to the 'rebel' figure identified by Camus. *Cocaine Nights* and *Super-Cannes* spell out the connection: Prentice tells Crawford that he is 'a new kind of Messiah' and describes him as the 'Imam of the marina, the Zoroaster of the beach umbrellas' (*CN* 289), while Sinclair's wife reproaches him for listening to Penrose, dismissing his ideas as 'Nietzsche on the beach – Philip Glass could set it to music' (*SC* 271). Both forms of phrasing suggest that it is not so much Nietzsche who is the target here as popularised versions of his thought and the *uses* to which it may be put (and there is, of course, a long and disturbing history here). The reference to Glass indicates that we are in the realm of pastiche and doubled texts. *Cocaine Nights, Super-Cannes* and *Millennium People* are all in fact structured around doubled and redoubled narratives; behind each central protagonist hovers an alter ego who lives out the former's hidden dreams, behind each alter ego are wider networks of power, and behind each detective story being recounted lie the philosophies of violence, crime and psychopathology that their representatives would unleash upon the world. In *Cocaine Nights* Crawford seeks to bind the community together and to regenerate it through criminal acts that release socially repressed instincts; Penrose in *Super-Cannes* sets out to foster individuals' most atavistic, transgressive desires with the aim of making them more healthy and more economically productive; and in *Millennium People* Gould preaches an annihilating gospel of apocalyptic destruction through which he plans to confront an absurd world.

Baudelaire's view that crime is of natural origin, whereas virtue is artificial is more or less Crawford's personal credo in *Cocaine Nights*. Confronting an administered society in which freedom of thought is circumscribed, he defends a philosophy of transgression through which individuals are energised and given the illusion that their lives are not completely determined. Crawford connects transgression with social health, arguing that the withering away of society feared by Nietzsche in *Human, All Too Human* has taken place; over-controlled, consumerist, and lacking in purpose, the Costa del Sol's retirement society is merely the site of enforced leisure and endless repetition. The self-conscious breaking of taboos (a rejection of the juridical and the symbolic law) is offered as a response to the problem of nihilism: 'Crime, and transgressive behaviour – by which I mean all activities that aren't necessarily illegal, but provoke us and tap our need for strong emotion, quicken the nervous system and jump the synapses deadened by leisure and inaction' (*CN* 180). This behaviour is conceived as lying outside ethical categories; in Estrella de Mar 'there is no remorse' because 'feelings of guilt, however old and deep-rooted, are assuaged' (*CN* 181) by the belief that transgression bolsters the community, making it healthy and strong. In this version of community members are bound together by their acceptance of the need for transgression, and residual feelings of shame are deflected through the ritual sacrifice of scapegoated victims.

Crawford considers that 'the psychopath plays a vital role. He meets the needs of the hour, touches our graceless lives with the only magic we know' (*CN* 271), and there is a clear link here between the text's deployment of a cinematic imaginary and the nihilism associated with the terminal zone of *post-histoire*: the ennui of a bleached existence lived off-camera is inseparable from the etiolation of a future-oriented horizon. *Super-Cannes'* Penrose transforms Crawford's invocation of psychopathy into a full-scale philosophy. The overseer of Eden-Olympia's psychic economy, he acknowledges that the corporate world is so streamlined and routinised that instinctual life has been virtually stamped out, leading to despair and anomie. The way to heal this deadened community is to permit individuals to express their desire for 'more violence and cruelty, more drama and rage' (*SC* 259), which Penrose sees as the prerequisites of health:

> Homo sapiens is a reformed hunter-killer of depraved appetites ... The deviant impulses coded into his central nervous system have been switched off. He can no longer harm himself or anyone else. But nature sensibly endowed him with a taste for cruelty and an intense curiosity about pain and death. Without them, he's trapped in the afternoon shopping malls of a limitless mediocrity. We need to revive him, give him back the killing eye and the dreams of death. Together they helped him to dominate this planet. (*SC* 263)

Penrose, of course, has no intention of unleashing the killing eye on a global scale. His aim is to institute a psychopathological regime in which transgressive and criminal acts function as a form of homeopathic medicine, lifting the lid on repression and re-energising society, but his reference to domination and death exposes the social and political underpinnings of this mode of thought and calls to mind its bloody histories.

In his interview with Alan Burns, Ballard noted of the 1960s that 'people were becoming dehumanized and overcerebralized; emotional responses to everything were becoming so stylized that we were moving into a kind of mad Nazi world'.[28] The observation is pertinent to the world projected in *Super-Cannes*, not least because Penrose's articulation of an aristocratic philosophy in which the ruling elite is free from social constraints is bound up with renascent National Front politics. Racism lies at the heart of the supposedly transgressive violence sanctioned by Penrose, which is in fact bound into French political agendas in relation to which he is a powerless dupe. Within the context of racism and imperialism, which is central to *Super-Cannes*, it is Conrad's Kurtz whom one recalls as the precursor of an apotheosis of the solipsistic self who places himself outside pre-existing categories and enfolds the darkness. Marlow says of him: 'There was nothing either above or below him, and I knew it. He had kicked himself loose of the earth.'²⁹ The security chief Halder calmly tells Sinclair: 'The people here have gone beyond God. Way beyond' (*SC* 202). In *Super-Cannes* Conrad's darkness is embraced as a source of benevolent truth to be discovered through a release of the self into psychopathology, but whereas Kurtz's methods are deemed unsound by the Company, already a rhetoric that construes human action in economic and pragmatic terms, Penrose's methods are approved as the means by which profit can be increased. His contention that the 'teams have to work harder, and learn to fight their way into the darkest heart of themselves' (*SC* 297) is justified by the fact that this strategy has already 'retuned the corporate nervous system and pushed profits to unprecedented heights' (*SC* 280).

Eden-Olympia stands for a highly advanced technological neo-imperialism. It upholds an economy based on the exploitation of cheap immigrant labour, a sub-structure predicated on racist assumptions that hark back to pre-war Germany, and an ideology of social engineering. One of Greenwood's murder victims is a business man with National Front allegiances whose walls are covered with photographs of immigrants he has had killed, and another character informs Sinclair that the entire corporation is built on neo-fascist lines: 'The top managements at Eden-Olympia are deeply racist, but in a new way. The corporate pecking order is all that counts ... We're back in Weimar Germany, with a weekend Freikorps fighting the Reds. Sooner or later some corporate raider with a messianic streak will turn up, backed by all the natural gas in Yakut, and decide that social Darwinism deserves another go' (*SC* 343–4). Penrose reveals the truth of these accusations when he claims that in an age of 'competing psychopathies' social control requires scapegoating mechanisms (driven by race) in which a slave-class (defined by colour) will be turned into the victims they deserve to be: 'We may need to play on deep-rooted masochistic needs built into the human sense of hierarchy. Nazi Germany and the old Soviet Union were Sadeian societies of torturers and willing victims. People no longer need enemies – in this Millennium their great dream is to become victims' (*SC* 365). There is a hint here of Nietzsche's assertion 'that egoism pertains to the essence of the noble soul', a view he derived from his 'immovable faith that to a being such as "we are" other beings have to be subordinate by their nature, and sacrifice themselves to us'.[30]

In *Super-Cannes* this line of thought is represented not as personal choice but as institutional logic, and this is where the book is at its brilliant best, since it shows how a will-to-power that is in Nietzsche's thought associated with the individual insinuates itself into enormously powerful dominative systems. Globalised, multinational interests take precedence here, and the individual is reduced to the despised role of abject *Untermensch*, a slave to a mastery that, in accordance with the logic of the profit-motive, situates itself in a space that is beyond good and evil. This is late capitalism as described by Deleuze: 'In capitalism only one thing is universal, the market. There's no universal state, precisely because there's a universal market of which states are the centers, the trading floors.'[31] In an ironic twist to Nietzsche's stress on self-overcoming, it is the corporation, not the individual, that becomes the higher entity in Ballard's text, and the present is colonised by the super-company: 'A giant multinational like Fuji or General Motors sets its own morality ... There are no more moral decisions than there are on a new superhighway ... We've achieved real freedom, the freedom from morality' (*SC* 95). Technocracy itself decides on all questions, but these are now conceived in terms of pre-planned technical processes that take them out of the realm of the ethical altogether: 'Thousands of people live and work here without making a single decision about right and wrong. The moral order is engineered into their lives along with the speed limits and the security systems' (*SC* 255). This is a view of reality marked by a failure of the imagination, which permits itself to be subjected to the productivist logic of an economy controlled from elsewhere. Deleuze, among others, has observed that what he terms 'control societies' are now 'taking over from disciplinary societies',[32] and this shift, already anticipated in Foucault's turn to a geopolitics orientated to the 'tactics and strategies deployed through implantations, distributions, demarcations, control of territories and organisations of domains',[33] is a key reference point for Ballard's late work.

The free imagination (always a touchstone for Ballard) offers one alternative to Eden-Olympia's programming of identity, while the haphazard events of the ordinary and the everyday provide another resource. References to contingent reality, to the 'everyday world where the human race still lives' (*SC* 378) run through *Super-Cannes*.

Sinclair's view of himself as 'too dull, too normal?' (SC 378) calls to mind Thomas Mann's anti-Nietzschean claim that ethics 'support life, and a man with good morals is an upright citizen of life, – perhaps a little boring, but extremely useful.'[34] Eden Olympia's dream of social engineering and complete order has a long history behind it, one that played a key role in the Nazi programme, although its roots lie further back in the Enlightenment.[35] Contingency is an affront to this dream, a disturbance to boundaries, classifications and structures – in short, a negation of the fully controlled, fully planned polity. Contingency permits the accidental, the unlooked for, the recalcitrant grit in the machine that it is impossible to extirpate. If it is affirmed as an inescapable feature of life, rather than blotted out in some fantasy of total symmetry and/or unity, then it may undermine the rage to rationalisation and the fantasy of transparent order. Thus it is significant that when Sinclair imagines himself defeating Eden-Olympia he considers that the 'winding-down of Penrose's therapeutic programme marked a defeat for him and the triumph of the contingent world' (SC 370), a triumph not unconnected with the re-awakening of his own powers of empathy. Richard Rorty's view of solidarity as 'created by increasing our sensitivity to the particular details of the pain and humiliation of other, unfamiliar sorts of people' offers one possible corrective to Eden-Olympia's systemic racism and its dream of a master–slave social hierarchy.[36]

But a different reading of contingency is offered in *Millennium People*. The doubled narrative in this novel tracks a path from the superficial middle-class revolt of disaffected professionals to the genuine despair of the nihilistic Gould, whose 'far more radical revolution', Markham acknowledges, is 'closer to my heart' (MP 4). This deeper revolt is primarily a metaphysical one, far removed from the farcical pseudo-politics of those who are 'completely detached from reality, with their naïve talk of overturning an entire century' (MP 65) and whose actions really mark the final dissolution of civic responsibility. This superficial rebellion is the expression of a deeper malaise – the problem of nihilism, which takes the form of millenarian despair. Gould's lack of belief in anything is the vacuum at the heart of this novel, which sucks everything else into it. Contingency is here associated here with suffering, disease, accidents and death, brute realities that culminate in a gospel of dread: 'Sadly, life is worth nothing. Or next to nothing ... The gods have died, and we distrust our dreams. We emerge from the void, stare back at it for a short while, and then rejoin the void. A young woman lies dead on her doorstep. A pointless crime, but the world pauses. We listen, and the universe has nothing to say. There's only silence, so we have to speak' (MP 261).

Gould's 'speech' is a euphemism for acts of terrorist violence in which meaninglessness is redeemed by being embraced through sympathetic identification. This is not a Nietzschean affirmation of all that is terrible in life but a profound revolt against that life, which declares its right to enact the violence and suffering endemic to existence. Meaning is not thereby discovered; on the contrary, it is negated again and again. Camus's description of the metaphysical rebel sums up Gould's motives: 'He attacks a shattered world to make it whole. He confronts the injustice at large in the world with his own principles of justice. Thus all he originally wants is to resolve this contradiction and establish a reign of justice, if he can, or of injustice if he is driven to the end of his tether.'[37] By inverting the Pascalian bet and refusing the lure of any possible theodicy, a kind of authenticity of being is asserted in the face of the world's irreducible pointlessness. The search for justification has been abandoned, to be replaced by the goal of freedom, which is associated with a radical voluntarism that functions as the guarantor of the only kind of authenticity to be had. The fact of meaninglessness is now accepted as non-negotiable, a brute datum that no philosophical system or religious theodicy can explain. It is the arbitrariness of violence, its lack of motive, that is its *raison d'être*, ensuring that 'the meaningless act is the only one that has any meaning' (MP 255). Markham's seduction by this way of thinking leads him to view the terrorist bomb as 'an inexplicable act of violence' which has 'a fierce authenticity that no reasoned behaviour could match' (MP 182).

As in *Cocaine Nights* and *Super-Cannes* this kind of rhetoric is underpinned by two assumptions, both of which have roots in romantic–expressive philosophies: firstly, that the self should take priority over society, and, secondly, that authenticity of self lies along the path of desire. What matters above all is that subjects are 'true' to the impulses that move them, and the more deeply these are deemed to lie within the self, the more tenaciously they are defended as ultimate grounds of value. In extreme cases, such as Stirnerian egoism, this way of thinking sees everything outside the self as an object to be appropriated, and nothing beyond the self as having value other than in relation to that self. By drawing attention to the link between

egoism and a monadic view of subjectivity Ballard suggests that a separation of the subject from others and a rejection of the external world
sanctions an instrumentalist view of those others and that this permits the unleashing of terrorist violence. In Stirner's words: 'I do not
want to recognize or respect in you any thing ... but to *use you* ... to me
you are only what you are for me,– to wit my object; and because *my*
object, therefore my property.'[38] The authenticity Markham locates in
the terrorist bomb derives its authority from antecedent assumptions
of this kind: the adrenalin-rush of violence overthrows the dull recti-
tude of rational behaviour. Liberation of the self is the good overrid-
ing all other goods. Thus when Markham reflects on his involvement
in the torching of the National Film Theatre he notes that the attack
'had unlocked the door of [his] cell' and that he had 'felt free again'
(*MP* 146); when he briefly returns home from his adventures with the
terrorists he considers that he 'had tasted freedom, and grasped how
unreal life in St John's Wood had become' (*MP* 192). Rejected as the
source of psychological repression and social constraint, mundane
existence is associated with the life-in-death of the ever same, while
the experiences of the desiring subject are held up as proofs of the
solid and true.

Nietzsche provided his own response to the question ('Why?') that
he claimed had not been answered. He sought 'a whole world of new
days' in 'a *revaluation of all values*, in a liberation from all moral values,
in saying Yes to and having confidence in all that has hitherto been
forbidden, despised, and damned'.[39] His refusal of moral criteria and
his advocacy of instinct inform ways of thinking that by apotheosising
the individual devalue the intersubjective world, loosen the bonds of
community, and sever the connection between acts and their consequences. The major protagonists in this trio of novels are caught up
in, and temporarily seduced by, systems of thought that not only
locate human authenticity in the expression of desire but also over-
value the right of the individual to act them out. The effects of living
out this logic are traced throughout the novels, while its avatars are
exposed. Crawford is likened to L-dopa: 'Cataleptic patients wake up
and begin to dance. They laugh, cry, speak and seem to recover their
real selves. But the dosage must be increased, to the point where it
will kill' (*CN* 304). Penrose's repressed desire for violence leads him
to create a system in which other people can 'be violent for him', thus
he 'sees himself as a new kind of messiah, and our role is to act out
his fantasies for him' (*SC* 351–2). Gould is the progenitor of a dis-

turbed spiritual modality in which the absence of belief will be met by future prophets: 'Congregations roamed the streets, hungry for a charismatic figure who would emerge sooner or later from the wilderness of a suburban shopping mall and scent a promising wind of passion and credulity' (*MP* 38).

These figures are symptomatic of wider socio-economic dynamics, which in Ballard's fiction press upon and exacerbate human instincts, encouraging them to flourish in fantasy and to find ever more flagrant modes of expression. Gould is typical in being described as one of those who 'use extreme violence to explore themselves, like some people use extreme sex' (*MP* 107), but Sinclair is no less drawn to violence, which is the spur to his sexuality, while Markham is so gripped by it that he is said to be 'like someone who's out-stared the sun' (*MP* 164), an image that harks back to the obsession with the apocalyptic implications of the atom bomb in *Empire of the Sun*. Violence is thus shown to be energising in precisely the ways its apologists in these novels suggest that it must be. But in the late novels the destructive element is so endemic to society that the notion of going beyond it seems to be a hopeless dream. It is violence that seems to preoccupy Ballard more than sex now, in fulfilment of Freud's premonition (at a different historical moment) in *Civilization and its Discontents* that the death-instinct was gaining in force: 'The fateful question for the human species seems to me to be whether and to what extent their cultural development will succeed in mastering the disturbance of their communal life by the human instinct of aggression and self-destruction.'[40] Penrose muses: 'Meaningless violence may be the true poetry of the new Millennium. Perhaps only gratuitous madness can define who we are' (*SC* 262). And for Gould: 'A pointless act has a special meaning of its own. Calmly carried out, untouched by any emotions, a meaningless act is an empty space larger than the universe around it' (*MP* 176). In pronouncements such as these, and in *Millennium People* as a whole, violence becomes the source of a negative sublime that seeks to out-bid the world itself: 'Yes! That would mean something. An empty space we could stare into with real awe. Senseless, inexplicable, as mysterious as the Grand Canyon' (*MP* 249). In these texts violence enthrals the individuals whose instincts for it have been developed to an intense pitch by a society that has eroded their sensitivity to it. If in one modality violence is the source of a sublime, world-defying, explosive rage against being, in another modality it is an empty gesture, an inconsequential act, a blank protest that is not *felt* in any way at all. No longer experienced as shocking, no longer understood as *real*, violence is in this latter sense just background noise. Violence as game, as voyeuristic spectacle, as side-show; violence as self-expression, as the road to psychic health, as release of tension. All of these. But not as pain caused to others, as suffering, as horror. A last example: 'I felt curiously uninvolved. I was an actor standing in for the real self who lay asleep beside Sally in St John's Wood. A dream of violence had escaped from my head into the surrounding streets, driven on by the promise of change' (*MP* 127). This dream of violence exists insofar as it is disconnected from reality, and this disconnection is itself the product of a banalisation of violence. Here the acting subject *must* fantasise himself as absent from the scene, as disengaged from the crimes he perpetrates and the terror he unleashes, as already somewhere else but certainly not here.

Notes

1 R. Girard, *Deceit, Desire, and the Novel: Self and Other in Literary Structure*, trans. Y. Freccero (Baltimore: The Johns Hopkins University Press, 1980), p. 6.
2 Girard, *Deceit, Desire, and the Novel*, pp. 4, 45.
3 J. Lacan, *The Four Fundamental Concepts of Psycho-Analysis*, trans. A. Sheridan, ed. J. A. Miller (Harmondsworth: Penguin, 1986), p. 34; S. Freud, *On Sexuality*, trans. J. Strachey (Harmondsworth: Penguin, 1977), p. 319.
4 G. Deleuze and F. Guattari, *Anti-Oedipus: Capitalism and Schizophrenia*, trans. R. Hurley, M. Seem and H. R. Lane (London: Athlone, 1984), p. 81.
5 K. Marx, *The Economic and Philosophic Manuscripts of 1844*, trans. M. Milligan, ed. D. J. Struik (New York: International, 1964), p. 114.
6 Marx, *The Economic and Philosophic Manuscripts*, pp. 112–13.
7 Marx, *The Economic and Philosophic Manuscripts*, pp. 115, 119.
8 H. Lefebvre, *Critique of Everyday Life*, trans. J. Moore (London: Verso, 1991), p. 58.
9 H. Lefebvre, 'Towards a Leftist Cultural Politics', in C. Nelson and L. Grossberg (eds), *Marxism and the Interpretation of Culture* (Chicago: University of Illinois Press, 1988): pp. 75–88, p. 79.
10 E. Luttwak, *Turbo-Capitalism: Winners and Losers in the Global Economy* (London: Orion, 1999), p. 27.
11 Luttwak, *Turbo-Capitalism*, p. 226.
12 A. Burns and C. Sugnet, 'J. G. Ballard', in A. Burns and C. Sugnet (eds), *The Imagination on Trial: British and American Writers Discuss their Working Methods* (London: Allison and Busby, 1981), p. 20.

13 M. Foucault, *Power/Knowledge: Selected Interviews and Other Writings, 1972–1977*, trans. C. Gordon, L. Marshall, J. Mepham and K. Soper, ed. C. Gordon (Brighton: Harvester, 1980), p. 98.

14 P. Breines, 'From Guru to Spectre: Marcuse and the Implosion of the Movement', in *Critical Interruptions: New Left Perspectives on Herbert Marcuse* (New York: Herder and Herder, 1970), p. 3.

15 H. Foster, 'Prosthetic Gods', *Modernism/Modernity*, 4. 2 (April 1997): 5–38, p. 7.

16 A. Satz, 'Puppets and Prosthesis', in *The Prosthetic Aesthetic, New Formations* 46 (spring 2002): 103–18, p. 111.

17 V. de l'Isle-Adam, *Axel*, trans. M. Gaddis Rose (London: Soho, 1986), p. 170. Thus Crawford: 'We're moving into the age of security grilles and defensible space. As for living, our surveillance cameras can do that for us' (*CN* 219).

18 Z. Bauman, *Modernity and Ambivalence* (Oxford: Polity, 1991), p. 226.

19 Marx, *The Economic and Philosophic Manuscripts*, p. 107.

20 F. Nietzsche, *On the Genealogy of Morals* and *Ecce Homo*, trans. W. Kaufman and R. J. Hollingdale (New York: Vintage, 1969), p. 44.

21 F. Nietzsche, *Twilight of the Idols/The Anti-Christ*, trans. R. J. Hollingdale (Harmondsworth: Penguin, 1990), pp. 127–8.

22 C. Taylor, *Sources of the Self: The Making of the Modern Identity* (Cambridge: Cambridge University Press, 1992), p. 343.

23 F. Nietzsche, *Beyond Good and Evil*, trans. R. J. Hollingdale (Harmondsworth: Penguin, 1990), pp. 54, 53.

24 Nietzsche, *Beyond Good and Evil*, p. 162.

25 Nietzsche, *Twilight of the Idols*, pp. 97, 101; Nietzsche, *Beyond Good and Evil*, p. 192.

26 F. Nietzsche, *Human, All Too Human*, trans. M. Faber and S. Lehmann (Harmondsworth: Penguin, 1994), pp. 74–6.

27 S. Freud, *Civilization, Society and Religion: Group Psychology, Civilization and its Discontents, and Other Works*, trans. J. Strachey, ed. A. Dickson (Harmondsworth: Penguin, 1991), p. 284; Nietzsche, *Human, All Too Human*, p. 145.

28 Burns and Sugnet, 'J. G. Ballard', p. 22.

29 J. Conrad, *Heart of Darkness*, ed. R. Hampson (Harmondsworth: Penguin, 1995), p. 107.

30 Nietzsche, *Beyond Good and Evil*, p. 204; Nietzsche *Twilight of the Idols*, pp. 125–6.

31 G. Deleuze, *Negotiations: 1972–1990*, trans. M. Joughin (New York: Columbia, 1995), p. 172.

32 Deleuze, *Negotiations*, p. 178.

33 Foucault, *Power/Knowledge*, p. 77.

34 T. Mann, 'Nietzsche's Philosophy in the Light of Contemporary Events', in R. Solomon (ed.), *Nietzsche: A Collection of Critical Essays* (New York: Anchor, 1973), p. 368.

35 For more on this genealogy, see Bauman, *Modernity and Ambivalence*, pp. 18–52.
36 R. Rorty, *Contingency, Irony, and Solidarity* (Cambridge: Cambridge University Press, 1989), p. xvi.
37 A. Camus, *The Rebel*, trans. A. Bower (Harmondsworth: Penguin, 1975), pp. 29–30.
38 M. Stirner, *The Ego and His Own* (London: Living Time Press, 2001), p. 106.
39 Nietzsche, *On the Genealogy of Morals*, p. 290.
40 Freud, *Civilization, Society and Religion*, pp. 339–40.

Coda

Violence and psychopathology

A dynamic of violence propels Ballard's late works. Violence drives their narratives, motivates their protagonists, and functions as a fantasised means of re-enchanting the world. And in *Millennium People* this is not even violence as a means to an end – however appalling a history this notion has had in the twentieth century – but violence as gratuitous act: pure destructiveness is asserted as the only possible response to a purely absurd universe. Violence has of course been a prevalent feature of Ballard's writing from the outset, visible in ruined landscapes, instrumental logics, programmed subjectivities, and dysfunctional psycho-social relations; it figures in his textual world as the sign of an irrational, instinctual perversity; a compulsion to undo, break up and annihilate. From small-scale and petty acts of destructiveness right through to global dreams of apocalypse, violence is depicted in his work as the *sine qua non* of social existence. But it is principally associated in this work with a masculine drive, which can be aligned with the mythic aggressivity Freud attributed to the sons of the primal horde, but which is also quite clearly associated with anxiety about male status in late twentieth-century Western life.[1] As Ballard has remarked: 'Men are going to have to cope with the huge task of deciding who they are. And they are going to have intense competition from the world of women'.[2]

Inasmuch as violence is endemic to society, it is in Ballard's work a characteristically male activity and obsession. When Ballard insists 'that violence is wholly bad whatever form it takes', adding that 'we're also *excited* by violence', his use of the inclusive 'we' elides the gendered nature of this 'excitement', which in his work is a *masculine* phenomenon that all too often follows a trajectory leading to the sublime terror of a cleansing apocalypse.[3] Nowhere is this more clear than

in the extraordinary zero-sum war-game played out in *Hello America*
(*HA*) – an archetypal fantasia of global violence as the ultimate form
of self-destructiveness – or in the nihilistic terrorism that is envisioned in *Millennium People* as a redemptive project. Throughout Ballard's writing masculinity is under threat, its social roles rendered
nugatory and its codes of behaviour presented as ineffectual. The
becalmed male protagonists who pass a desultory existence in Vermilion Sands are the passive dupes of an overwhelming female sexuality; the questing characters of the early novels are insignificant
ciphers in post-technological landscapes that dwarf them; the aggressive figures who identify with the car (that parody of thrusting phallic
prowess) are folded into and then destroyed by the machine they glo-
rify; and the bewildered narrators of the last novels are adrift in a late
capitalist zone in which they are the puppets of systems that have
turned masculinity into a relic of a superseded age. Inasmuch as all
Ballard's characters notoriously lack psychological 'depth', it is above
all the male protagonists who are represented as outmoded or half-
alive, as lacking any viable models for the development of a new gendered subjectivity and thus as particularly vulnerable to a remoulding
or a programming that is instituted from elsewhere. In the late writing the almost compulsive repetition of oedipal scenarios (with their
ambiguous substitute father figures) points up this absence and
leaves the male subject trapped in a border-zone between the restrictions demanded by the law and the liberation offered by desire. This
is the stasis out of which masculinity cannot move, caught as it is in
a Never-Never Land between a simultaneous yearning both for the
missing father and for freedom from his tyrannical authority. It is no
accident that Gould, the most psychopathic of these substitute figures, is himself the archetypal fatherless child whose refusal to confront (in Freud's terms, to reality-test) the external world marks him
out as the leader of a new tribe of permanently infantilised adults, all
of whom cannot make any accommodation with a symbolic realm
they perceive as pure threat: 'Gould was Peter Pan, mentally
marooned on his asylum island, searching for his lost boys as reality
moved towards him in the menacing form of a thousand starter
homes' (*MP* 166).

An early Ballard story, 'Deep End' (1961), offers a haunting proleptic insight into the violent themes that he explores in his late writing.
The story depicts a dying world, abandoned by most of the human
race, which, with the exception of a few seemingly misguided misfits,

has migrated to Mars. Holliday is one such dissident; determined 'to stay behind and keep watch over a forgotten Earth' (*CS* 236), he is a Crusoe-like *bricoleur* trying to salvage something from the wreckage of a species existence that has been characterised by a global destructiveness that has turned the earth into a gigantic waste-ground. Holliday's is an existential choice, a decision to remain out of loyalty to a human project that may, despite all appearances, have some redeeming features; thus although he acknowledges the devastation wrought by *homo sapiens*, he views the colonisation of a distant planet as a refusal to face up to the consequences of what has taken place on earth, which in all likelihood means that exactly the same history will repeat itself on Mars. Holliday's loyalty to earth is not to be construed as nostalgia but as an attempt to confront and work through a destructive history. 'Deep End' is particularly chilling because it insists that the pollution of earth which has necessitated its evacuation is the result of an environmental violence that cannot be left behind by way of a physical removal to somewhere else. When Holliday discovers a single fish – a powerful symbol of rebirth and regeneration – he realises that the earth 'isn't dead and exhausted after all' because 'new forms of life' (*CS* 241) could be bred from it. But in a shocking ending to the story his hopes are dashed by the mindless act of violence with which a group of adolescent boys who are themselves headed for Mars kill the helpless creature. Told that this senseless act does not betoken 'the end of the world' (*CS* 243) – which is precisely what is symbolically being suggested – and that he should have the fish stuffed, Holliday furiously retorts that this would be akin to embalming himself and, by implication, the rest of what is left of the human race.

There are several possible imaginative responses to the disgust occasioned by this kind of violence. In Ballard's work two predominate. On the one hand a powerful redemptive strain of almost mystical proportions characterises some of his work, envisaging the transfiguration of both the world and the humans who desecrate it.[4] On the other hand, a strong urge to escape from and even to destroy a world seen as irredeemable is also manifested in his writing; in this vein he produces works which, as David Pringle observes, recognise 'that we long for an empty world, a total cataclysm'.[5] The works that are orientated to visions of metamorphosis destabilise the familiar lineaments of the visible world by interpreting it in terms of the unconscious, thereby prising open the habitually closed portals to the

inner psyche and thus ensuring that empirical reality is no longer
seen in conventional terms.[6] This process requires a radical break
with history and with previous psychological investments: the old
models of subjectivity must be destroyed, an emergent reality
accepted, and a new identity – described in *The Drowned World* as 'a
total reorientation of the personality' (*DW* 44) – re-assembled.

The flip-side of this transfigurative dream is a pessimistic reading
of human life that is characterised by biomorphic horror and existential dread. A profound alienation of the subject from its physical
being, its identity, and the public realm in which it must perforce live
are the features of a complete turning away from sociality and inter-
subjectivity. Here it is the theme of escape that predominates. Take,
for example, 'The Enormous Space' (1989). In this text the man who
cuts himself off from external reality is endeavouring to resist the
tyranny of a routinised bourgeois existence that has taken over the
entirety of the social lifeworld. His decision to retreat from the world
is motivated by the desire for liberation from public and private relationships. As in 'The Overloaded Man' there is a desire here to access
a more significant realm of being. Thus the narrator sees himself as
'a reductive Crusoe paring away exactly those elements of bourgeois
life which the original Crusoe so dutifully reconstituted' and aiming
by this process to banish these elements from his purified life so as to
'find in their place a far richer realm formed from the elements of
light, time and space' (*CS* 1132). The story's principal target is the
banality and boredom of everyday life – themes that play such a key
role in Ballard's late novels – which is cluttered with so much conventional rubbish that original perception is destroyed at source. The
protagonist's rejection of the pointless encumbrances that thwart his
access to a different realm of being represents his attempt to pass
from one domain to another in the belief that his 'conventional suburban villa is in fact the junction between our small illusory world and
another larger and more real one' (*CS* 1136). Yet this passage from a
prosaic realm to a visionary one results in a death-dealing solipsism,
which claims two lives and leaves the narrator to speculate that his
belief in a purer realm may be nothing more than a figment of his
own imagination.

Stories such as 'The Enormous Space' not only depict profound
states of alienation but also explore the dangerous consequences of
the attempt to overcome it through strategies of negation. In these
stories, as in *Millennium People*, alienation gives rise to a derealisation

of the world so extreme that it either appears as a realm without value or is reduced to the lineaments of the solipsistic mind. In both cases it is not just the perceiving subject that becomes an other to itself. The world and those who inhabit it become spectral figures whose obliteration is viewed with equanimity. This alienation is phenomenological, a revolt against the limitations of the space -time continuum and the imperfections of humanity, but it is also a response to social and technological pressures, and is thus a refusal of the ways in which subjectivity is constructed and constrained under late twentieth-century capitalism. Stories such as 'The Overloaded Man' and 'The Enormous Room' hauntingly evoke a longing to resist coercive and exploitative socio-economic systems, but instead of looking for ways of overturning them try to bypass them by means of an escape to a purer, higher realm beyond the grubby dissonances of the material world. Praxis does not figure in Ballard's writing, which, however angry, engaged, and committed it is, figures a resolutely post-political world. Politics is sidelined in Ballard's texts because it is seen to have little purchase on the economic, technological and social circuits that incessantly decode and recode twentieth-century life. If Ballard's texts at times appear as contorted, fragmented narratives this is in no small measure the result of their attempts to trace the often bizarre patterns and loops made by this ramifying circuitry.[7]

Back in 1985, David Punter noted that 'the long tradition of enclosed and unitary subjectivity comes to mean less and less to [Ballard] as he explores the ways in which person is increasingly controlled by landscape and machine, increasingly becomes a point of intersection for overloaded scripts and processes which have effectively concealed their distant origins in human agency.'[8] This observation has been amply borne out by his work since the 1980s, and inasmuch as alienation continues to figure prominently in this work, it needs to be seen in relation to the colonisation of economic and social life by systems that have progressively eroded the very possibility of human agency. It is not for nothing that Ballard's texts displace human subjects from the centre of his narratives, which are taken over by the now dominant features of the urban environment: road networks, car parks, high-rises, airport concourses, business parks, suburban estates, waste-grounds, gated communities, retirement pueblos. The subject is in Ballard's works not just dwarfed by urban space and rendered insignificant by it, but is also moulded and constrained by it in ways that show up the appeal to agency as a nostalgic dream. Elizabeth Grosz's suggestion that the city should now be seen as 'the site for the body's cultural saturation, its takeover and transformation by images, representational systems, the mass media, and the arts – the place where the body is representationally reexplored [sic], transformed, contested, reinscribed', draws attention to the view of subjectivity that is operative in Ballard's texts.[9] There is also a gradual stripping away of temporality (history both past and yet to come) in this focus on space, which hollows out human life and reduces it to an interminable present of the ever-same. The past no longer exists as a repository of values upon which it is possible to draw or in relation to which one can define oneself, while the future is an abandoned enterprise: 'nothing exciting or new or interesting is ever going to happen again ... the future is just going to be a vast, conforming *suburb of the soul* ... nothing new will happen, no breakouts will take place.'[10] Writing of an earlier moment, Perry Anderson uses language that is similar to Ballard's. Anderson traces the shutting down of modernism's radical potential back to World War Two. He argues that since then

> all the basic institutional coordinates of the major industrial countries have remained fixed, as capitalism has anchored itself in the structures ... of liberal democracy and consumer prosperity, to become a self-reproducing order such as it very rarely was before 1945 ... . The critical distance of art from commerce and publicity has narrowed enormously; the capacity of the established order for absorption and corruption has increased vertiginously. In these conditions, any generalized break-out of the kind that marked modernism is difficult to conceive.[11]

Referring to an 'implosion of space into time' in late twentieth-century life, Grosz suggests that the body does not so much locate itself in relation to the 'spatiotemporal layout' of the metropolis but is rather defined and determined through an 'interface with the computer, forming part of an information machine in which the body's limbs and organs will become interchangeable parts', a situation in which body and machine cross-breed, machines becoming anthropomorphised and humans becoming machinic.[12] In Ballard's work this results in versions of identity that construe it either as prosthetic or as programmed or as an amalgam of the two. There is here a powerful sense that the machinic subject destroys all distinctions between the 'human' and the 'technological', which conceive the latter as a detachable addition – either ornament or excrescence. As Marquand Smith has argued, 'to designate and define the form of the prosthetic body is to show that the organic and the artificial, meat and machinery ... are always and already *of* one another: an originary technicity.'[13] In Ballard's work, whichever of these two subject-conceptions (the programmed or the prosthetic) takes precedence, the result is always the same: the notion of an identity thought of as centrally composed around a human 'core' is here displaced by a view of the subject as a functional mechanism to be engineered and/or coded. Attempts to resist the reduction of the subject to the status of an automaton are often grounded in appeals to the 'core' that is seen to have been overlaid by inauthentic demands.[14] This move is never made in Ballard's writing. Even the early works have nothing to do with discovering an already present 'self', but rather emphasise the need to assemble a self out of the materials of a radically transformed world. The late texts, in turn, describe a subjectivity so thoroughly imbricated in technological networks of power that no meaning exists in the concept of an authentic self. Martin Bax sums up this aspect of Ballard's work under the sign of a third stage to the industrial revolution:

> the microchip, the home computer, the television itself – is actually *invading people*, impinging on people's behavior, taking over their lives ... All of us are now, in fact, *bio-robots* – we can't exist without the equipment which we have around us, like cars, telephones, tape recorders, contact lenses, so we're no longer just biological organisms, we're *bio-robotical* organisms.[15]

On this view, the subject may then be seen as essentially prosthetic; as David Wills has suggested, it is 'always already imperfect, mechanical, in relations of dependence, originarily disabled or incomplete ... in short ... prosthetic.'[16]

The novels of the early 1970s are all in different ways attempts to grasp the nature of the dominative regimes that were recoding the human being as a bio-mechanical entity. But as I argued in my second chapter the attempt to decode the operative technological and social logics meets with limited success, primarily because a system that is, in Deleuzian terms, deterritorialising and reterritorialising with great adaptability and speed cannot decisively be caught in narrative form. The turn to the techniques of Surrealist collage, Pop Art assemblages, Dalían critical-paranoia, and the rhizomatic 'map' rather than the axiomatic 'tracing' discloses the need to shatter narrative form and to produce a textuality that does not look for a premature resolution but

rather remains fugitive, open-ended, aware of the numerous unad-
dressed issues that naggingly remain outside the textual frame. The
kind of cognitive mapping called for by Fredric Jameson, which rests
on 'the conception of some (unrepresentable, imaginary) global social
totality' is precisely what is called into question in works such as *The
Atrocity Exhibition* or *Crash*, which offer hypothetical explanations for
the inner logics of the period but make no claim to completeness or
objectivity.[17] There is, in short, no longer any totality to be grasped
here any more than there is a critical vantage-point outside the system
of representations within which the critique is offered. Thus Ballard
argues that before the advent of the telecommunications industries
all the cultural and political events of the day were 'part of one *whole
– sort of graspable* in a way. And it may be that that's going to end. Sections of the landscape will have no connection whatsoever with each
other ... probably nobody will ever again be fully engaged with a sort
of *central experience*'.[18]

This resistance to totalisation is beautifully exemplified in 'The
Index' (1977), a brilliantly economical story that demonstrates the
impossibility of the eagle-eye overview and foregrounds the
inescapable relation between conceptual systems and the 'truths' they
articulate. 'The Index' comprises nothing more than an index to a
planned autobiography that was never actually written and a note
explaining that the only thing remaining of this work, by 'one of the
most remarkable figures of the 20th century' (*CS* 940), is the index
itself. An internal recursiveness thus draws everything back to this
alphabetised list of entries, which gestures tantalisingly to a world of
events, relationships and contacts that can only be inferred by cross-
referencing the entries, but that remain resolutely fragmentary and
elliptical. At the same time, the index discloses a classificatory system
that is conventional and arbitrary. Because it is alphabetical, it orders
the events of the life that never actually gets to be narrated (and is thus
forever beyond the textual frame) not in terms of chronology but in
terms of a linguistic system that arbitrarily imposes a certain kind of
order. This not only calls into question its own classificatory system
but also provokes reflection on the chronological one that would have
controlled the narrative of the absent text: the viability of all classificatory and narrative systems is in this way problematised, leaving
unresolved the issue of how a life or an epoch is to be described.
Although the index can to a degree be decoded, this decoding cannot
be complete because the lacunae embedded in its very structure

thwart all final reconstructions or interpretations. The story functions as a lovely formal reminder of the impossibility of unification or total-isation; its structure and form blazon forth the paradigmatic nature of all conceptualisations and the limited insights of all narrative models.

The problem of totalisation at the level of narrative is then inextri-cable from that of subjectivity as it is represented within narrative. This is seen most clearly in *The Atrocity Exhibition* in the representa-tion of Traven as a fragmented cipher who exists as a series of textual moduli, but it is also evident in the mimetic and/or programmed sub-jectivities of the main characters in works such as *Crash*, *Cocaine Nights*, *Super-Cannes* and *Millennium People*. Michel de Certeau's use of Saussure's *langue/parole* distinction is pertinent in this context. *Langue* in this schema relates to the technocratic and socio-cultural system within which various forms of *parole* (speech, action) must unfold, and de Certeau envisages the ways in which individuals can resist this constraining and dominative system through the 'tactic' of *poeisis* and *bricolage*, a kind of fugitive reappropriation of an otherwise seemingly monolithic set of structures and relations.[19] But in Bal-lard's late writing *langue* is so restrictively organised that new combi-nations of its elements are precluded from the outset. The circuitry is hardwired, the code already written, and the messages to be relayed already programmed. The subject is a conduit or a nodal point in a *langue* that fixes its place in advance. Thus if 'The Index' calls into question the idea of a life unified along the axis of chronologically conceived time, then Ballard's late novels problematise the idea that a life can be authored in and through narrative. What de Certeau sees as 'a *therapeutics for deteriorating social relations*', through which the oppositional practices of everyday life interrupt and break up tech-nocracy before reassembling aspects of it in some oppositional form, is ruled out of court here.[20]

What happens when the machinic subject – an interface between networks of relays, or a prosthetic bio-entity – is no longer conceivable as an autonomous self capable of agency? I have suggested earlier in this book that one consequence of the collision in subjectivity of tech-nology, informatics and the visual media is that the realm of the spec-tacular comes to predominate over all else in Ballard's writing. Of particular interest in Ballard's late works is the fact that the systema-tisation of the subject has as its counterpart the etiolation of inter-subjectivity; isolated from human contact with others, the subject now exists in some derealised, depersonalised space. Yet the result of this attempted reduction of the subject to a programmed bio-robot is a return of the repressed, which transforms it into a raging solipsistic entity that is identified with the self-asserting *id*, that which Freud evocatively described as 'a chaos, a cauldron full of seething excitations.'[21] If the social system is so hegemonic that it cannot be adapted or broken up, and if politics appears to offer no viable way of restructuring or overthrowing it, then it can at least be rejected *in toto*. This is the bleak conclusion come to in *Millennium People*. The desire for the complete negation of life itself articulated in this novel exemplifies a nihilism that David Levin, in the context of a more general philosophical discussion, describes as 'a rage against Being', which demands 'the destruction of Being ... including that way of being which we call "human" and consider to be our own.'[22] *Millennium People* embodies an all-consuming *passion* for destruction that construcs violence as the only valid response to a world from which meaning has been expunged. This violence is seen as a form of authenticity, a defiant post-humanist *non serviam* in which it is not the deity that is abominated but a cosmos that refuses to succumb to any and every structure of meaning. It is only by bringing about an identification of the subject with the violence it enacts that a form of 'selfhood' is in fantasy recovered. In the Freudian model the ego represents reality to the id (which implies at least a degree of agency) but here the ego has been *colonised* by the technocratic world, leaving the id, 'filled with energy reaching it from the instincts', to redouble its assault on this version of the subject and this domination of its lifeworld.'[23] A 'new kind of fanatic' then emerges from the disaster zone, one who needs 'the fantasy of absolute power' and who only seems 'fully alive when he [can] imagine himself as the perpetrator of appalling crimes' (*MP* 271).

Ballard has repeatedly invoked Conrad in his claims that the individual and society need to confront everything that is questionable about the human species and the modes of existence it has forged: 'I feel we should immerse ourselves in the most destructive element, ourselves, and swim. I take it that the final destination of the 20th century, and the best we can hope for in the circumstances, is the attainment of a moral and just psychopathology' (*AE* 37). He has insisted that it is by way of an *imaginative*, and not a physically *enacted*, thinking through of human destructiveness that a path beyond it may be discoverable. But the late works return again and again to the difference between exploring the speculative mindscapes of the imagination and the translation of such mindscapes (a disastrous category mistake) into the realm of the real. What Ballard defends as the 'morally free psychopathology of *metaphor*, as an element in one's dreams', is, when carried over by those who literalise metaphor into the domain where it has no place, an id-driven psychopathology that lays waste to human life.[24] This is less Nietzsche's 'beyond good and evil', and more Freud's: 'The id of course knows no judgements of value: no good and evil, no morality'.[25] Conrad was no less aware of this psychopathology than Ballard, except that the text which exemplifies it is not *Lord Jim* but *The Secret Agent*. As in *Millennium People*, in which Gould insists that acts of terror only have the power to disturb if they are pointless, so in *The Secret Agent* the Professor argues that 'madness and despair are a force' and that with such a force he can 'move the world'.[26] In both texts the apparent *pointlessness* of terror is its *point*: it is a brutal manifestation of the refusal of all moral and social categories in the belief that senseless destruction opens up the channel to an authenticity of the solitary will and a meaning defying sublimity. By blowing a hole in space-time, terror announces in as visceral and public manner as possible its revolt against sociality itself.[27] Neither the Professor nor Gould has any political programme, and both are driven by monologic and deeply infantile conceptions of the world that refuse to acknowledge the inescapability of contingency and shun the claims of intersubjectivity. All that is then left are solitary id-driven wills proclaiming their right to assert themselves through acts of motiveless violence in which any notion of ethical truth or programmatic social change has long since been obliterated.

Notes

1 For the first point, the locus classicus is S. Freud, *Totem and Taboo: Some Points of Agreement between the Mental Lives of Savages and Neurotics*, trans. J. Strachey (London and New York: Routledge, 2002).
2 W. Self, 'Conversations: J. G. Ballard', in *Junk Mail* (London: Penguin, 1996), pp. 329–71, p. 355.
3 V. Vale and A. Juno (eds), *RE/Search* 8. 9 (1984), p. 161.
4 G. Revell, 'Interview with J. G. Ballard', *RE/Search* 8. 9 (1984): pp. 42–52, p. 45.
5 J. Goddard and D. Pringle 'An Interview with J. G. Ballard', in J. Goddard and D. Pringle (eds), *J. G. Ballard: The First Twenty Years* (Hayes, Middlesex: Bran's Head, 1976), pp. 8–35, p. 65.

6 W. Blake, *The Complete Poems*, ed. W. H. Stevenson (London: Longman, 1990), p. 114; J. G. Ballard, 'Foreword' to Aldous Huxley, *The Doors of Perception* and *Heaven and Hell* (London: Flamingo, 1994), no pagination.

7 For a good description of this aspect of capitalism, see G. Deleuze and F. Guattari, *Anti-Oedipus: Capitalism and Schizophrenia*, trans. R. Hurley, M. Seem and H. R. Lane (London: Athlone, 1984), p. 374.

8 D. Punter, *The Hidden Script: Writing and the Unconscious* (London: Routledge and Kegan Paul, 1985), p. 9.

9 E. Grosz, *Space, Time, and Perversion: Essays on the Politics of Bodies* (London: Routledge, 1995), p. 108.

10 A. Juno and V. Vale, 'Interview with J. G. Ballard', *RE/Search* 8. 9 (1984): 6–35, p. 8.

11 P. Anderson, *A Zone of Engagement* (London: Verso, 1992), p. 54.

12 Grosz, *Space, Time, and Perversion*, p. 110. See also S. Bukatman, *Terminal Identity: The Virtual Subject in Postmodern Science Fiction* (Durham and London: Duke University Press, 1993), pp. 8–9.

13 M. Smith, 'The Uncertainty of Placing: Prosthetic Bodies, Sculptural Design, and Unhomely Dwelling in Marc Quinn, James Gillingham, and Sigmund Freud', in *The Prosthetic Aesthetic*, New Formations 46 (spring 2002): 85–102, p. 86.

14 See J. Dollimore, *Sexual Dissidence: Augustine to Wilde, Freud to Foucault* (Oxford: Clarendon, 1991), p. 39.

15 Vale and Juno (eds), *RE/Search*, p. 36.

16 Quoted in Smith, 'The Uncertainty of Placing', p. 85.

17 F. Jameson, 'Cognitive Mapping', in C. Nelson and L. Grossberg (eds), *Marxism and the Interpretation of Culture* (London: Macmillan, 1988): pp. 347–57, p. 356.

18 Juno and Vale, 'Interview with J. G. Ballard', p. 29.

19 M. de Certeau, *The Practice of Everyday Life*, trans. S. Rendall (Berkeley: University of California Press, 1988), pp. xii–xix.

20 de Certeau, *The Practice of Everyday Life*, p. xxiv.

21 S. Freud, *New Introductory Lectures on Psychoanalysis*, trans. J. Strachey (Harmondsworth: Penguin, 1975), p. 106.

22 D. M. Levin, *The Opening of Vision: Nihilism and the Postmodern Situation* (New York and London: Routledge, 1988), p. 5.

23 Freud, *New Introductory Lectures*, p. 106. For the ego and 'reality-testing', see p. 108.

24 Revell, 'Interview with J. G. Ballard', p. 47.

25 Freud, *New Introductory Lectures*, p. 107.

26 J. Conrad, *The Secret Agent* (Harmondsworth: Penguin, 1975), p. 248.

27 In *The Secret Agent* there is a reference to 'sudden holes in space and time' that permit terrorist explosions to take place: see p. 76. In *Millennium*

People the terrorist bomb is that which 'force[s] a violent rift through time and space, and rupture[s] the logic that [holds] the world together' (*MP* 182).

Bibliography

Works by J. G. Ballard

The Drowned World (1962) (London: Victor Gollancz, 2001).
The Voices of Time and Other Stories (1962) (London: Phoenix, 1974).
The Wind From Nowhere (1962) (Harmondsworth: Penguin, 1967).
The Four-Dimensional Nightmare (1963) (London: Victor Gollancz, 1974).
Passport to Eternity (1963) (New York: Berkley, 1963).
The Terminal Beach (1964) (London: Phoenix, 2001).
The Drought (1965) (London: Flamingo, 2001).
The Crystal World (1966) London: Flamingo, 2000).
The Disaster Area (1967) (London: Flamingo, 1992).
The Atrocity Exhibition (1970) (London: Flamingo, 2001).
Vermilion Sands (1971) (London: Vintage, 2001).
Concrete Island (1973) (London: Vintage, 1994).
Crash (1973) (London: Vintage, 1975).
High-Rise (1975) (London, Flamingo, 2000).
Low-Flying Aircraft and Other Stories (1976) (London: Jonathan Cape, 1976).
The Best of J. G. Ballard (1977) (London: Futura, 1977).
The Best Short Stories of J. G. Ballard (1978) (New York: Holt, Rinehart, Winston, 1978).
The Unlimited Dream Company (1979) (London: Flamingo, 2000).
The Venus Hunters (1980) (London: Granada, 1980).
Hello America (1981) (Reading: Triad, 1983).
Myths of the Near Future (1982) (London: Vintage, 1999).
Empire of the Sun (1984) (London: Flamingo, 1994).
The Day of Creation (1987) (London: Flamingo, 1993).
Running Wild (1988) (London: Flamingo, 2002).
War Fever (1990) (London: William Collins, 1990).
The Kindness of Women (1991) (London: Flamingo, 1994).
Rushing to Paradise (1994) (London: Flamingo, 1995).

'Foreword' to Aldous Huxley, *The Doors of Perception* and *Heaven and Hell* (London: Flamingo, 1994): no pagination.
Cocaine Nights (1996) (London: Flamingo, 1997).
A User's Guide to the Millennium: Essays and Reviews (1996) (New York: Picador, 1996).
'J. G. Ballard's Comments on His Own Fiction', *Interzone* (April 1996): 19–25.
Super-Cannes (2000) (London: Flamingo, 2001).
The Complete Short Stories (London: Flamingo, 2001).
Millennium People (2003) (London: Flamingo, 2003).

Interviews

Bresson, C. 'J. G. Ballard at Home', *Metaphores* 7 (March 1982): 5–29.
Burns, A. and C. Sugnet, 'J. G. Ballard', in A. Burns and C. Sugnet (eds), *The Imagination on Trial: British and American Writers Discuss their Working Methods* (London: Allison and Busby, 1981), pp. 16–30.
Frick, T. 'J. G. Ballard', *Paris Review* 94 (1984): 132–60.
Goddard, J. and D. Pringle, 'An Interview with J. G. Ballard', in J. Goddard and D. Pringle (eds), *J. G. Ballard: The First Twenty Years* (Hayes, Middlesex: Bran's Head, 1976), pp. 8–35.
Juno, A. and V. Vale, 'Interview with J. G. Ballard', *RE/Search* 8. 9 (1984): 6–35.
Pringle, D. 'From Shanghai to Shepperton', *Foundation: The Review of Science Fiction* 24 (1982): 5–23.
——, 'J. G. Ballard', *Interzone* (April 1996): 12–16.
Revell, G. 'Interview with J. G. Ballard', *RE/Search* 8. 9 (1984): 42–52.
Self, W. 'Conversations: J. G. Ballard', in *Junk Mail* (London: Penguin, 1996), pp. 329–71.

Critical works

Adamowicz, E. *Surrealist Collage in Text and Image: Dissecting the Exquisite Corpse* (Cambridge: Cambridge University Press, 1998).
Adams, P. 'Death Drive', in M. Grant (ed.), *The Modern Fantastic: The Films of David Cronenberg* (Westport CT: Praeger, 2000): 102–22.
Adorno, T. *Minima Moralia: Reflections from Damaged Life* (London: Verso, 1999).
—— and M. Horkheimer, *Dialectic of Enlightenment*, trans. J. Cumming (London: Verso, 1973).
Anderson, P. *A Zone of Engagement* (London: Verso, 1992).
Apollonio, U. (ed.), *Futurist Manifestoes* (London: Thames and Hudson, 1973).
Armstrong, A. *The Radical Aesthetic* (Oxford: Blackwell, 2000).

Artaud, A. *Artaud on Theatre*, ed. C. Schumacher and B. Singleton (London: Methuen, 1989).

Augé, M. *Non-Places: Introduction to an Anthropology of Supermodernity*, trans. J. Howe (London: Verso, 1995).

Banham, R. *The New Brutalism: Ethic or Aesthetic?* (London: The Architectural Press, 1966).

Barthes, R. *Sade Fourier Loyola*, trans. R. Miller (London: Jonathan Cape, 1977).

Baudrillard, J. *Simulations*, trans. P. Foss, P. Patton and P. Beitchman (New York: Semiotext[e], 1983).

——, 'Two Essays', *Science Fiction Studies* 55. 18: 3 (November 1991): 309–19.

——, *The Consumer Society: Myths and Structures*, trans. C. Turner (London: Sage, 2003).

Bauman, Z. *Modernity and Ambivalence* (Oxford: Polity, 1991).

Benjamin, W. *Illuminations*, trans. H. Zohn (New York: Schocken, 1978).

Benko, G. 'Introduction: Modernity, Postmodernity and the Social Sciences', in G. Benko and U. Strohmeyer (eds), *Space and Social Theory: Interpreting Modernity and Postmodernity* (Oxford: Blackwell, 1997), pp. 1–44.

Bergson, H. *Laughter: An Essay on the Meaning of the Comic*, trans. C. Brereton and F. Rothwell (London: Macmillan, 1911).

Blake, W. *The Complete Poems*, ed. W. H. Stevenson (London: Longman, 1990).

Bollas, C. *Cracking Up: The Work of Unconscious Experience* (London: Routledge, 1997).

Borch-Jacobsen, M. 'The Laughter of Being', in F. Botting and S. Wilson (eds), *Bataille: A Critical Reader* (Oxford: Blackwell, 1998).

Bradbury, M. *No, Not Bloomsbury* (London: André Deutsch, 1987).

Breines, P. 'From Guru to Spectre: Marcuse and the Implosion of the Movement', in *Critical Interruptions: New Left Perspectives on Herbert Marcuse* (New York: Herder and Herder, 1970).

Breton, A. *Manifestoes of Surrealism*, trans. R. Seaver and H. R. Lane (Ann Arbor: University of Michigan Press, 1972).

——, *What is Surrealism? Selected Writings*, ed. F. Rosemont (London: Pluto, 1978).

——, *Mad Love*, trans. M. A. Caws (Lincoln: University of Nebraska Press, 1988).

Brigg, P. *J. G. Ballard* (Mercer Island WA: Starmont House, 1985).

Brokotman, M. (ed.), *Car Crash Culture* (New York: Palgrave, 2001).

Bukatman, S. *Terminal Identity: The Virtual Subject in Postmodern Science Fiction* (Durham and London: Duke University Press, 1993).

Burroughs, W. *Naked Lunch* (London: Flamingo, 1993).

Camus, A. *The Rebel*, trans. A. Bower (Harmondsworth: Penguin, 1975).

——, *The Myth of Sisyphus*, trans. J. O'Brien (Harmondsworth: Penguin, 1980).

Caws, M. A. *The Surrealist Look: An Erotics of Encounter* (Cambridge MA: MIT Press, 1997).

Certeau, M. de, *The Practice of Everyday Life*, trans. S. Rendall (Berkeley: University of California Press, 1988).

Cheyfitz, E. *The Poetics of Imperialism: Translation and Colonization from The Tempest to Tarzan* (Oxford: Oxford University Press, 1991).

Conrad, J. *The Secret Agent: A Simple Tale* (Harmondsworth: Penguin, 1975).

——, *Heart of Darkness*, ed. R. Hampson (Harmondsworth: Penguin, 1995).

Dalí, S. *The Collected Writings of Salvador Dalí*, trans. H. Finkelstein (Cambridge: Cambridge University Press, 1998).

Debord, G. *The Society of the Spectacle*, trans. D. Nicholson-Smith (New York: Zone, 1995).

Deleuze, G. *The Logic of Sense*, trans. M. Lester with C. Stivale, ed. C. V. Boundas (London: Athlone Press, 1990).

——, *Negotiations: 1972–1990*, trans. M. Joughin (New York: Columbia University Press, 1995).

—— and F. Guattari, *Anti-Oedipus: Capitalism and Schizophrenia*, trans. R. Hurley, M. Seem and H. R. Lane (London: Athlone, 1984).

—— and F. Guattari, *A Thousand Plateaus: Capitalism and Schizophrenia*, trans. B. Massumi (Minneapolis and London: University of Minnesota Press, 1996).

—— and C. Parnet, *Dialogues II*, trans. H. Tomlinson and B. Habberjam (London and New York: Continuum, 1987).

Delville, M. *J. G. Ballard* (Plymouth: Northcote House, 1998).

Dentith, S. *Parody* (London: Routledge, 2000).

Descombes, V. *Modern French Philosophy*, trans. L. Scott-Fox and J. M. Harding (Cambridge: Cambridge University Press, 1988).

Dollimore, J. *Sexual Dissidence: Augustine to Wilde, Freud to Foucault* (Oxford: Clarendon, 1991).

Donald, J. *Imagining the Modern City* (London: Athlone, 1999).

Ehrenburg, I. *The Life of the Automobile*, trans. J. Neugroschel (London: Serpent's Tail, 1999).

Ellul, J. *The Technological Society*, trans. J. Wilkinson (London: Jonathan Cape, 1965).

Finch, C. *Pop Art: Object and Language* (London: Studio Vista/Dutton Pictureback, 1968).

Foster, D. A. 'J. G. Ballard's Empire of the Senses: Perversion and the Failure of Authority', *PMLA* 108:3 (May 1993): 519–32.

Foster, H. 'Prosthetic Gods', *Modernism/Modernity* 4: 2 (April 1997): 5–38.

Foucault, M. *The Order of Things: An Archaeology of the Human Sciences* (New York: Vintage, 1973).

——, *The History of Sexuality: Volume One: An Introduction*, trans. R. Hurley (Harmondsworth: Penguin, 1978).

——, *Power/Knowledge: Selected Interviews and Other Writings, 1972–1977*, trans. C. Gordon, L. Marshall, J. Mepham and K. Soper, ed. C. Gordon (Brighton: Harvester, 1980).

Fredericks, C. *The Future of Eternity: Mythologies of Science Fiction and Fantasy* (Bloomington: Indiana University Press, 1982).

Freud, S. *Introductory Lectures on Psychoanalysis*, trans. J. Strachey (Harmondsworth: Penguin, 1974).

——, *New Introductory Lectures on Psychoanalysis*, trans. J. Strachey (Harmondsworth: Penguin, 1975).

——, *On Sexuality*, trans. J. Strachey (Harmondsworth: Penguin, 1977).

——, *On Metapsychology: The Theory of Psychoanalysis*, trans. J. Strachey (Harmondsworth, Penguin, 1984).

——, *Civilization, Society and Religion: Group Psychology, Civilization and its Discontents, and Other Works*, trans. J. Strachey, ed. A. Dickson (Harmondsworth: Penguin, 1991).

——, *Totem and Taboo: Some Points of Agreement between the Mental Lives of Savages and Neurotics*, trans. J. Strachey (London and New York: Routledge, 2002).

Galt Harpham, G. *On the Grotesque: Strategies of Contradiction in Art and Literature* (Princeton: Princeton University Press, 1982).

Girard, R. *Deceit, Desire, and the Novel: Self and Other in Literary Structure*, trans. Y. Freccero (Baltimore: The Johns Hopkins University Press, 1980).

Goddard, J. *J. G. Ballard: A Bibliography* (Lymington, Hampshire: Cypher Press, 1970).

—— and D. Pringle (eds), *J. G. Ballard: The First Twenty Years* (Hayes, Middlesex: Bran's Head Books, 1976).

Goodchild, P., *Deleuze and Guattari: An Introduction to the Politics of Desire* (London: Sage, 1996).

Greenland, C. *The Entropy Exhibition: Michael Moorcock and the British 'New Wave' in Science Fiction* (London: Routledge, 1983).

Grosz, E. *Space, Time, and Perversion: Essays on the Politics of Bodies* (London: Routledge, 1995).

Guattari, F. *The Guattari Reader*, ed. G. Genosko (Oxford: Blackwell, 1996).

Hegarty, P. *Georges Bataille: Core Cultural Theorist* (London: Sage, 2000).

Highmore, B. *Everyday Life and Cultural Theory: An Introduction* (London: Routledge, 2002).

James, H. *What Maisie Knew* (Harmondsworth: Penguin, 1971).

Jameson, F. 'Cognitive Mapping', in C. Nelson and L. Grossberg (eds), *Marxism and the Interpretation of Culture* (London: Macmillan, 1988), pp. 347–57.

Jolas, E. 'Super-Occident', *transition* 15 (February 1929): 11–16.

Jouffroy, A. *Bellmer*, trans. B. Frechtman (n.p.: William and Norma Copley Foundation, n.d.).

Kalsched, D. *The Inner World of Trauma: Archetypal Defenses of the Personal Spirit* (London: Routledge, 1999).

Lacan, J. *The Four Fundamental Concepts of Psycho-Analysis*, trans. A. Sheridan, ed. J. A. Miller (Harmondsworth: Penguin, 1986).

Landon, B. *Science Fiction After 1900: From the Steam Man to the Stars* (New York and London: Routledge, 2002).

Larkin, P. *The Whitsun Weddings* (London: Faber and Faber, 1990).

Le Corbusier, *Towards a New Architecture*, trans. F. Etchells (London: The Architectural Press, 1948).

Lefebvre, H. 'Towards a Leftist Cultural Politics' in C. Nelson and L. Grossberg (eds), *Marxism and the Interpretation of Culture* (London: Macmillan, 1988): pp. 75–88.

——, *Critique of Everyday Life*, trans. J. Moore (London: Verso, 1991).

Levin, D. M. *The Opening of Vision: Nihilism and the Postmodern Situation* (New York and London: Routledge, 1988).

Lewis, W. *The Wild Body* (London: Chatto and Windus, 1927).

——, *Blasting and Bombardiering: An Autobiography* (London: John Calder, 1982).

Leys, R. *Trauma: A Genealogy* (Chicago: University of Chicago Press, 2000).

l'Isle-Adam, V. de *Axel*, trans. M. Gaddis Rose (London: Soho, 1986).

Luckhurst, R. 'The Many Deaths of Science Fiction: A Polemic', *Science Fiction Studies* 21: 1 (March 1994): 35–50.

——, 'The Angle Between Two Walls': The Fiction of J. G. Ballard (Liverpool: Liverpool University Press, 1997).

Luttwak, E. *Turbo-Capitalism: Winners and Losers in the Global Economy* (London: Orion, 1999).

Mahon, A. 'Hans Bellmer's Libidinal Politics', in R. Spiteri and D. LaCoss (eds), *Surrealism, Politics and Culture* (Aldershot: Ashgate, 2003).

Mann, T. 'Nietzsche's Philosophy in the Light of Contemporary Events', in R. Solomon (ed.), *Nietzsche: A Collection of Critical Essays* (New York: Anchor, 1973).

Marinetti, F. T. *Mafarka the Futurist: An African Novel*, trans. C. Diethe and S. Cox (London: Middlesex University Press, 1998).

Marx, K. *The Economic and Philosophic Manuscripts of 1844*, trans. M. Milligan, ed. D. J. Struik (New York: International, 1964).

—— and F. Engels, *Manifesto of the Communist Party*, trans. S. Moore (Moscow: Progress Publishers, 1977 [1848]).

McCaffery, L. (ed.), *Storming the Reality Studio: A Casebook of Cyberpunk and Postmodern Science Fiction* (Durham and London: Duke University Press, 1991).

McEwan, I. *The Comfort of Strangers* (London: Picador, 1981).

Nadeau, M. *The History of Surrealism*, trans. R. Howard (London: Jonathan Cape, 1968).

Niethammer, L. in collaboration with D. Van Laak, *Posthistoire: Has History Come to an End?*, trans. P. Camiller (London: Verso, 1992).

Nietzsche, F. *On the Genealogy of Morals* and *Ecce Homo*, trans. W. Kaufman and R. J. Hollingdale (New York: Vintage, 1969).

——, *Beyond Good and Evil*, trans. R. J. Hollingdale (Harmondsworth: Penguin, 1990).

——, *Twilight of the Idols/The Anti-Christ*, trans. R. J. Hollingdale (Harmondsworth: Penguin, 1990).

——, *The Birth of Tragedy*, trans. S. Whiteside, ed. M. Tanner (Harmondsworth: Penguin, 1993).

——, *Human, All Too Human*, trans. M. Faber and S. Lehmann (Harmondsworth: Penguin, 1994).

Ollman, B. *Alienation: Marx's Conception of Man in Capitalist Society* (Cambridge: Cambridge University Press, 1973).

Orwell, G. *Homage to Catalonia* (Harmondsworth: Penguin, 1978).

Paolozzi, E. *The Metallization of a Dream* (London: Lion and Unicorn Press, 1963).

——, *Writings and Interviews*, ed. Robin Spencer (Oxford: Oxford University Press, 2000).

Parrinder, P. (ed.), *Science Fiction: A Critical Guide* (London and New York: Longman, 1979).

Pick, D. *War Machine: The Rationalisation of Slaughter in the Modern Age* (New Haven: Yale University Press, 1996).

Pirandello, L. *On Humour*, trans. A. Illiano and D. P. Testa (Chapel Hill NC: University of North Carolina Press, 1960).

Platt, C. *Dream Makers: Science Fiction and Fantasy Writers at Work* (London: Xanadu, 1987).

Plotinus, *The Enneads*, trans. S. MacKenna (Harmondsworth: Penguin, 1991).

Pringle, D. *Earth is the Alien Planet: J. G. Ballard's Four-Dimensional Nightmare* (San Bernardino CA: Borgo Press, 1979).

——, *J. G. Ballard: A Primary and Secondary Bibliography* (Boston: G. K. Hall, 1984).

Punter, D. *The Hidden Script: Writing and the Unconscious* (London: Routledge and Kegan Paul, 1985).

Rorty, R. *Contingency, Irony, and Solidarity* (Cambridge: Cambridge University Press, 1989).

Ruddick, N. 'Ballard/Crash/Baudrillard', *Science Fiction Studies* 58. 19: 3 (November 1992): 354–60.

Ruskin, J. *The Stones of Venice Vol. 3* (London: George Allen, 1898).

Sade, Marquis de *Justine, Philosophy in the Bedroom and Other Writings*, trans. R. Seaver and A. Wainhouse (New York: Grove Press, 1966).

Samuels, A. *Jung and the Post-Jungians* (London: Routledge, 1997).

Satz, A. 'Puppets and Prosthesis', in *The Prosthetic Aesthetic, New Formations* 46 (spring 2002): 103–18.

Sayer, K. and J. Moore (eds), *Science Fiction, Critical Frontiers* (London: Macmillan, 2000).

Schiller, F. *Naïve and Sentimental Poetry* and *On the Sublime*, trans. J. A. Elias (New York: Frederick Ungar, 1980).

Scholes, R. and E. S. Rabkin, *Science Fiction: History, Science, Vision* (Oxford: Oxford University Press, 1977).

Seltzer, M. *Bodies and Machines* (New York and London: Routledge, 1992).

Sennett, R. *The Corrosion of Character: The Personal Consequences of Work in the New Capitalism* (New York: W. W. Norton, 1998).

Shakespeare, W. *The Tempest*, ed. F. Kermode (London: Routledge, 1992).

Shelley, P. B. *Poetical Works*, ed. T. Hutchinson (Oxford: Oxford University Press, 1978).

Sinclair, I. *Crash* (London: British Film Institute, 1999).

Smith, M. 'The Uncertainty of Placing: Prosthetic Bodies, Sculptural Design, and Unhomely Dwelling in Marc Quinn, James Gillingham, and Sigmund Freud', *The Prosthetic Aesthetic, New Formations* 46 (Spring 2002): 85–102.

Sobchak, V. 'Baudrillard's Obscenity', *Science Fiction Studies* 55. 18: 3 (November 1991): 327–9.

Sontag, S. *Against Interpretation* (London: Eyre and Spottiswoode, 1967).

——, *A Susan Sontag Reader* (Harmondsworth: Penguin, 1982).

Steiner, J. *Psychic Retreats: Pathological Organizations in Psychotic, Neurotic and Borderline Patients* (London: Routledge, 1999).

Stephenson, G. *Out of the Night and Into the Dream: A Thematic Study of the Fiction of J. G. Ballard* (Westport CT: Greenwood Press, 1991).

Stirner, M. *The Ego and His Own* (London: Living Time Press, 2001).

Suvin, S. *Metamorphoses of Science Fiction: On the Poetics and History of a Literary Genre* (New Haven and London: Yale University Press, 1979).

——, 'Novum is as Novum Does', in K. Sayer and J. Moore (eds), *Science Fiction, Critical Frontiers* (London: Macmillan, 2000): pp. 3–22.

Taylor, C. *Sources of the Self: The Making of the Modern Identity* (Cambridge: Cambridge University Press, 1992).

Todorov, T. *Hope and Memory: Reflections on the Twentieth Century*, trans. D. Bellos (London: Atlantic, 2003).

Vale, V. and A. Juno (eds), *RE/Search* 8. 9 (1984). Special J. G. Ballard issue.

Vattimo, G. *The End of Modernity: Nihilism and Hermeneutics in Post-modern Culture*, trans. J. R. Snyder (London: Polity, 1988).

Virilio, P. *The Lost Dimension*, trans. D. Moshenberg (New York: Semiotext(e), 1991).

Whitehead, A. N. *Process and Reality: An Essay in Cosmology* (New York: Harper, 1957).

Williams, R. *The Politics of Modernism: Against the New Conformists* (London: Verso, 1990).

Wilson, A. *No Laughing Matter* (London: Secker and Warburg, 1967).

Wollen, P. and J. Kerr (eds), *Autopia. Cars and Culture* (London: Reaktion, 2002).

Woolf, V. *The Common Reader Vol. 1* (New York: Harcourt, Brace and Company, 1953).

Yeats, W. B. *Collected Poems* (London: Macmillan, 1981).

Žižek, S. *On Belief* (London and New York: Routledge, 2001).

Index